STECK-VAUGHN

ATLAS OF THE WORLD

Written by Keith Lye

STECK-VAUGHN
ELEMENTARY · SECONDARY · ADULT · LIBRARY

A Harcourt Company

www.steck-vaughn.com

ABOUT THE ATLAS

Maps are essential tools for anyone who wants to understand the planet Earth. Their use goes back several thousand years. For example, in ancient Egypt, officials used maps to calculate taxes on property. From the days of the ancient Greeks, maps were a way of summarizing information about the known world.

Topographic and thematic maps

Topographic maps incorporate many features, including the height of the land, political boundaries, and cities and towns. They are a form of abbreviation. One map often contains such a vast amount of information that it would take an entire book to put it in words. Today, maps that portray one particular aspect of the changing world have become increasingly useful aids. These thematic maps help us to compare information about one place with that of another.

Flat maps of a round world

Because most maps depict the earth's curved surface on a flat paper surface, no map can be completely accurate. For this reason cartographers have devised different map projections – mathematical ways of projecting the earth's curvature onto a flat surface. Each projection preserves accurately some of the following features: shape, size, distance, and direction. Only a globe can preserve all of them accurately at the same time. But even the largest globes are far less detailed than most maps – and less convenient to carry about.

The six essential elements of geography

The Geographic Education Standards Project has developed six essential elements that every geographically informed person should know and understand. The *Steck-Vaughn Atlas of the World* provides the regional and thematic maps necessary to address these national geographic standards:

1. The World in Spatial Terms
2. Places and Regions
3. Physical Systems
4. Human Systems
5. Environment and Society
6. The Uses of Geography

Regional maps

Following a world overview, the atlas then takes an in-depth view of the world, which for this purpose is divided into 23 regions. These regions and the countries included in them are listed below. Each regional section contains topographic and political maps. The maps are supplemented by ready-reference fact panels with data that adds to the information on the maps. Basic data and flags are also provided for every independent country in the world, taking account of the many changes to the world map that have occurred in recent years.

Abbreviations

GDP = Gross Domestic Product
(The total value of a country's annual output of goods and services.)

GNP = Gross National Product
(A country's GDP plus income from abroad.)

sq km = square kilometers
sq mi = square miles

REGIONS OF THE WORLD

Canada and Greenland Canada, Greenland (dependency of Denmark)
United States of America United States of America
Mexico, Central America, and the Caribbean Antigua and Barbuda, Bahamas, Barbados, Belize, Costa Rica, Cuba, Dominica, Dominican Republic, El Salvador, Grenada, Guatemala, Haiti, Honduras, Jamaica, Mexico, Nicaragua, Panama, St. Kitts-Nevis, St. Lucia, St. Vincent and the Grenadines, Trinidad and Tobago
South America Argentina, Bolivia, Brazil, Chile, Colombia, Ecuador, Guyana, Paraguay, Peru, Suriname, Uruguay, Venezuela
Nordic Countries Denmark, Finland, Iceland, Norway, Sweden
British Isles Ireland, United Kingdom
France Andorra, France, Monaco
Spain and Portugal Portugal, Spain
Italy and Greece Cyprus, Greece, Italy, Malta, San Marino, Vatican City
Central Europe and the Low Countries Austria, Belgium, Germany, Liechtenstein, Luxembourg, Netherlands, Switzerland
Eastern Europe Albania, Bosnia and Herzegovina, Bulgaria, Croatia, Czech Republic, Hungary, Macedonia, Poland, Romania, Slovakia, Slovenia, Yugoslavia
Russia and Its Neighbors Armenia, Azerbaijan, Belarus, Estonia, Georgia, Kazakhstan, Kyrgyzstan, Latvia, Lithuania, Moldova, Mongolia, Russia, Tajikistan, Turkmenistan, Ukraine, Uzbekistan
Southwest Asia Afghanistan, Bahrain, Iran, Iraq, Israel, Jordan, Kuwait, Lebanon, Oman, Qatar, Saudi Arabia, Syria, Turkey, United Arab Emirates, Yemen
Northern Africa Algeria, Chad, Djibouti, Egypt, Eritrea, Ethiopia, Libya, Mali, Mauritania, Morocco, Niger, Somalia, Sudan, Tunisia
Central Africa Benin, Burkina Faso, Burundi, Cameroon, Cape Verde Islands, Central African Republic, Côte d'Ivoire, Democratic Republic of the Congo, Equatorial Guinea, Gabon, Gambia, Ghana, Guinea, Guinea-Bissau, Kenya, Liberia, Nigeria, Republic of the Congo, Rwanda, São Tomé and Príncipe, Senegal, Seychelles, Sierra Leone, Tanzania, Togo, Uganda
Southern Africa Angola, Botswana, Comoros, Lesotho, Madagascar, Malawi, Mauritius, Mozambique, Namibia, South Africa, Swaziland, Zambia, Zimbabwe
Indian Subcontinent Bangladesh, Bhutan, India, Maldives, Nepal, Pakistan, Sri Lanka
China and Taiwan The People's Republic of China, Taiwan
Southeast Asia Brunei, Cambodia, East Timor, Indonesia, Laos, Malaysia, Myanmar, Philippines, Singapore, Thailand, Vietnam
Japan and Korea Japan, North Korea, South Korea
Australia and Its Neighbors Australia, Papua New Guinea
New Zealand and Its Neighbors Federated States of Micronesia, Fiji, Kiribati, Marshall Islands, Nauru, New Zealand, Palau, Samoa, Solomon Islands, Tonga, Tuvalu, Vanuatu
Antarctica

Published in 2002 in the United States of America by:
Steck-Vaughn Publishers
10801 N. MoPac Expy., Bldg. #3, Austin, Texas 78759, USA.

AN ANDROMEDA BOOK
Copyright © 2002 Andromeda Oxford Ltd; first printed 1994, updated 2001.
Devised and produced by:
Andromeda Oxford Ltd, 11-13 The Vineyard, Abingdon, Oxfordshire OX13 5BL, England.
Editors: Ruth Hooper and Jenny Fry.
Design: Craig Eaton.
Cartography: Richard Watts and Tim Williams.
Flags produced by Lovell Johns, Oxford, U.K. and authenticated by the Flag Research center, Winchester, Mass.

ISBN: 0-7398-5001-6
Printed in the United States of America
1 2 3 4 5 6 7 8 9 10 05 04 03 02 01

CONTENTS

World: Physical and Political   4
World: Climate and Habitats   6
World: Environmental Issues and Population   8
World: Resources and Agriculture   10
Canada and Greenland   12
United States of America   14
Mexico, Central America, and the Caribbean   16
South America   18
Nordic Countries   20
British Isles   22
France   24
Spain and Portugal   26
Italy and Greece   28
Central Europe and the Low Countries   30
Eastern Europe   32
Russia and Its Neighbors   34
Southwest Asia   36
Northern Africa   38
Central Africa   40
Southern Africa   42
Indian Subcontinent   44
China and Taiwan   46
Southeast Asia   48
Japan and Korea   50
Australia and Its Neighbors   52
New Zealand and Its Neighbors   54
Antarctica   56

Glossary   58
Gazetteer and Index   59

THE WORLD

PHYSICAL

Land covers about 57,259,000 square miles (148,300,000 sq km) of the earth's surface. The land can be divided broadly into physical regions that are distinguished by the topography (surface features) and the climate.

The changing land

Land features such as mountains are constantly changing. While earthquakes and volcanic eruptions cause sudden and catastrophic change, other forces, such as weathering, are slow.

Worn fragments of rock are removed by the forces of erosion. These include running water, particularly in wet regions; glaciers (moving bodies of ice) in cold regions; winds, especially in deserts; and sea waves along coasts. Much of the worn rock is dumped onto sea or lake beds, where it piles up and eventually over many years forms new rock layers. This is part of the rock cycle, which has continued throughout the earth's history.

The changing map

Other forces operate inside the earth. Movements in the partly molten mantle affect parts of the overlying lithosphere, the planet's hard outer shell. As these huge blocks, or tectonic plates, move, they cause volcanic eruptions, earthquakes, and mountain building. New rock is formed from molten material from the mantle.

Around 280 million years ago, all the world's land areas were joined together in one supercontinent, which geologists call Pangea. About 200 million years ago, this super-continent started to separate, and the continents we know today gradually drifted to their present positions. Along the ocean ridges on the deep sea floor, plates are moving apart. These slow but unceasing movements continue today.

POLITICAL

While natural forces constantly change physical maps, human factors, such as wars, change political maps. For example, the world map in 1946 was substantially different from that of 1939, when World War II began. Another upheaval occurred in the 1950s and 1960s when many European colonies in Africa and Asia achieved their independence. Many of the independent nations adopted new names for cities and even physical features.

New nations

An upheaval occurred in the early 1990s, when the collapse of many communist governments changed the political map of Europe and Asia. For example, when in 1991 the Soviet Union was dissolved, 15 separate nations were born. The former Yugoslavia also has split up into five new nations.

Sovereignty

By 1999 the world contained 192 independent nations. Despite boundary disputes between some neighboring countries, each nation has a defined territory, which is recognized internationally, and a government that is responsible for making and implementing laws. The independent nations are often called sovereign states, because, unlike dependencies or states and provinces within nations, they recognize no authority higher than their own.

Sovereignty has nothing to do with size. The world's five smallest sovereign states have a combined area of about 42 square miles (110 sq km) and a population of about 72,000. Yet they are all sovereign states, unlike Texas, a state within the United States, which covers 267,340 square miles (692,407 sq km) and had a population of 20.85 million by 2000.

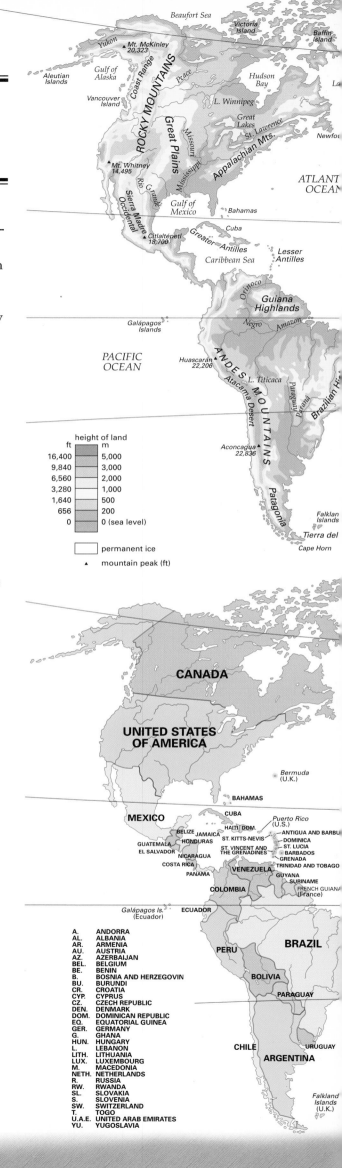

A. ANDORRA
AL. ALBANIA
AR. ARMENIA
AU. AUSTRIA
AZ. AZERBAIJAN
BEL. BELGIUM
BE. BENIN
B. BOSNIA AND HERZEGOVIN
BU. BURUNDI
CR. CROATIA
CYP. CYPRUS
CZ. CZECH REPUBLIC
DEN. DENMARK
DOM. DOMINICAN REPUBLIC
EQ. EQUATORIAL GUINEA
GER. GERMANY
G. GHANA
HUN. HUNGARY
L. LEBANON
LITH. LITHUANIA
LUX. LUXEMBOURG
M. MACEDONIA
NETH. NETHERLANDS
R. RUSSIA
RW. RWANDA
SL. SLOVAKIA
S. SLOVENIA
SW. SWITZERLAND
T. TOGO
U.A.E. UNITED ARAB EMIRATES
YU. YUGOSLAVIA

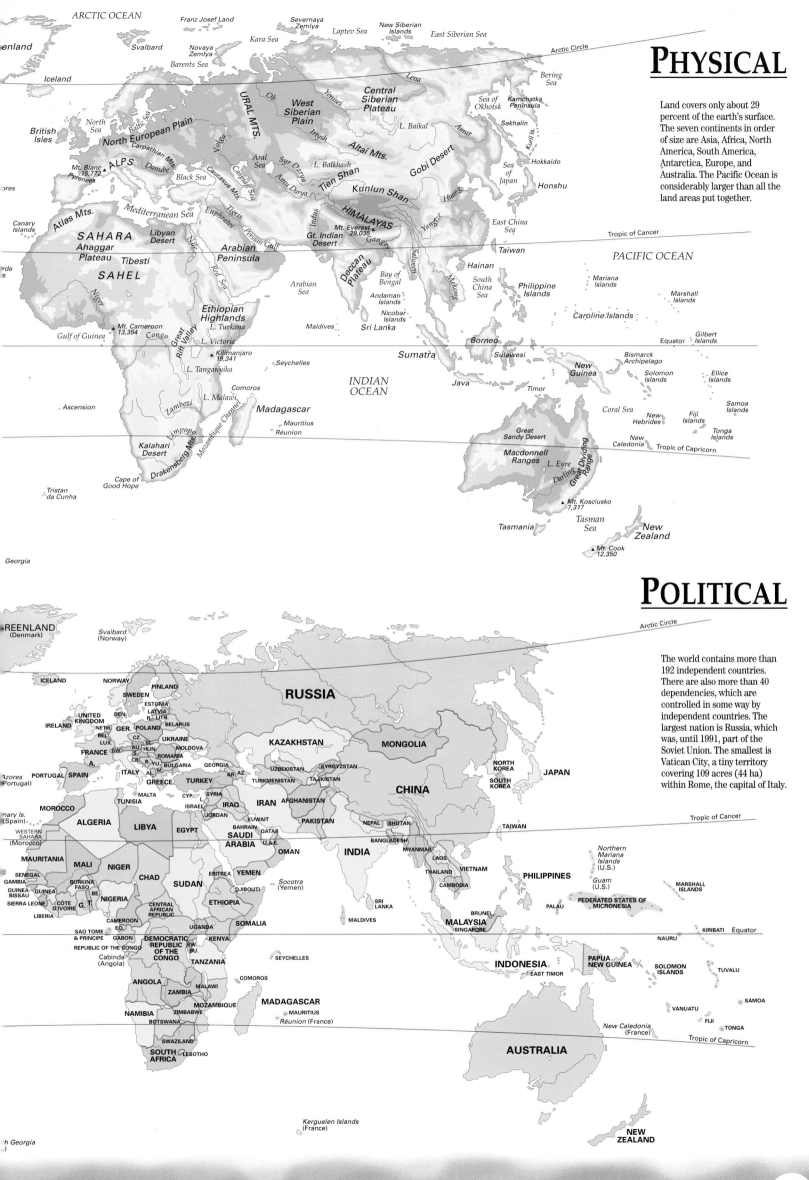

PHYSICAL

Land covers only about 29 percent of the earth's surface. The seven continents in order of size are Asia, Africa, North America, South America, Antarctica, Europe, and Australia. The Pacific Ocean is considerably larger than all the land areas put together.

POLITICAL

The world contains more than 192 independent countries. There are also more than 40 dependencies, which are controlled in some way by independent countries. The largest nation is Russia, which was, until 1991, part of the Soviet Union. The smallest is Vatican City, a tiny territory covering 109 acres (44 ha) within Rome, the capital of Italy.

THE WORLD

CLIMATE

While weather is the day-to-day, or hour-to-hour, condition of the air, climate is the long-term pattern of weather of a place.

Latitude and climate

The earth's atmosphere is always on the move. The reason for the movement of air is the sun, whose rays are most concentrated in tropical zones and least concentrated at the poles. The difference in temperature is mostly responsible for the planetary winds – the trade winds, westerlies, and polar easterlies – which constantly exchange air between hot tropical and cold polar regions.

Terrain and climate

While latitude is a major factor affecting climate, several other factors determine the pattern of world climates. First, winds are affected by the terrain. Warm, moist winds from the ocean pass over a mountain range and are chilled. Because their capacity to retain water vapor is reduced by cooling, the water vapor is turned into tiny droplets, which form rain clouds. It rains on the side of the mountain where the clouds rise. Beyond the mountain peaks, the winds become warmer as they descend, picking up moisture and creating a dry region, called a rain shadow.

The influence of the sea

The sea often has a moderating influence on the climate, and moist winds from the ocean usually bring plenty of rain. These moderating effects are felt less and less the farther one travels inland. Warm ocean currents, such as the Gulf Stream and its extension, the North Atlantic Current, have a warming effect on northwestern Europe. By contrast, eastern Canada in the same latitude is chilled by the cold Labrador Current.

HABITATS

The type of climate a region has determines broadly the kinds of plants and animals that live there. But many factors influence a species' habitat – topographical features, soil, and availability of oxygen, water, and food. A species' total physical, biological, and chemical surroundings make up its habitat. Similar habitats have like temperature and precipitation ranges, and can be classified into zones that follow lines of latitude.

Rain forests and savanna

Tropical rain forests flourish where it is hot and wet all year. They occur around the globe mostly in areas close to the equator. Savannas occur in tropical regions with a dry season.

Arid regions

Deserts are places with an average annual rainfall of less than 10 inches (25 cm). Deserts cover about one-seventh of the earth's land surface and center on a zone between the tropics and middle latitudes.

Forests and grasslands

In the latitudes on either side of the tropics are the temperate zones, or middle latitudes. Deciduous forests of maples, oaks, and beeches give way to grasslands. In North America and Eurasia, coniferous forests grow in the higher latitudes.

Cold zones

Cold zones include the ice sheets of Antarctica and Greenland and the treeless tundra regions, where plants grow only during the short summer.

Mountain habitats

Mountain habitats are determined largely by altitude rather than latitude. The difference in habitats is caused by temperature differences, which decrease by $1^{\circ}F$ ($0.55^{\circ}C$) every 300 feet (100m) in altitude.

Hot tropical climates are hot and wet all year.	Tropical
Tropical monsoon climates have wet and dry seasons.	
Tropical steppe has a short, unreliable rainy season.	
Summers are wet and warm; winters wet and mild.	subtropical
Summers are dry and warm; winters wet and mild.	
Desert areas have little rain and no cold season.	
It rains all year with no great temperature variation.	temperate
These climates have warm summers and cold winters.	
Little rain with no great temperature variation.	
Subarctic winters are very cold; summers are short.	cold
Arctic or ice-cap climates are freezing all year round.	

The world's climatic zones are affected by latitude, prevailing winds, terrain (especially high mountain ranges that lie in the path of winds), distance from the sea, and ocean currents.

Surface currents have a marked effect on the climate of coastal regions. Onshore winds passing over cold currents are chilled. Winds passing over warm currents are warmed.

Physical zones
- ice and snow
- tundra
- mountains/barren land
- forest
- grassland
- semidesert
- desert

▲ mountain peak (ft)

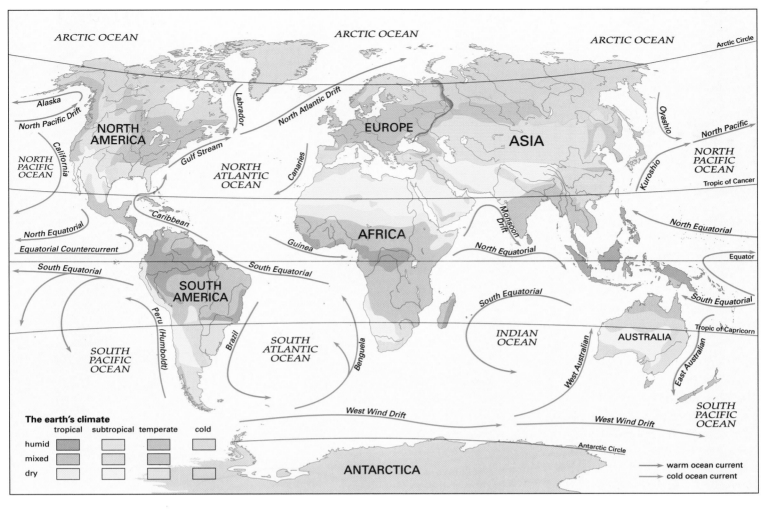

The earth's climate

	tropical	subtropical	temperate	cold
humid				
mixed				
dry				

→ warm ocean current
→ cold ocean current

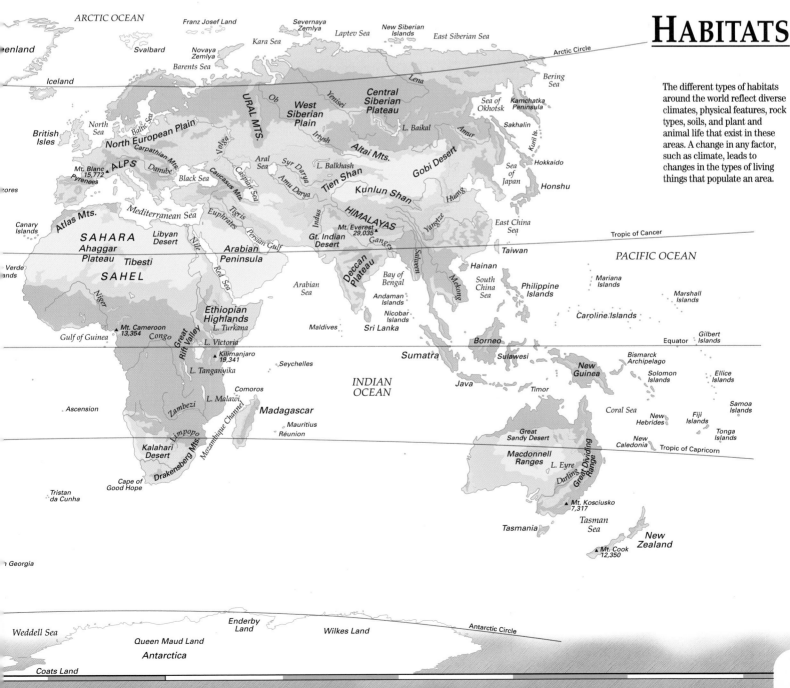

HABITATS

The different types of habitats around the world reflect diverse climates, physical features, rock types, soils, and plant and animal life that exist in these areas. A change in any factor, such as climate, leads to changes in the types of living things that populate an area.

THE WORLD

ENVIRONMENTAL ISSUES

Natural habitats around the world are always undergoing change with variations in climate. These changes occur gradually over hundreds of years. In addition to natural changes, however, many habitats are being greatly modified by increasing human activity.

Deforestation

The temperate middle latitudes were once largely covered by deciduous forests of ash, beech, elm, oak, and maple. However, much of the original deciduous forests have been cut down to provide fuel, timber, and farmland.

Perhaps the most serious environmental issue in the world today is the destruction of the rain forests in South America, Central Africa, and Southeast Asia. These forests contain more than half of the world's species of plants and animals, many of which are rapidly becoming extinct. Rain forest destruction may cause climatic change and contribute to global warming.

Desertification

Soil erosion often occurs when deforestation, overgrazing, and poor farming lays the land bare to wind and rain. In arid regions, soil erosion can turn fertile land into barren desert. The desertification of semiarid grasslands, such as the Sahel region south of the Sahara, is another major environmental issue.

Other problems

Many environmental problems arise from pollution. Major issues include smog, caused by industrial smoke or motor exhaust fumes, acid rain, the pollution of rivers and lakes by industrial wastes or untreated sewage, discharges of nuclear radiation, and the depletion of freshwater resources.

POPULATION

In 2000, the world's population reached 6.055 billion. It is estimated that this total will reach 7 billion in 2013 and 8 billion in 2028. Predictions show that by 2050 the world population could reach as high as 9.3 billion.

The population explosion

Around 10,000 years ago, when people began to grow crops and live in permanent settlements, the world was thinly populated. From around 5 million people in 8000 B.C., the population increased steadily to reach 500 million in A.D. 1650. The population then doubled in only 200 years, reaching 1 billion in 1850. The acceleration of population growth continued. By the mid-1920s, world population had reached nearly 2 billion, and it passed the 4 billion mark in the 1970s.

The increases in the last 200 years occurred first in nations that were industrializing. But the rates of population growth in the developed industrial world have recently declined. Today, the highest growth rates are in the developing world.

Where people live

At the turn of the twentieth century, about half of the world's people lived on only 5 percent of the world's land area, while about half of the world's land area contained only about 5 percent of the world's population. The population explosion in areas attractive to settlement and the consequent expansion of city populations have all contributed to pollution, while urban living has contributed to many of the environmental problems that exist today.

Population pressure also affects rural areas, where the increasing demand for land to grow food has led to the destruction of natural habitats.

ATLANTIC OCEAN

PACIFIC OCEAN

The map depicts two regions where natural habitats are at risk. These are the equatorial rain forests, which are being cut down at an alarmingly rapid rate, and semiarid regions, which are being turned into deserts by deforestation and overgrazing.

ATLANTIC OCEAN

PACIFIC OCEAN

The world's population is distributed unevenly around the planet. Vast areas, including the Sahara in North Africa, the Australian interior, northern Canada and Siberia, and the Amazon basin in South America are sparsely populated. Other areas in India, Southeast Asia, Western Europe, and the northeastern United States are extremely crowded.

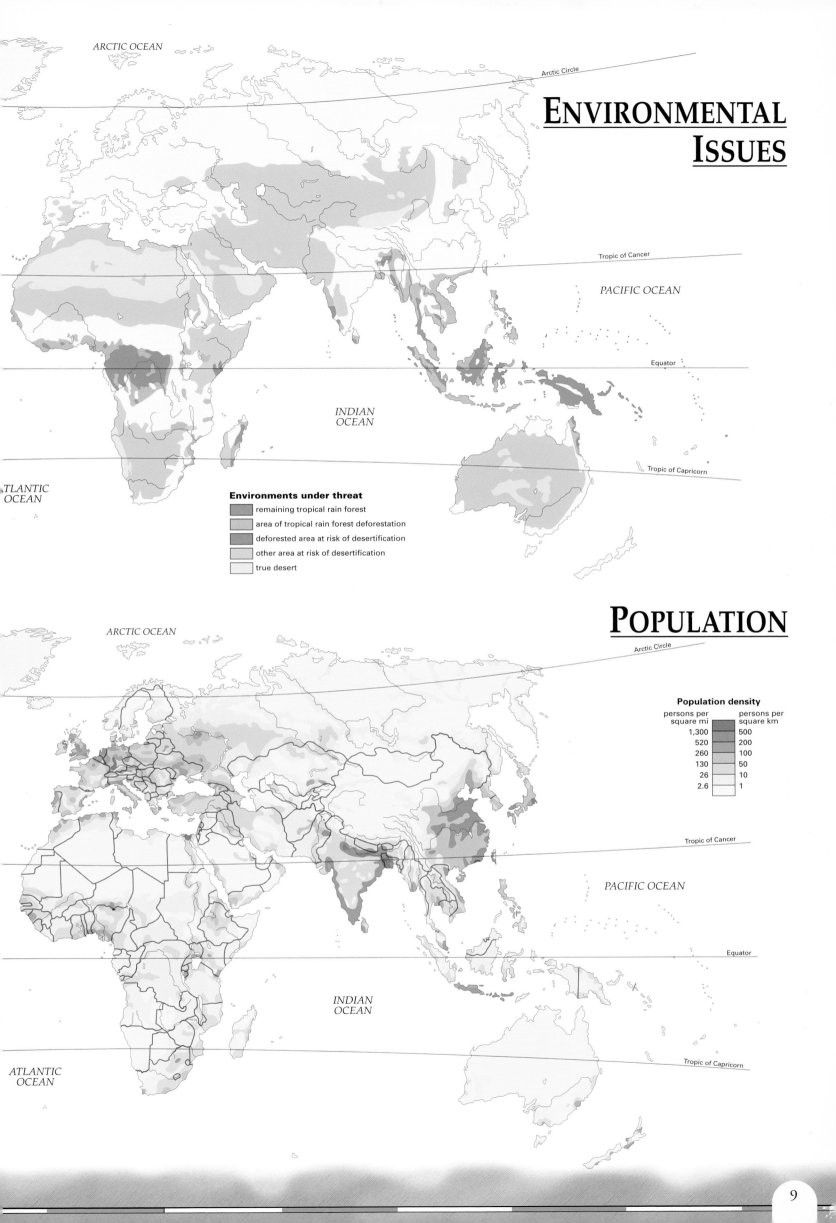

ENVIRONMENTAL ISSUES

ARCTIC OCEAN

Arctic Circle

Tropic of Cancer

PACIFIC OCEAN

Equator

INDIAN OCEAN

ATLANTIC OCEAN

Tropic of Capricorn

Environments under threat

- remaining tropical rain forest
- area of tropical rain forest deforestation
- deforested area at risk of desertification
- other area at risk of desertification
- true desert

POPULATION

ARCTIC OCEAN

Arctic Circle

Population density

persons per square mi	persons per square km
1,300	500
520	200
260	100
130	50
26	10
2.6	1

Tropic of Cancer

PACIFIC OCEAN

Equator

INDIAN OCEAN

ATLANTIC OCEAN

Tropic of Capricorn

THE WORLD

RESOURCES

The world's leading resources include those that provide fuel, together with metals and nonmetallic minerals used in industry.

Energy resources

Coal, oil, and natural gas are called fossil fuels because they were formed from once-living organisms. Coal was the main fuel during the industrial revolution in the nineteenth century. Today, however, oil and natural gas provide about three-fifths of the world's energy.

Fossil fuels are nonrenewable resources, and some experts estimate that, at present drilling rates, the world's oil reserves will run out by 2035.

Nuclear power continues to be controversial, and so it seems likely that such renewable energy resources as water and solar power will be increasingly used in the future. Also important is the fact that the use of water and solar power, unlike that of fossil fuels, does not cause pollution.

Mineral reserves

Most metals are extracted from ores, which are combinations of minerals. Iron, which is used to make steel, is the most widely used metal. Other major metallic minerals include aluminum, which is obtained from the ore bauxite; copper; lead; tin; and zinc. Uranium is also a metal. It has become important because of its use as a nuclear fuel. Nonmetallic minerals include some building materials, diamonds, phosphates, and sulfur.

Metals are also nonrenewable resources and some are becoming scarce. As a result, recycling is becoming increasingly common. About half of the iron and one-third of the aluminum now used by industry comes from scrap.

AGRICULTURE

Agriculture is the world's leading industry. Not only does it provide food, but it also produces those materials used to make clothing, prepare paints and inks, or make soaps, for example. Forestry and fishing also produce materials used in industry as well as provide food.

The development of agriculture

The deliberate planting and harvesting of crops began around 10,000 years ago, and, soon afterward, farming communities began to displace the traditional hunting and gathering economies. Other early developments were the domestication of animals and irrigation. As of the eighteenth century, farming became increasingly mechanized and scientific. Today, agriculture employs only a small proportion of people in the prosperous developed countries. For example, the United States leads the world in agricultural production, yet agriculture employs only about 3 percent of its work force. By contrast, a high proportion of people in most developing countries work on the land. Much of the agriculture is carried out at subsistence level—that is, farmers produce enough for their families, with comparatively little left over for sale.

Modern transportation methods, especially the use of refrigeration, have made it possible to move perishable goods around the world. Agriculture is big business.

Forestry and fishing

Forests cover about 30 percent of the earth's land area. Forestry is the commercial utilization and management of forests. Wood is a major raw material in industry.

The fishing industry is particularly important in countries such as Japan, where other protein-rich foods are in short supply.

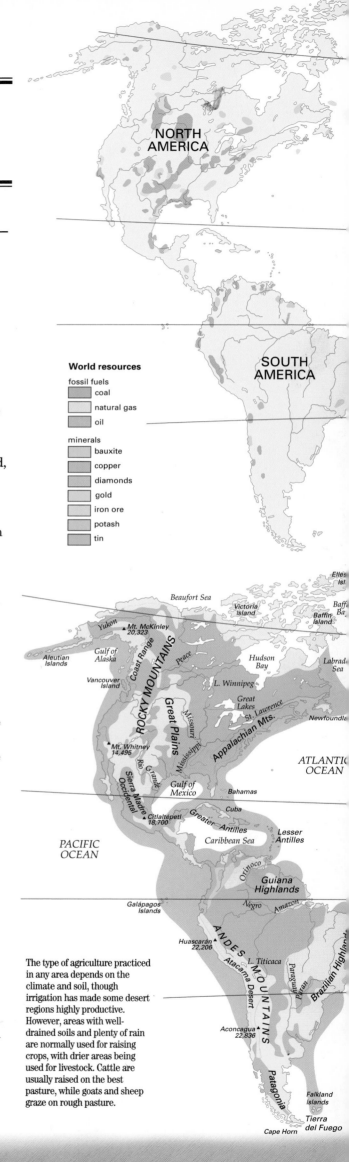

World resources

fossil fuels
- coal
- natural gas
- oil

minerals
- bauxite
- copper
- diamonds
- gold
- iron ore
- potash
- tin

The type of agriculture practiced in any area depends on the climate and soil, though irrigation has made some desert regions highly productive. However, areas with well-drained soils and plenty of rain are normally used for raising crops, with drier areas being used for livestock. Cattle are usually raised on the best pasture, while goats and sheep graze on rough pasture.

RESOURCES

The map shows that fossil fuels, particularly oil and gas, are concentrated in the Northern Hemisphere. North America is especially rich in energy reserves. On the other hand, reserves of metals and other minerals are spread far more evenly around the world.

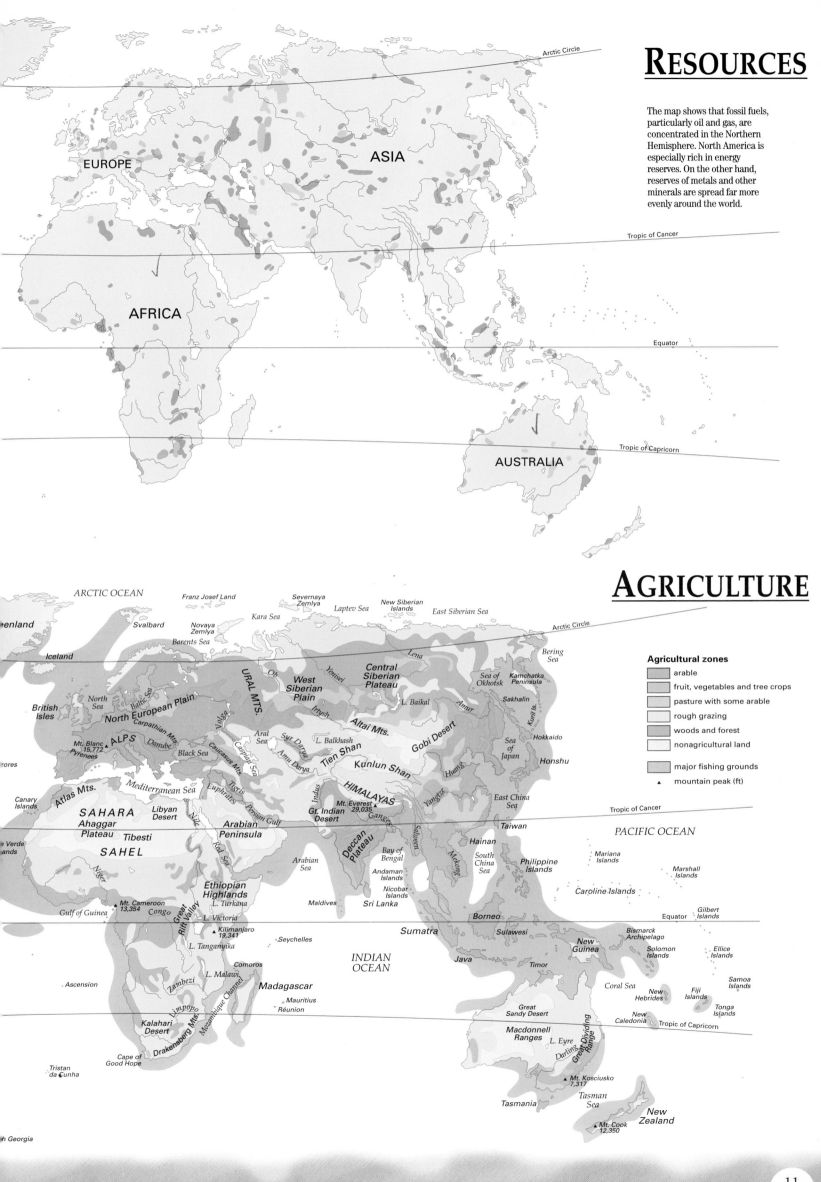

EUROPE

ASIA

AFRICA

AUSTRALIA

Arctic Circle

Tropic of Cancer

Equator

Tropic of Capricorn

AGRICULTURE

Agricultural zones
- arable
- fruit, vegetables and tree crops
- pasture with some arable
- rough grazing
- woods and forest
- nonagricultural land
- major fishing grounds
- ▲ mountain peak (ft)

ARCTIC OCEAN

Franz Josef Land

Severnaya Zemlya

Laptev Sea

New Siberian Islands

East Siberian Sea

Kara Sea

enland

Svalbard

Novaya Zemlya

Barents Sea

Lena

Bering Sea

Iceland

Central Siberian Plateau

Ob

Yenisei

West Siberian Plain

Sea of Okhotsk

Kamchatka Peninsula

British Isles

North Sea

Baltic Sea

North European Plain

URAL MTS.

Irtysh

L. Baikal

Amur

Sakhalin

Kuril Is.

Carpathian Mts.

Volga

Altai Mts.

Hokkaido

Mt. Blanc 15,772 ▲ ALPS

Danube

Aral Sea

Sur Darya

L. Balkhash

Tien Shan

Gobi Desert

Sea of Japan

Honshu

Pyrenees

Black Sea

Caucasus Mts.

Caspian Sea

Amu Darya

Kunlun Shan

ores

Mediterranean Sea

Tigris

Euphrates

HIMALAYAS

Huang

East China Sea

Canary Islands

Atlas Mts.

Persian Gulf

Indus

Mt. Everest 29,035 ▲

Ganges

Yangtze

Tropic of Cancer

ands

SAHARA

Libyan Desert

Nile

Arabian Peninsula

Gt. Indian Desert

Salween

Taiwan

PACIFIC OCEAN

Ahaggar Plateau

Tibesti

Red Sea

Deccan Plateau

Bay of Bengal

Hainan

Mariana Islands

Verde ands

SAHEL

Arabian Sea

Andaman Islands

South China Sea

Philippine Islands

Marshall Islands

Niger

Ethiopian Highlands

Maldives

Nicobar Islands

Sri Lanka

Mekong

Caroline Islands

Mt. Cameroon 13,354

Congo

L. Turkana

Gulf of Guinea

Great Rift Valley

Borneo

Equator

Gilbert Islands

Kilimanjaro 19,341

L. Victoria

Sumatra

Sulawesi

Bismarck Archipelago

Seychelles

New Guinea

Solomon Islands

Ellice Islands

L. Tanganyika

INDIAN OCEAN

Java

Timor

Comoros

Mauritius

Réunion

Coral Sea

New Hebrides

Fiji Islands

Samoa Islands

Ascension

Zambezi

L. Malawi

Madagascar

Great Sandy Desert

New Caledonia

Tonga Islands

Tropic of Capricorn

Kalahari Desert

Limpopo

Drakensberg Mts.

Mozambique Channel

Macdonnell Ranges

L. Eyre

Darling

Great Dividing Range

Cape of Good Hope

Tristan da Cunha

▲ Mt. Kosciusko 7,317

Tasmania

Tasman Sea

New Zealand

h Georgia

▲ Mt. Cook 12,350

CANADA AND GREENLAND

Northern North America includes Canada, the world's second largest country, and Greenland, the world's largest island. The Arctic islands of Canada are a cold tundra region that contain many glaciers. Two of these islands—Baffin and Ellesmere—are also among the world's ten largest islands. About six-sevenths of Greenland is buried under a thick ice sheet, the world's second largest body of ice after the ice sheet of Antarctica.

Canada's most prominent features include the western mountains, the interior plains, the Canadian Shield, the St. Lawrence lowlands, and, in the southeast, an extension of the Appalachian region. Canada also shares with the United States the world's largest expanse of fresh water—the Great Lakes.

Because of the climate, about 80 percent of Canadians live within 186 miles (300 km) of their southern border. Canada is one of the world's leading mineral exporters and manufacturing nations. Its farming and fishing industries are highly efficient.

Canada has a diverse population. The earliest inhabitants, the Native Americans, entered Canada about 30,000 years ago. They were followed by the Inuits, whose descendants now also live in Greenland. These two peoples make up a small minority of the population. Nearly two-thirds of the people today are English and French-speaking descendants of European settlers, though Canada also has communities from other parts of Europe, notably Germany, Italy, and Ukraine, and from Asia.

Canada and Greenland make up about half of North America. Northern Canada and most of Greenland lie north of the Arctic Circle, while the northern tip of Greenland is about 441 miles (710 km) from the North Pole. Canada's greatest east-west distance is nearly 3,230 miles (5,200 km). This vast distance is reflected by its six time zones. When it is 8:30 a.m. in St. John's, Newfoundland, it is 4.00 a.m. in Vancouver, British Columbia.

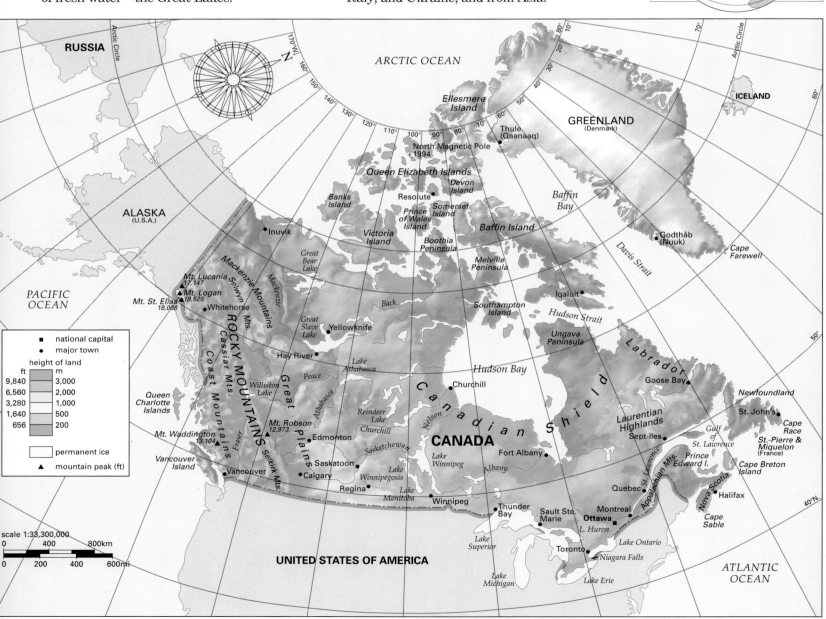

THE POLITICAL AND CULTURAL WORLD

Canada has a federal system of government, but it faces problems arising from its ethnic diversity. One problem is reconciling the aspirations of the French-speaking people, who form the majority in Quebec, with the different traditions of the English-speaking Canadians. Another problem is how to integrate Native American and Inuit peoples in the modern state.

Greenland is a self-governing province of Denmark, though it is 50 times bigger than the rest of the country. To assert its independence, Greenland left the European Community in 1985, though it continued its relationship with Denmark.

COUNTRIES IN THE REGION

Canada (Greenland, dependency of Denmark)

RELIGION

Roman Catholic 46.5%; Protestant 41%; Eastern Orthodox 1.5%; Jewish 1.2%; Muslim 0.4%; Hindu 0.3%; Sikh 0.3%; nonreligious 7.4%; others 1.4%

ETHNIC ORIGIN

French 27%; British 40%; other European 20%; Indigenous Indian and Inuit (known as First Nations) 1.5%; others 11.5%

FORM OF GOVERNMENT

Federal multiparty parliamentary monarchy with two legislative houses

ECONOMIC INDICATORS

	Canada
GDP (US$ billions)	603.1
GNP per capita (US$)	21,860
Annual rate of growth of GDP, 1990–1997	2.2%
Manufacturing as % of GDP	21.7%
Central government spending as % of GDP	20%
Merchandise exports (US$ billions)	214.4
Merchandise imports (US$ billions)	200.9
Aid given as % of GDP	0.34%

WELFARE INDICATORS

	Canada
Infant mortality rate (per 1,000 live births)	
1978	12
1998	6
Population per physician (1996)	476
Expected years of schooling (1995)	16.8
(males 16.5, females 17.1)	
Health expenditure as % of GDP (1995)	9.2%
Adult literacy (1995)	98.8%
(males 99%, females 98.7%)	

Constitutional changes
In the 1990s, Canadians debated the future of their country. Many French Canadians wanted to create a French Canadian state in Quebec. In 1999, the long campaign of the Inuit people for a homeland found success in the creation of Nunavut from a partition of the Northwest Territories.

Area 3,851,791 sq mi (9,976,140 sq km)
Population 31,281,092
Capital Ottawa
Chief languages English, French
Currency 1 Canadian dollar (Can $) = 100 cents

Canada

UNITED STATES OF AMERICA

The bulk of the United States, comprising 48 of the 50 states, lies between Canada to the north and Mexico to the south. The forty-ninth state, Alaska, is in the northwestern corner of North America. The fiftieth state, Hawaii, is an island chain situated in the Pacific Ocean.

The United States, the world's fourth largest country, is a land of towering mountain ranges and extensive plains. Prominent land features include the Grand Canyon, great rivers that lead into the interior, deserts, explosive volcanoes in the Cascade Range, and wetlands in the southeast. The climate ranges from the icy shores of the Arctic Ocean to the intense heat of the dry Death Valley in California.

The first inhabitants of the United States, the Native Americans, came from Eurasia about 30,000 years ago across a land bridge over what is now the Bering Strait. They were followed about 6,000 years ago by the ancestors of the Inuit. Since the early sixteenth century, Europeans and, later, people from almost every part of the world, have migrated to and made their homes in the United States.

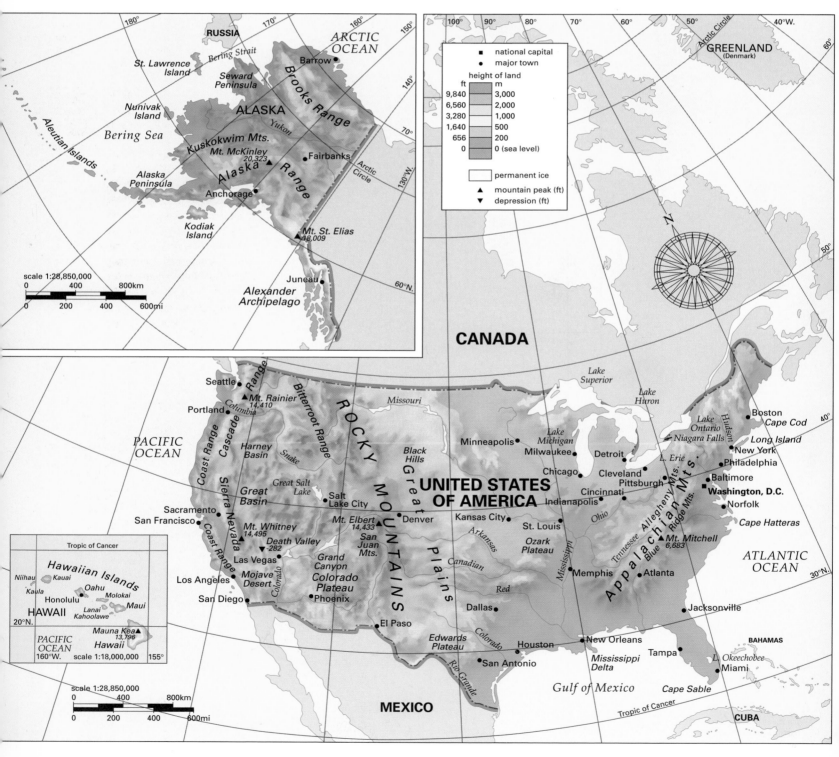

THE POLITICAL AND CULTURAL WORLD

The United States was born during the American Revolution (1775–1783), when the people of the 13 British colonies in the east overthrew British rule. The country expanded westward during the nineteenth century. Alaska was purchased from Russia in 1867, while Hawaii was annexed in 1898. Both territories became states in 1959.

The United States is a federal republic, whose government has three branches. The executive branch is headed by the president, who is also head of state. The legislative branch includes Congress, which consists of the Senate and House of Representatives. The judicial branch is headed by the Supreme Court.

COUNTRIES IN THE REGION

United States of America

Territories outside the region American Samoa, Guam, Johnston Atoll, Midway Islands, Northern Marianas, Puerto Rico, U.S. Virgin Islands, Wake Island, Howland, Jarvis, Baker, Palmyra

The U.S.A. is composed of 50 states, including Alaska and Hawaii.

LANGUAGE

Official language English
Percentage of population by first language
English (79%), Spanish (11%), German (3%), Italian (2%), French (1.3%), Polish (1.2%)

IMMIGRATION

Percentage of foreign born 9.5
Total immigrants (1996) 915,900
Regions sending most immigrants (1996) Mexico (163,743), Russia (19,668), Ukraine (21,079), Philippines (54,588), Africa (52,889), China (50,981), India (42,819), Vietnam (39,922), Cuba (26,166), Canada (21,751), Poland (15,504), Yugoslavia (former) (10,755)

RELIGION

Protestant (56%), Roman Catholic (28%), nonreligious and atheist (6.8%), Jewish (2%), Eastern Orthodox (2.3%), Muslim (1.9%), Hindu (0.2%)

MEMBERSHIP OF INTERNATIONAL ORGANIZATIONS

Colombo Plan
North Atlantic Treaty Organization (NATO)
Organization of American States (OAS)
Organization for Economic Cooperation and Development (OECD)
World Trade Organization (WTO)

STYLE OF GOVERNMENT

Multiparty federal republic with two-chamber assembly

ECONOMIC INDICATORS

	United States
GDP (US$ trillions)	7.819
GNP per capita (US$)	28,740
Annual rate of growth of GDP, 1990-1997	4.1%
Manufacturing as % of GDP	17%
Central government spending as % of GNP	21.1%
Merchandise exports (US$ billions)	681.3
Merchandise imports (US$ billions)	877.3
Aid given as % of GNP	0.12%

WELFARE INDICATORS

	United States
Infant mortality rate (per 1,000 live births)	
1965	25
2000	7
Daily food supply available	
(calories per capita, 1995)	3,603
Population per physician (1995)	470
Teacher–pupil ratio (primary school, 1995)	1 : 21

Area 3,618,770 sq mi (9,368,900 sq km)
Population 275,562,673
Armed forces army 495,000; navy 388,760; air force 390,000; marines 174,000
Ethnic composition White 80.3%; African-American 12.1%; Asian 2.8%; Native American 0.8%; other 3.9% (Hispanics comprise 11% and are included in White and African-American percentages.)
Currency 1 United States dollar (US$) = 100 cents
Life expectancy males 72.9 yrs; females 79.7 yrs

United States of America

- ◼ national capital
- ■ state capital
- ● other town

D.C. DISTRICT OF COLUMBIA
MISS. MISSISSIPPI
W.VA. WEST VIRGINIA

The national flag of the United States is popularly called the "Stars and Stripes." The 13 alternating red and white stripes represent the original 13 colonies that declared themselves states in 1776. The 50 white stars on a blue background represent the 50 states of today.

MEXICO, CENTRAL AMERICA, AND THE CARIBBEAN

Mexico and Central America together form a land bridge that extends to the northwest tip of South America. The region also includes 13 independent island nations in the Caribbean, two U.S. territories, and a number of European dependencies. Rugged scenery, active volcanoes, and subtropical and tropical climates are the main characteristics of the region.

The first inhabitants of the region were the Native Americans, who founded such cultures as the Mayan and Aztec empires. Spain conquered the region in the sixteenth century, and Spanish culture dominates to this day. Other people in this complex cultural mix are Africans, other Europeans, and some Asians, who were introduced as laborers.

The islands of the Greater Antilles (Cuba, Jamaica, Hispaniola, and Puerto Rico) formed a single landmass about 100 million years ago. Mexico and Central America became joined to South America between 5 million and 2 million years ago. The region was broken up by earth movements.

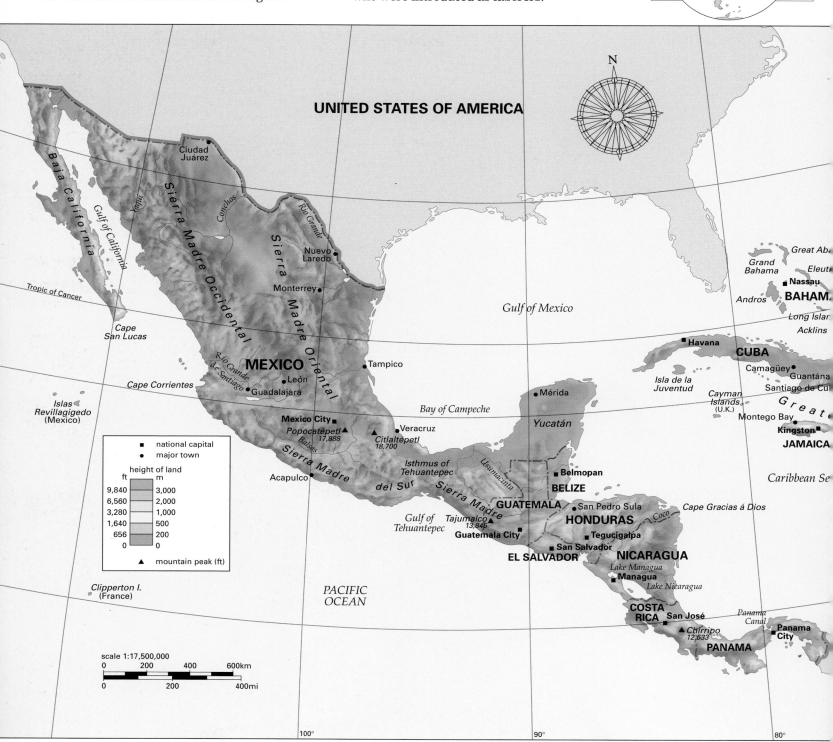

THE POLITICAL AND CULTURAL WORLD

Although geographically part of North America, most of the region belongs culturally to Latin America. Spanish is the chief language, and Roman Catholicism the main religion, though some Native Americans and Africans combine the Christian faith with some of their own traditional beliefs.

In the past the region has suffered much instability. Civilian governments have been overthrown by military groups, while brutal dictatorships and civil war have hampered the region's progress. Cuba is the only communist regime. Its policies were unaffected by the changes in its former ally, the Soviet Union.

COUNTRIES IN THE REGION

Antigua and Barbuda, Bahamas, Barbados, Belize, Costa Rica, Cuba, Dominica, Dominican Republic, El Salvador, Grenada, Guatemala, Haiti, Honduras, Jamaica, Mexico, Nicaragua, Panama, St. Kitts-Nevis, St. Lucia, St. Vincent and the Grenadines, Trinidad and Tobago

Dependencies of other states Anguilla, Bermuda, British Virgin Islands, Cayman Islands, Montserrat, Turks and Caicos Islands (UK); Aruba, Netherlands Antilles (Netherlands); Guadeloupe, Martinique (France); Puerto Rico, US Virgin Islands (USA)

LANGUAGE

Countries with one official language
(English) Antigua and Barbuda, Bahamas, Barbados, Belize, Dominica, Grenada, Jamaica, St. Kitts-Nevis, St. Lucia, St. Vincent and the Grenadines, Trinidad and Tobago; (Spanish) Costa Rica, Cuba, Dominican Republic, El Salvador, Guatemala, Honduras, Mexico, Nicaragua, Panama
Country with two official languages
(Creole, French) Haiti

Other languages spoken in the region include Carib, Nahua and other indigenous languages; Creoles and French patois; and Hindi (Trinidad and Tobago).

RELIGION

Countries with one major religion (P) Antigua and Barbuda; (RC) Costa Rica, Cuba, Dominica, Dominican Republic, El Salvador, Honduras, Mexico, Nicaragua
Countries with more than one major religion (P, RC) Bahamas, Barbados, Belize, Grenada, Jamaica, St. Kitts-Nevis, St. Lucia, St. Vincent and the Grenadines; (P, RC, V) Haiti; (H, M, P, RC) Trinidad and Tobago
Key: H–Hindu, M–Muslim, P–Protestant, RC–Roman Catholic, V–Voodoo

STYLES OF GOVERNMENT

Republics Costa Rica, Cuba, Dominica, Dominican Republic, El Salvador, Guatemala, Haiti, Honduras, Mexico, Nicaragua, Panama, Trinidad and Tobago
Monarchies All other countries in the region
Multiparty states All countries except Cuba, Haiti
One-party states Cuba, Haiti
Military influence Guatemala, Haiti, Honduras

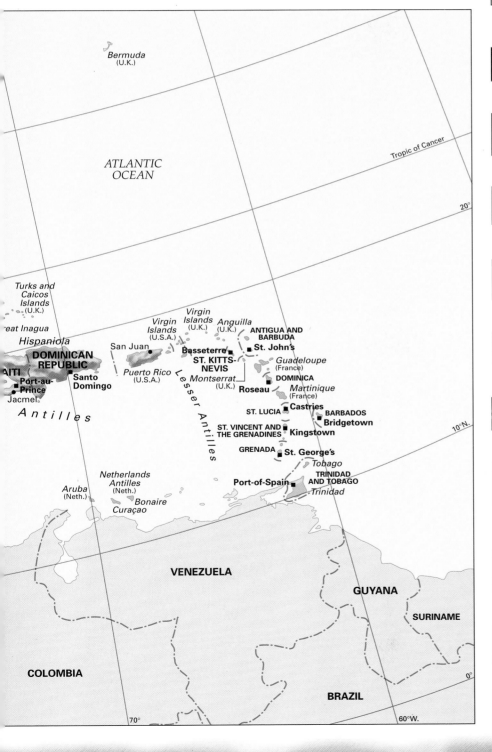

Antigua and Barbuda
Area 171 sq mi (442 sq km)
Pop. 66,422

Bahamas
Area 5,382 sq mi (13,939 sq km)
Pop. 294,982

Barbados
Area 166 sq mi (430 sq km)
Pop. 274,540

Belize
Area 8,867 sq mi (22,965 sq km)
Pop. 249,183

Costa Rica
Area 19,730 sq mi (51,100 sq km)
Pop. 3,710,558

Cuba
Area 42,804 sq mi (110,861 sq km)
Pop. 11,141,997

Dominica
Area 290 sq mi (750 sq km)
Pop. 71,540

Dominican Republic
Area 18,704 sq mi (48,443 sq km)
Pop. 8,442,533

El Salvador
Area 8,124 sq mi (21,041 sq km)
Pop. 6,122,515

Grenada
Area 133 sq mi (345 sq km)
Pop. 89,018

Guatemala
Area 42,042 sq mi (108,889 sq km)
Pop. 12,639,939

Haiti
Area 10,579 sq mi (27,400 sq km)
Pop. 6,867,995

Honduras
Area 43,277 sq mi (112,088 sq km)
Pop. 6,249,598

Jamaica
Area 4,244 sq mi (10,991 sq km)
Pop. 2,652,689

Mexico
Area 756,066 sq mi (1,958,201 sq km)
Pop. 100,349,766

Nicaragua
Area 46,467 sq mi (120,349 sq km)
Pop. 4,812,569

Panama
Area 29,762 sq mi (77,082 sq km)
Pop. 2,808,268

St. Kitts-Nevis
Area 104 sq mi (269 sq km)
Pop. 38,819

St. Lucia
Area 238 sq mi (617 sq km)
Pop. 156,260

St. Vincent and the Grenadines
Area 150 sq mi (389 sq km)
Pop. 115,461

Trinidad and Tobago
Area 1,980 sq mi (5,128 sq km)
Pop. 1,175,523

SOUTH AMERICA

South America, the fourth largest continent, contains the Andes, the world's longest unbroken mountain range, and the mighty Amazon River, which discharges one-fifth of the world's flow of fresh water into the sea.

Extending from the equatorial lands in the north to Cape Horn, which is just 500 miles (800 km) from Antarctica, the continent has a wide range of climates and habitats.

Native Americans migrating from North America reached the southern tip of South America about 8,000 years ago. One group, the Incas, founded a major civilization in the Andes, but it was crushed by Spanish soldiers in the 1530s. The predominant culture in South America today is Latin American. Roman Catholicism is the main religion, and Spanish and Portuguese are the chief languages.

South America was once joined to Africa, forming part of the supercontinent of Gondwanaland. When the two continents began to move apart about 150 million years ago, the South Atlantic Ocean opened up between them. Plate movements are still going on, further widening the Atlantic.

| | national capital |
| ● | major town |

height of land

ft	m
16,400	5,000
9,840	3,000
6,560	2,000
3,280	1,000
1,640	500
656	200
0	0

▲ mountain peak (ft)

scale 1:39,000,000

THE POLITICAL AND CULTURAL WORLD

L atin American culture is a complex blend of Native American, European, and African influences. The carnivals held in Rio de Janeiro combine Christian and African traditions, while many Native American Roman Catholics combine Christian dogma with some of the beliefs of their ancestors.

Deep divisions exist between rural people, who are often Native Americans, and urban societies, which are often dominated by people of European or of mixed European and Native American descent. In Peru, for example, such differences have led to civil war. Political instability and the suppression of human rights are occasionally still happening in South America.

COUNTRIES IN THE REGION

Argentina, Bolivia, Brazil, Chile, Colombia, Ecuador, Guyana, Paraguay, Peru, Suriname, Uruguay, Venezuela

Island territories Easter Island, Juan Fernández (Chile); Galápagos (Ecuador); Tierra del Fuego (Argentina/Chile)
Disputed borders Guyana/Venezuela; Peru/Ecuador
Dependencies of other states Falkland Islands, South Georgia, South Sandwich Islands (U.K.); French Guiana (France)

LANGUAGE

Countries with one official language (Dutch) Suriname; (English) Guyana; (Portuguese) Brazil; (Spanish) Argentina, Chile, Colombia, Ecuador, Paraguay, Uruguay, Venezuela
Country with two official languages (Quechua, Spanish) Peru
Country with three official languages (Aymara, Quechua, Spanish) Bolivia

Other languages spoken in the region include Arawak, Carib, Jivaro, Lengua, Mapuche, Sranang Tongo, Toba, and numerous other indigenous languages.

RELIGION

Countries with one major religion (RC) Argentina, Bolivia, Brazil, Chile, Colombia, Ecuador, Paraguay, Peru, Venezuela
Countries with more than one major religion (A, N, P, RC) Uruguay; (H, I, M, P, RC) Guyana, Suriname

Key: A–Atheist, H–Hindu, I–Indigenous religions, M–Muslim, N–Nonreligious, P–Protestant, RC–Roman Catholic

STYLES OF GOVERNMENT

Republics All countries of the region
Federal states Argentina, Brazil, Venezuela
Multiparty states All countries of the region

ECONOMIC INDICATORS

	Brazil	Colombia	Bolivia
GDP (US$ billions)	786.4	96.4	8.1
GNP per capita (US$)	6,240	6,720	3,280
Annual rate of growth of GDP, 1990-97	3.4%	4.4%	4.0%
Manufacturing as % of GDP	19.7%	9.6%	16.4%
Central government spending as % of GNP	39.6%	17.2%	19.6%
Merchandise exports (US$ billions)	47.7	10.6	1.1
Merchandise imports (US$ billions)	53.2	12.8	1.4
Aid received as % of GNP	0.1%	0.3%	13.3%
Total external debt as % of GDP	24.1%	34.9%	64.7%

WELFARE INDICATORS

	Brazil	Colombia	Bolivia
Infant mortality rate (per 1,000 live births)			
1965	104	86	160
2000	38.04	24.7	60.44
Malnutrition in children under 5	10.5%	15%	29.1%
Population per physician (1993)	844	1,105	2,348
Teacher-pupil ratio (primary school, 1998)	1 : 25	1 : 25	1 : 25

- ▣ national capital
- • other town

Area 292,135 sq mi (756,626 sq km)
Population 14,973,843 **Chile**

Area 440,831 sq mi (1,141,748 sq km)
Population 39,309,422 **Colombia**

Area 103,930 sq mi (269,178 sq km)
Population 12,562,496 **Ecuador**

Area 83,044 sq mi (215,083 sq km)
Population 705,156 **Guyana**

Area 157,048 sq mi (406,752 sq km)
Population 5,434,095 **Paraguay**

Area 496,225 sq mi (1,285,216 sq km)
Population 26,624,582 **Peru**

Area 63,251 sq mi (163,820 sq km)
Population 431,156 **Suriname**

Area 67,574 sq mi (175,016 sq km)
Population 3,308,523 **Uruguay**

Area 352,144 sq mi (912,050 sq km)
Population 23,203,466 **Venezuela**

Area 1,073,399 sq mi (2,780,092 sq km)
Population 36,737,664 **Argentina**

Area 424,164 sq mi (1,098,581 sq km)
Population 7,982,850 **Bolivia**

Area 3,265,076 sq mi (8,456,508 sq km)
Population 171,853,126 **Brazil**

Like many former European colonies, the countries of South America have made slow progress toward democracy and have seen much political upheaval in recent times. There have been periods of military rule in most countries in the region, with resulting human rights abuses. Chile and Paraguay have recently ended rule by the military.

NORDIC COUNTRIES

The Nordic countries include Norway, Sweden, Denmark, Finland, and Iceland. Glacial erosion has shaped the land, sculpting rugged mountain scenery, deep fjords, and many ice-scoured basins that now contain lakes.

Iceland has icecaps and volcanoes. Because it straddles the Atlantic ridge, new crustal rock is being formed in Iceland as the plates on either side of the ridge slowly move apart.

Except for Finnish and Lapp, the Nordic peoples speak closely related languages. Their historic Viking traditions have given them a distinctive personality and sense of adventure.

Natural resources, including North Sea oil and hydroelectric power supplies in Norway, iron ore in Sweden, and fisheries and forests, support the economies of the Nordic countries. Farming is important in the south.

The Nordic countries occupy the northwestern corner of Europe. They include various islands. The Faeroe Islands and Greenland are Danish, the Jan Mayen Islands, Bear Island, and Svalbard are Norwegian, and the Åland Islands in the Baltic are Finnish.

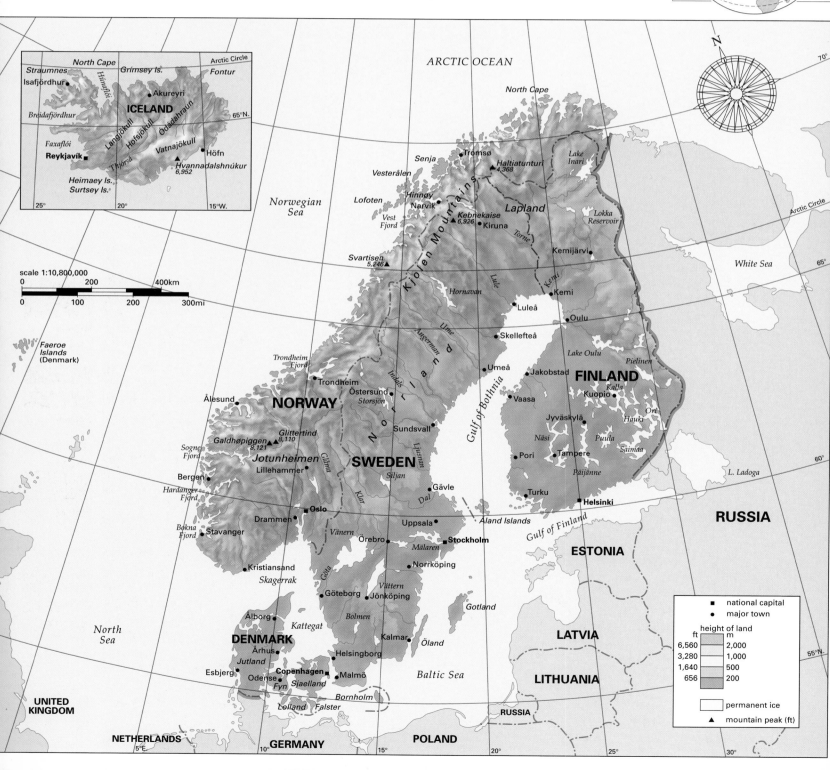

THE POLITICAL AND CULTURAL WORLD

The modern Nordic states began to evolve in the early nineteenth century. Norway became an independent country in 1905, when it broke away from its union with Sweden. In 1944 Iceland broke away from Denmark, which had lost Schleswig and Holstein in a war with Prussia in 1864. Finland declared its independence from Russia in 1917, though it lost land to the Soviet Union in 1944.

Because of their cultural affinity, the Nordic countries collaborate through the Nordic Council of Ministers. Established in 1971, it provides funds for joint institutions. The related Nordic Council is an advisory body.

COUNTRIES IN THE REGION

Denmark, Finland, Iceland, Norway, Sweden

Island territories Åland Islands (Finland); Faeroe Islands (Denmark); Jan Mayen, Svalbard Islands (Norway)
Territories outside region Greenland (Denmark)

Norway has a territorial claim in Antarctica.

LANGUAGE

Countries with one official language (Danish) Denmark; (Icelandic) Iceland; (Norwegian) Norway; (Swedish) Sweden
Country with two official languages (Finnish, Swedish) Finland

Faeroese is recognized with Danish as an official language in the Faeroe Islands.

RELIGION

Denmark Protestant (95%), nonreligious and atheist (3%)
Finland Protestant (92%), nonreligious and atheist (5%), Eastern Orthodox (1%)
Iceland Protestant (96%), nonreligious and atheist (2%), Roman Catholic (1%)
Norway Protestant (98%), nonreligious and atheist (1%)
Sweden Protestant (68%), nonreligious and atheist (28%), Eastern Orthodox (1%)

STYLES OF GOVERNMENT

Republics Finland, Iceland
Monarchies Denmark, Norway, Sweden
Multiparty states Denmark, Finland, Iceland, Norway, Sweden
One-chamber assembly Denmark, Finland, Norway, Sweden
Two-chamber assembly Iceland

MEMBERSHIP OF INTERNATIONAL ORGANIZATIONS

Council of Europe Denmark, Iceland, Norway, Sweden
European Union (EU) Denmark, Finland, Sweden
European Free Trade Association (EFTA) Iceland, Norway
North Atlantic Treaty Organization (NATO) Denmark, Iceland, Norway
Nordic Council Denmark, Finland, Iceland, Norway, Sweden
Organization for Economic Cooperation and Development (OECD) Denmark, Finland, Iceland, Norway, Sweden

Iceland has no military forces and is not a member of NATO Military Command.

ECONOMIC INDICATORS

	Denmark	Norway	Sweden
GDP (US$ billions)	163	153.4	227.8
GNP per capita (US$)	22,740	23,940	19,030
Annual rate of growth of GDP, 1990–1997	2.5%	4.0%	0.9%
Manufacturing as % of GDP	20.2%	12.6%	24.3%
Central government spending as % of GNP	59.6%	45.8%	63.8%
Merchandise exports (US$ billions)	48.5	48.8	83.1
Merchandise imports (US$ billions)	43.0	37.7	65.2
Aid given as % of GNP	1.04%	0.85%	0.84%

WELFARE INDICATORS

	Denmark	Norway	Sweden
Infant mortality rate (per 1,000 live births)			
1965	19	17	13
2000	7	5	5
Daily food supply available (calories per capita)	3,704	3,274	2,117
Population per physician (1996)	345	357	323
Teacher-pupil ratio (primary school, 1995)	1 : 11	1 : 12	1 : 13

Iceland
Area 39,769 sq mi (103,000 sq km)
Population 276,365
Currency 1 Icelandic króna (IsK) = 100 aurar

- ■ national capital
- • other town

Norway
Area 125,182 sq mi (324,220 sq km)
Population 4,481,162
Currency 1 Norwegian krone (NKr) = 100 øre

Sweden
Area 173,732 sq mi (449,964 sq km)
Population 8,873,052
Currency 1 Swedish krona (SKr) = 100 öre

Finland
Area 130,128 sq mi (337,030 sq km)
Population 5,167,486
Currency 1 markka (Fmk) = 100 pennia
Euro (€) also in use
€ = 100 cents

Denmark
Area 16,639 sq mi (43,094 sq km)
Population 5,336,394
Currency 1 Danish krone (DKr) = 100 øre

Denmark, Norway, and Sweden are constitutional monarchies, whose governments are led by elected prime ministers and cabinets. The monarchs have little real power. Finland and Iceland are democratic republics. Finland's president is the country's chief executive. In Iceland, the president's power is limited.

BRITISH ISLES

The British Isles contain a great variety of geology and a wide range of highland and lowland scenery that is unusual in such a small area. The climate is mild, mainly because of the influence of the North Atlantic Current, the northern extension of the warm Gulf Stream. The weather is also distinguished by its variability, caused by the depressions that regularly cross the islands from west to east.

Celts settled in the region about 450 B.C. But the population also owes its ancestry to invaders, such as the Romans, Vikings, and Normans. There has recently been further diversification with the arrival of immigrants from Africa, Asia, and the West Indies.

The United Kingdom once ruled the largest empire in history. Though the imperial era has ended, the country remains a world power.

The British Isles consists of two large islands and more than 5,000 smaller ones, rising from the continental shelf off the coast of northwest Europe. It was cut off from the mainland about 7,500 years ago when melting ice sheets filled the North Sea and English Channel.

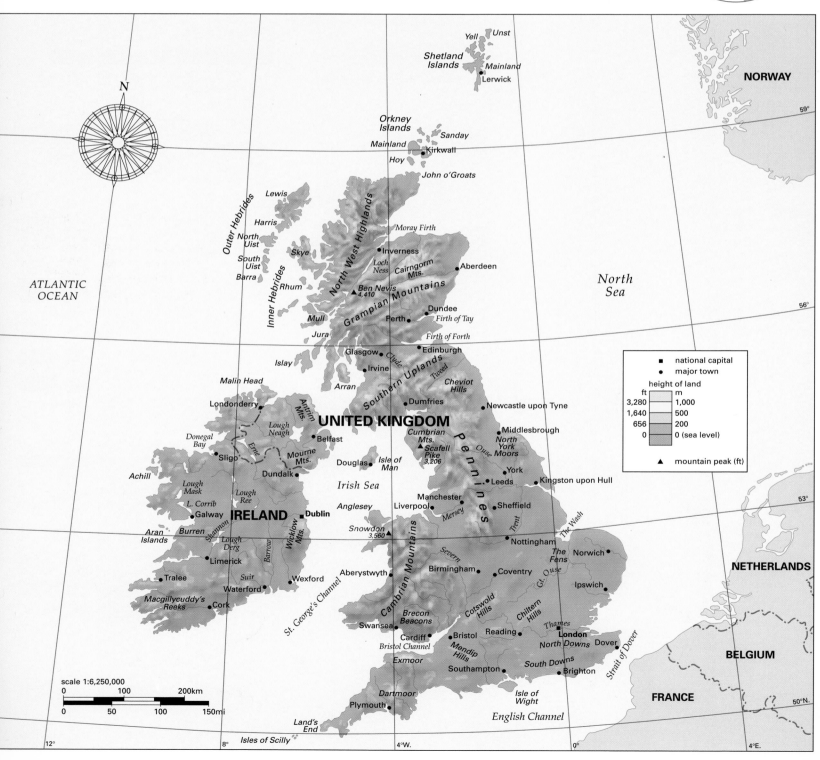

THE POLITICAL AND CULTURAL WORLD

The United Kingdom of Great Britain and Northern Ireland is often called Britain. Great Britain consists of England; Wales, which was absorbed by England in 1277; and Scotland, which was formally united with England under the Act of Union of 1707.

Ireland was united with Great Britain in 1801, but it became independent in 1921, with the exception of the six counties of Northern Ireland, which stayed in the United Kingdom.

The rest of Ireland is now a republic, while Britain is a constitutional monarchy. The Channel Islands and the Isle of Man are self-governing territories under the British Crown.

COUNTRIES IN THE REGION

Ireland, United Kingdom

Island territories Channel Islands, Isle of Man (U.K.)
Territories outside the region Anguilla, Ascension, Bermuda, British Indian Ocean Territory, British Virgin Islands, Cayman Islands, Falkland Islands, Gibraltar, Montserrat, Pitcairn Island, St. Helena, South Georgia, South Sandwich Islands, Tristan de Cunha, Turks and Caicos Islands (U.K.)

RELIGION

Ireland Roman Catholic (93.1%), Anglican (2.8%), Protestant (0.4%), others (3.7%)
United Kingdom Anglican (56.8%), Roman Catholic (13.1%), Protestant (12.7%), nonreligious (8.8%), Muslim (1.4%), Jewish (0.8%), Hindu (0.7%), Sikh (0.4%)

LANGUAGE

Country with one official language (English) U.K.
Country with two official languages (English, Irish) Ireland

Local minority languages are Gaelic, Irish, and Welsh. Significant immigrant languages include Bengali, Chinese, Greek, Gujarati, Italian, Polish, and Punjabi.

STYLES OF GOVERNMENT

Republic Ireland
Monarchy United Kingdom
Multiparty states Ireland, U.K.
Two-chamber assembly Ireland, U.K.

MEMBERSHIP OF INTERNATIONAL ORGANIZATIONS

Council of Europe Ireland, U.K.
Colombo Plan U.K.
European Union (EU) Ireland, U.K.
North Atlantic Treaty Organization (NATO) U.K.
Organization for Economic Cooperation and Development (OECD) Ireland, U.K.

ECONOMIC INDICATORS

	Ireland	United Kingdom
GDP (US$ billions)	72.7	1,278.4
GNP per capita (US$)	16,740	20,520
Annual rate of growth of GDP, 1988–1998	7.3%	1.7%
Manufacturing as % of GDP	n/a	19.9%
Central government spending as % of GNP	36.3%	41.4%
Merchandise exports (US$ billions)	45.5	259.0
Merchandise imports (US$ billions)	35.7	283.7
Aid given as % of GDP	0.3%	0.27%

WELFARE INDICATORS

	Ireland	United Kingdom
Infant mortality rate (per 1,000 live births)		
1965	25	20
1998	7	7
Daily food supply available (calories per capita, 1996)	3,636	3,237
Teacher–pupil ratio (primary school, 1995)	1 : 23.5	1 : 21.2

Shetland
Islands
●Lerwick

■ national capital
▪ regional capital
● other town

Orkney
Islands ●Kirkwall

Ireland
Area 27,135 sq mi (70,280 sq km)
Population 3,797,257
Capital Dublin
Currency 1 Irish pound (Ir£) = 100 new pence
Euro (€) also in use
€ = 100 cents

United Kingdom
Area 94,526 sq mi (244,820 sq km)
Population 59,511,464
Capital London
Currency 1 pound sterling (£) = 100 new pence

Outer Hebrides
Lewis
Inner Hebrides
Skye ●Inverness
●Aberdeen
SCOTLAND
Mull
Jura
Perth● ●Dundee
Islay Greenock● ●Edinburgh
Glasgow● ●Motherwell
●Irvine
Arran
Dumfries● Newcastle upon Tyne●
●Londonderry
NORTHERN IRELAND ■Belfast Middlesbrough●
●Sligo Isle of Man ●Douglas **UNITED KINGDOM**
Achill Island
Dundalk● York●
Drogheda● Leeds● ●Kingston upon Hull
Bradford●
Manchester●
Anglesey ●Liverpool ●Sheffield
●Galway **Dublin**■ Holyhead●
Aran Islands **IRELAND** Stoke on Trent● Derby● ●Nottingham
●Limerick **ENGLAND** ●Norwich
Birmingham● ●Coventry
●Wexford Aberystwyth● ●Cambridge
Waterford● Northampton● ●Ipswich
●Cork **WALES** Gloucester●
Swansea● Newport● ●Oxford
Cardiff■ ●Bristol **London**■
Reading● Dover●
Southampton● ●Brighton
●Exeter Portsmouth●
Isle of Wight
Plymouth● ●Torbay

Regional loyalties are strong throughout the British Isles. Both Scotland and Wales have nationalist movements that have demanded a greater degree of home rule and local parliaments.

FRANCE

France is the largest country in Western Europe. Its varied landscapes include rolling plains, hills, beautiful river valleys, the remains of ancient volcanoes, and dramatic mountain scenery in the Alps and Pyrenees.

The north has a cool temperate climate, while the south has the typical hot summers and mild, moist winters of Mediterranean lands. Other variations occur from west to east. While the west comes under the moderating influence of the Atlantic, to the east the climate becomes increasingly continental. Summers are hotter and winters are much colder.

The French have a strong sense of identity, a pride in their culture, and a firm belief in the preeminence of their capital, Paris, as a world center of art and learning. Yet the French owe their origins to many diverse groups, including Celts, Romans, Franks, and Vikings. Recent immigration has been from North Africa, Southeast Asia, and other parts of Europe.

France is a major industrial power, with an increasingly urbanized population. It is also the largest producer of farm products in Western Europe. It is especially famous for its fine wines and wide range of cheeses.

Northern France lies at the western end of the North European Plain – an ancient pathway of human migrations – that extends from the Ural Mountains of Russia to southeastern England. The south and southeast lie in a zone where the African and Eurasian plates have collided, thrusting up young ranges, including the snow-capped Pyrenees and Alps.

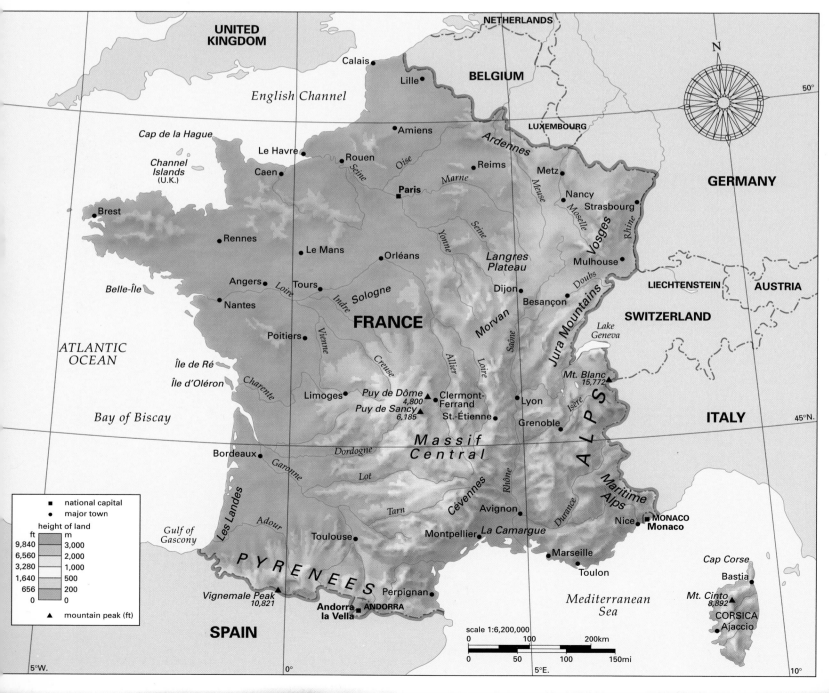

THE POLITICAL AND CULTURAL WORLD

Modern France owes its origins to the French Revolution of 1789 and its principles of liberty, equality, and fraternity, which have been incorporated into the constitutions of many other countries. Today France is a parliamentary democracy, whose executive branch is headed by the president and the prime minister.

France has two of Europe's ministates as neighbors. Nestling in the Pyrenees is the tiny state of Andorra, a principality whose heads of state are the president of France and the bishop of Urgel in Spain. The other ministate is Monaco, a principality ruled by the House of Grimaldi since 1308.

COUNTRIES IN THE REGION

Andorra, France, Monaco

Island provinces Corsica (France)
Territories outside the region French Guiana, French Polynesia, Guadeloupe, Martinique, Mayotte, New Caledonia, Réunion, St. Pierre and Miquelon, Wallis and Futuna (France)

France has a territorial claim in Antarctica.

LANGUAGE

Countries with one official language (Catalan) Andorra; (French) France, Monaco

Local minority languages in France are Basque, Breton, Catalan, Corsican, Flemish, German (Alsatian), and Provençal. Significant immigrant languages include Arabic, Italian, Polish, Portuguese, Spanish, and Turkish. English, Italian, and Monégasque are spoken in Monaco; Spanish in Andorra.

RELIGION

Andorra Roman Catholic (94.2%)
France Roman Catholic (76%), Muslim (3%), non-religious and atheist (3%) Protestant (2%), Jewish (1%)
Monaco Roman Catholic (91%), Anglican (1%), Protestant (1%), Eastern Orthodox (1%)

STYLES OF GOVERNMENT

Republic France
Principalities Andorra, Monaco
Multiparty state France
States without parties Andorra, Monaco
One-chamber assembly Andorra
Two-chamber assembly France, Monaco

MEMBERSHIP OF INTERNATIONAL ORGANIZATIONS

Council of Europe France
European Union (EU) France
North Atlantic Treaty Organization (NATO) France
Organization for Economic Cooperation and Development (OECD) France

ECONOMIC INDICATORS

	France
GDP (US$ trillions)	1.394
GNP per capita (US$)	21,860
Annual rate of growth of GDP, 1990–1997	1.3%
Manufacturing as % of GDP	21.8%
Central government spending as % of GDP	51.6%
Merchandise exports (US$ billions)	284.2
Merchandise imports (US$ billions)	256.1
Aid given as % of GNP (France)	0.46%

WELFARE INDICATORS

	France
Infant mortality rate (per 1,000 live births)	
1965	22
1997	6
Daily food supply available (calories per capita, 1995)	3,588
Population per physician (1996)	345
Internet users (million, 1998)	2.5

France
Area 211,210 sq mi (547,030 sq km)
Population 59,329,691
Currency 1 franc (f) = 100 centimes
Euro (€) also in use
€ = 100 cents

Andorra
Area 181 sq mi (468 sq km)
Population 66,824
Currency 1 French franc (f) = 100 centimes
1 Spanish peseta (Pts) = 100 céntimos

Monaco
Area 0.75 sq mi (1.95 sq km)
Population 31,693
Currency 1 French franc (f) = 100 centimes

- national capital
- regional capital
- other town

France is divided into 22 metropolitan regions, each governed by an elected council and its own president. The regions are responsible for their own economic planning. The regions are divided into 96 metropolitan departments, each with its own elected council. These councils are responsible for local social services.

SPAIN AND PORTUGAL

Spain, Portugal, and the tiny British dependency of Gibraltar, which occupies a strategic position near the Strait of Gibraltar, form the Iberian Peninsula, isolated from the rest of Europe by the Pyrenees Mountains.

Much of the peninsula is a high plateau, called the Meseta. The Meseta is bordered not only by the Pyrenees, but also by the Cantabrian Mountains in the northwest and the Sierra Nevada in the southeast. Because of its altitude, the Meseta has a severe climate, with hot summers and bitterly cold winters. The Meseta is arid, and parts of the southeast are semidesert. Lowland Portugal's climate is moderated by moist Atlantic winds. Other lowlands include the Ebro and Guadalquivir river valleys in Spain.

From early times, Iberia was invaded by waves of colonizers, including Celts, Phoenicians, Greeks, Carthaginians, Romans, and Visigoths, each of whom left their imprint on Iberian culture. The last invaders were the Moors (Muslim Arabs), who entered the peninsula in the year 711. Their last bastion, the Alhambra palace in Granada, did not fall until 1492, the year Columbus sailed from Spain.

Although Spain and Portugal were both leaders in terms of world exploration, both countries were, by the early twentieth century, among Europe's poorest. Today, as members of the European Union, their economies have been expanding quickly, and Spain is growing especially rapidly. Tourism plays a major part in the economies of both countries.

The Iberian Peninsula occupies the south-western corner of Europe. Separated from North Africa by the Strait of Gibraltar, Iberia often seems to visitors to be almost as much African as European. Spain also includes the Balearic Islands in the Mediterranean and the Canary Islands in the Atlantic. Portugal has two autonomous regions, the Azores in the North Atlantic and the Madeira Islands off the northwest coast of Africa.

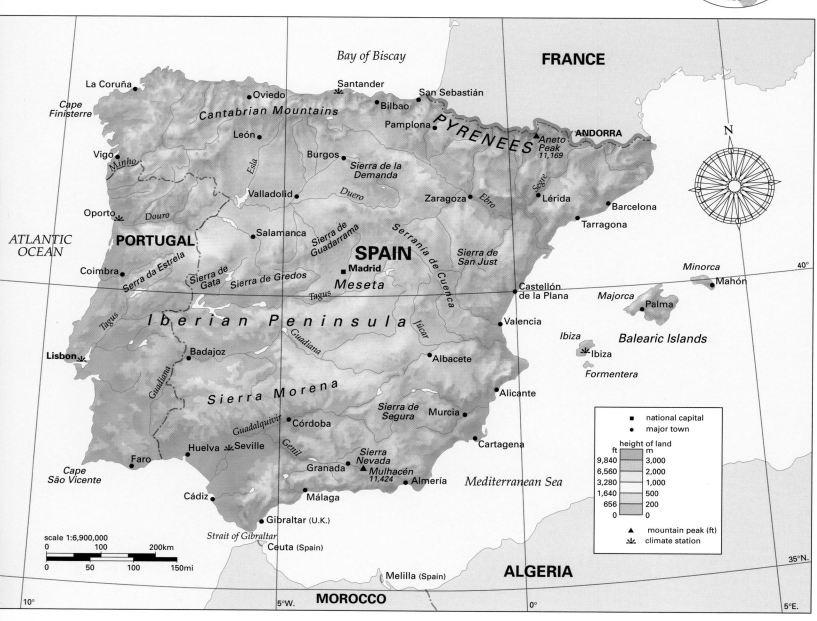

THE POLITICAL AND CULTURAL WORLD

After the Spanish civil war (1936–1939), Spain became a dictatorship under General Franco. When he died in 1975, the monarchy was restored, and Spain became a parliamentary democracy. Between 1928 and 1974, Portugal was also a dictatorship. But after the overthrow of its military leaders, it became a democratic republic.

Spain claims Gibraltar, the world's smallest colony, but Britain justifies its control over the territory by arguing that the majority of Gibraltarians want to remain British. Despite the lack of agreement over sovereignty, cooperation over such matters as the shared use of Gibraltar's airport has increased.

Portugal

Area 35,672 sq mi
(92,389 sq km)
Population 10,048,000
Capital Lisbon
Currency 1 escudo
(Esc) = 100 centavos
Euro (€) also in use
€ = 100 cents

Both Spain and Portugal are now democracies; Spain was governed by General Franco until 1975 and Portugal by the dictator Salazar until 1968. Spain's head of state is King Juan Carlos, who came to the throne in 1975.

COUNTRIES IN THE REGION

Portugal, Spain

Territories outside the region Azores, Madeira (Portugal); Balearic Islands, Canary Islands, Ceuta, Melilla (Spain)

LAND

Highest point on mainland, Mulhacén, 11,424 ft (3,482 m); Pico de Teide on Tenerife in the Canary Islands, 12,195 ft (3,718 m)
Lowest point sea level
Major features Meseta plateau in center, Cantabrian Mountains and Pyrenees in north, Sierra Nevada in south

WATER

Longest river Tagus, 630 mi (1,010 km)
Largest basin Duero, 38,000 sq mi (98,000 sq km)
Highest average flow Duero, 11,000 cu ft/sec (312 cu m/sec)

CLIMATE

	Temperature °F (°C) January	July	Altitude ft (m)
Oporto	48 (9)	68 (20)	239 (73)
Lisbon	52 (11)	72 (22)	361 (110)
Santander	48 (9)	66 (19)	210 (64)
Seville	50 (10)	79 (26)	43 (13)
Ibiza	52 (11)	75 (24)	23 (7)

	Precipitation inches (mm) January	July	Year
Oporto	6.3 (159)	0.8 (20)	45.3 (1,150)
Lisbon	4.4 (111)	0.1 (3)	27.9 (708)
Santander	4.9 (124)	2.5 (64)	47.6 (1,208)
Seville	2.9 (73)	0.4 (1)	22.0 (559)
Ibiza	1.7 (42)	0.2 (5)	17.5 (444)

LANGUAGE

Countries with one official language
(Portuguese) Portugal; (Spanish) Spain

Local minority languages spoken in Spain are Basque, Catalan, and Galician.

RELIGION

Portugal Roman Catholic (94%), nonreligious and atheist (3.8%)
Spain Roman Catholic (97%), nonreligious and atheist (2.6%), Protestant (0.4%)

STYLES OF GOVERNMENT

Republic Portugal
Monarchy Spain
Multiparty states Portugal, Spain
One-chamber assembly Portugal
Two-chamber assembly Spain

ECONOMIC INDICATORS

	Spain	Portugal
GDP (US$ billions)	531.3	97.5
GNP per capita (US$)	15,720	13,840
Annual rate of growth of GDP, 1990–1997	1.6%	2.1%
Manufacturing as % of GDP	23.7%*	25.8%
Central government spending as % of GDP	38.2%	44.2%
Merchandise exports (US$ billions)	104.5	24.7
Merchandise imports (US$ billions)	117.8	34.3
Aid given as % of GNP	0.22%	0.21%

* Includes mining and public utilities.

WELFARE INDICATORS

	Spain	Portugal
Infant mortality rate (per 1,000 live births)		
1965	38	65
2000	4.99	6.05
Daily food supply available (calories per capita, 1995)	3,338	3,639
Population per physician (1996)	238	333
Teacher-pupil ratio (primary school, 1995)	1 : 17.8	1 : 12.4

■ national capital
● other town

(map of Spain and Portugal with cities: La Coruña, Gijón, Santander, Oviedo, Bilbao, San Sebastián, Santiago de Compostela, Vitoria, Pamplona, León, Logroño, Vigo, Burgos, Figueras, Braga, Valladolid, Soria, Zaragoza, Lérida, Gerona, Vila Real, Calatayud, Barcelona, Oporto, Salamanca, Segovia, Tortosa, Tarragona, Aveiro, Viseu, Ciudad Rodrigo, Ávila, Coimbra, Guarda, Madrid, PORTUGAL, Castelo Branco, Cuenca, Castellón de la Plana, Balearic Islands, Palma, Minorca, Toledo, Valencia, Majorca, Santarém, Portalegre, Cáceres, SPAIN, Ibiza, Lisbon, Badajoz, Mérida, Ciudad Real, Albacete, Formentera, Setúbal, Évora, Elche, Alicante, Beja, Linares, Murcia, Córdoba, Cartagena, Portimão, Faro, Huelva, Seville, Granada, Jerez de la Frontera, Málaga, Almería, Cádiz, Gibraltar (U.K.))

Area 194,885 sq mi
(504,750 sq km)
Population 39,996,671
Capital Madrid
Currency 1 peseta
(Pta) = 100 centimos
Euro (€) also in use
€ = 100 cents

Spain

ITALY AND GREECE

Italy and Greece occupy a region where the earth's crust is unstable; there are frequent earthquakes and spectacular volcanic eruptions, especially in southern Italy. The snow-capped Alps in northern Italy were raised up as the result of a collision between the northward-moving African plate and the Eurasian plate.

About 40 percent of the land is mountainous, the Po valley being the most extensive lowland.

The coastlands, with their hot, dry summers and mild, wet winters, are tourist magnets for north Europeans. But the mountains of southern Italy and Greece can be bitterly cold and snowy in the winter months.

The ancient ruins of Greece and Italy are testimony to two major civilizations, whose art, philosophy, and politics lie at the heart of European culture.

Italy and Greece are on two peninsulas that jut into the Mediterranean Sea. Both countries include many islands. Around 440 islands make up about one-fifth of Greece's area. Malta is an island republic south of Sicily. Cyprus is another island republic in the east.

THE POLITICAL AND CULTURAL WORLD

Italy and Greece both underwent periods of instability and dictatorship in the twentieth century, though today they are democratic republics.

Greece has a long-standing dispute with Turkey over Cyprus, an island with a Greek majority and a Turkish minority. In 1974 Greece's military regime was implicated in moves to unite Cyprus with Greece. (Cyprus had been independent since 1960.) Turkey invaded northern Cyprus and set up the Turkish Republic of Northern Cyprus, a state that is recognized only by Turkey.

Cyprus
Area 3,572 sq mi
(9,251 sq km)
Population 758,363
Capital Nicosia
Currency 1 Cyprus pound
(C£) = 100 cents
[1 Turkish lira (TL) = 100 kurus]

Greece
Area 50,949 sq mi
(131,957 sq km)
Population 10,601,527
Capital Athens
Currency 1 drachma
(Dr) = 100 lepta
Euro (€) also in use
€ = 100 cents

- ▪ national capital
- • other town

COUNTRIES IN THE REGION

Cyprus, Greece, Italy, Malta, San Marino, Vatican City

Island areas Aegean Islands, Crete, Ionian Islands, (Greece); Egadi Islands, Elba, Capri, Ischia, Lipari Islands, Pantelleria, Ponza, Sardinia, Sicily (Italy)

LAND

Highest point Monte Rosa, 15,204 ft (4,634 m)
Lowest point sea level
Major features Alps, Apennines, Pindus Mountains, Po valley, islands including Sardinia, Crete, Greek archipelago, and Cyprus

WATER

Longest river Po, 380 mi (620 km)
Largest basin Po, 29,000 sq mi (75,000 sq km)
Highest average flow Po, 54,000 cu ft/sec (1,540 cu m/sec)
Largest lake Garda, 140 sq mi (370 sq km)

CLIMATE

	Temperature °F (°C)		Altitude
	January	July	ft (m)
Genoa	46 (8)	75 (24)	69 (21)
Venice	36 (2)	73 (23)	7 (2)
Messina	52 (11)	79 (26)	177 (54)
Salonika	42 (6)	82 (28)	226 (69)
Athens	48 (9)	82 (28)	351 (107)

	Precipitation inches (mm)		
	January	July	Year
Genoa	3.1 (79)	1.6 (40)	50 (1,270)
Venice	2.0 (50)	2.6 (67)	33.6 (854)
Messina	5.7 (146)	0.7 (19)	38.3 (974)
Salonika	1.7 (45)	0.9 (23)	18.3 (465)
Athens	2.4 (62)	0.4 (1)	13.3 (339)

LANGUAGE

Countries with one official language : Greece (Greek); Italy, San Marino (Italian)
Countries with two official languages Malta (English, Maltese); Cyprus (Greek, Turkish); Vatican City (Italian, Latin)

Other languages spoken in the region include Albanian, Macedonian, and Turkish (Greece); Albanian, Catalan, French, German, Greek, Ladin, Sardinian, and Slovenian (Italy).

RELIGION

Cyprus Greek Orthodox (80%), Muslim (19%)
Greece Greek Orthodox (97.6%), Muslim (1.5%), other Christian (0.5%)
Italy Roman Catholic (81.7%), nonreligious and atheist (13.6%), Muslim (1.2%), others (3.5%)
Malta Roman Catholic (97.3%), Anglican (1.2%), others (1.5%)
San Marino Roman Catholic (95%), nonreligious and atheist (3%)
Vatican City Roman Catholic (100%)

STYLES OF GOVERNMENT

Republics Cyprus, Greece, Italy, Malta, San Marino
City state Vatican City
Multiparty states Cyprus, Greece, Italy, Malta, San Marino
State without parties Vatican City
One-chamber assembly Cyprus, Greece, Malta, San Marino
Two-chamber assembly Italy

ECONOMIC INDICATORS

	Greece	Italy
GDP (US$ billions)	119.1	1.212 trillion
GNP per capita (US$)	13,080	20,060
Annual rate of growth of GDP, 1990–1997	1.6%	1.1%
Manufacturing as % of GDP	13.9%	16.4%
Central government spending as % of GDP	33.6%	48.6%
Merchandise exports (US$ billions)	5.6	238.2
Merchandise imports (US$ billions)	21	191.5
Aid given as % of GNP	0.16%	

WELFARE INDICATORS

	Greece	Italy
Infant mortality rate (per 1,000 live births)		
1965	34	36
2000	8	7
Daily food supply available (calories per capita, 1995)	3,825	3,216
Population per physician (1995)	256	182
Teacher-pupil ratio (primary school, 1995)	1 : 22	1 : 12

Italy
Area 116,324 sq mi
(301,277 sq km)
Population 57,634,327
Capital Rome
Currency 1 lira
(Lit) = 100 centesimi
Euro (€) also in use
€ = 100 cents

Malta
Area 122 sq mi
(316 sq km)
Population 391,670
Capital Valletta
Currency 1 Maltese lira
(Lm) = 100 cents = 1,000 mils

San Marino
Area 24 sq mi
(61 sq km)
Population 26,937
Capital San Marino
Currency 1 Italian lira
(Lit) = 100 centesimi

Vatican City
Area 0.17 sq mi
(0.44 sq km)
Population 900
Currency 1 Vatican lira
(VL) = 1 Italian lira = 100 centesimi

Both Italy and Greece are republics that once had monarchies and abolished them. Both are highly centralized states. Malta has been a democratic republic within the British Commonwealth since 1964. San Marino claims to be the world's oldest republic.

CENTRAL EUROPE AND THE LOW COUNTRIES

The Low Countries—Belgium, Luxembourg, and the Netherlands—together with northern Germany are part of the North European Plain. The flat land of the north contrasts with the spectacular rugged Alpine scenery in the south, which includes Switzerland, Liechtenstein, and Austria.

Most people of the region speak Germanic languages, notably Dutch and German, though French is spoken in Belgium and Switzerland. Highly efficient farms are found throughout the region. Manufacturing is the main source of wealth, and products include chemicals, electronic goods, and vehicles.

The Low Countries and their neighbors in Central Europe form part of the world's temperate zone. In the Low Countries, large areas are below sea level—much of the Netherlands has been reclaimed from the sea. The Alps in the south contain majestic peaks and sparkling lakes.

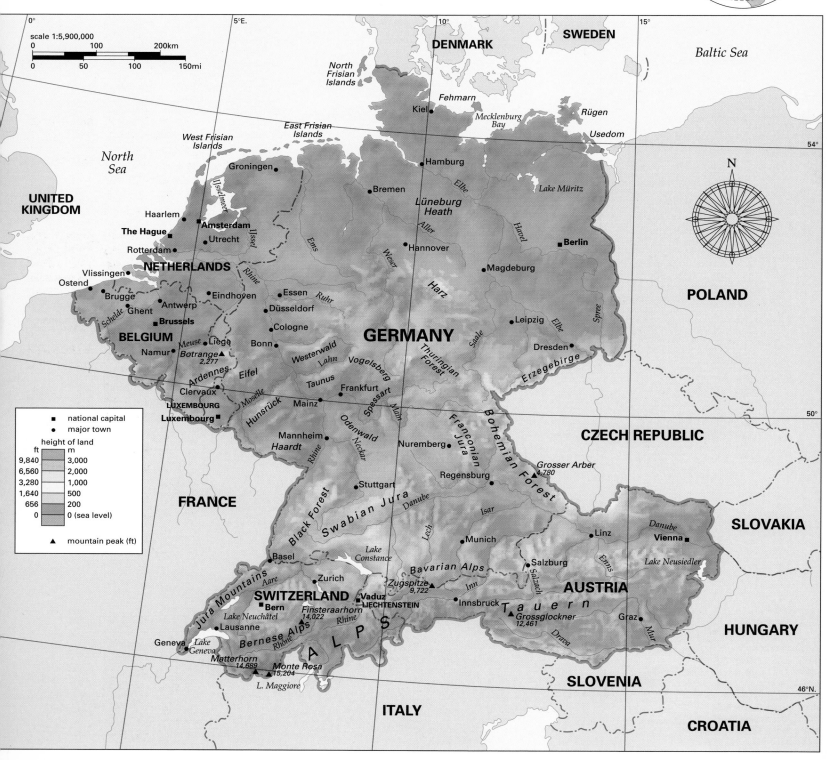

scale 1:5,900,000

| national capital |
| major town |

height of land

ft	m
9,840	3,000
6,560	2,000
3,280	1,000
1,640	500
656	200
0	0 (sea level)

▲ mountain peak (ft)

THE POLITICAL AND CULTURAL WORLD

Of the seven countries in the region, four are parliamentary democracies with monarchs as heads of state. They are the kingdoms of Belgium and the Netherlands, the Grand Duchy of Luxembourg, and the Principality of Liechtenstein. The other three countries—Austria, Germany, and Switzerland—are federal republics.

After World War II, Central Europe played an important part in the Cold War. But communism collapsed in Eastern Europe in 1990. West and East Germany, which were divided in 1945, were reunified politically. The task of economic integration, however, proved to be more costly than many Germans had expected.

COUNTRIES IN THE REGION

Austria, Belgium, Germany, Liechtenstein, Luxembourg, Netherlands, Switzerland

Territories outside the region
Aruba, Netherlands Antilles (Netherlands)

LANGUAGE

Countries with one official language (Dutch) Netherlands; (German) Austria, Germany, Liechtenstein
Country with two official languages (French, German) Luxembourg
Countries with three official languages (Dutch, French, German) Belgium; (French, German, Italian) Switzerland

RELIGION

Austria Roman Catholic (85%), Protestant (6%), other (9%)
Belgium Roman Catholic (90%), nonreligious and atheist (7.5%), Muslim (1.1%), Protestant (0.4%)
Germany Protestant (40.8%), Roman Catholic (33.9%), nonreligious and atheist (3.6%), Muslim (2.1%), other (19.6%)
Liechtenstein Roman Catholic (87.3%), Protestant (8.3%), other (4.4%)
Luxembourg Roman Catholic (97%), Protestant (1.3%)
Netherlands Roman Catholic (32%), nonreligious and atheist (38%), Dutch Reformed (15%), Muslim (4.3%)
Switzerland Roman Catholic (47.6%), Protestant (44.3%)

STYLES OF GOVERNMENT

Republics Austria, Germany, Switzerland
Monarchies Belgium, Liechtenstein, Luxembourg, Netherlands
Federal states Austria, Germany, Switzerland
Multiparty states Austria, Belgium, Germany, Liechtenstein, Luxembourg, Netherlands, Switzerland
One-chamber assembly Liechtenstein
Two-chamber assembly Austria, Belgium, Germany, Netherlands, Switzerland

ECONOMIC INDICATORS

	Belguim	Netherlands
GDP (US$ billions)	242.5	360.5
GNP per capita (US$)	22,370	21,340
Annual rate of growth of GDP, 1990–1997	1.4%	2.4%
Manufacturing as % of GDP	19%	18%
Central government spending as % of GDP	49.4%	50.8%
Merchandise exports (US$ billions)	150.4	163.7
Merchandise imports (US$ billions)	142.9	146.0
Aid given as % of GNP	0.34%	0.81%

WELFARE INDICATORS

	Belgium	Netherlands
Infant mortality rate (per 1,000 live births)		
1965	24	14
2000	4.76	4.42
Daily food supply available (calories per capita, 1995)	3,530	3,230
Population per physician (1995)	267	394
Teacher-pupil ratio (primary school, 1995)	1 : 13	1 : 16

Austria
Area 32,377 sq mi (83,857 sq km)
Population 8,131,111
Currency 1 Schilling (S) = 100 Groschen
Euro (€) also in use
€ = 100 cents

Belgium
Area 11,782 sq mi (30,518 sq km)
Population 10,241,506
Currency 1 Belgian franc (BF) = 100 centimes
Euro (€) also in use
€ = 100 cents

■ national capital
• other town

Germany
Area 137,821 sq mi (356,954 sq km)
Population 82,797,408
Currency 1 Deutsche mark (DM) = 100 Pfennig
Euro (€) also in use
€ = 100 cents

Liechtenstein
Area 62 sq mi (160 sq km)
Population 32,207
Currency 1 Swiss franc (SF) = 100 centimes

Luxembourg
Area 998 sq mi (2,586 sq km)
Population 437,389
Currency 1 Luxembourg franc (LuxF) = 100 centimes
Euro (€) also in use
€ = 100 cents

Netherlands
Area 16,163 sq mi (41,863 sq km)
Population 15,892,237
Currency 1 guilder (G) = 100 cents
Euro (€) also in use
€ = 100 cents

Belgium, Luxembourg, Netherlands, and former West Germany were founder members in the 1950s of what is now the European Union. Both Switzerland and Liechtenstein were politically neutral during both world wars, while Austria was allied to Germany. After its defeat in 1945, Germany was divided, and its eastern part came under Soviet influence. The two parts of the country were reunited in October 1990.

Switzerland
Area 15,943 sq mi (41,293 sq km)
Population 7,262,372
Currency 1 Swiss franc (SF) = 100 centimes

Map labels

North Frisian Islands
Flensburg
Kiel
Fehmarn
East Frisian Islands
Rostock
West Frisian Islands
Lübeck
Schwerin
Bremerhaven
Hamburg
Groningen
Oldenburg
Bremen
NETHERLANDS
Zwolle
Haarlem
Amsterdam
Enschede
Osnabrück
Hannover
Brunswick
Berlin
The Hague
Utrecht
Rotterdam
Arnhem
Bielefeld
Hildesheim
Potsdam
Magdeburg
Nijmegen
Münster
Vlissingen
Eindhoven
Essen
Dortmund
Göttingen
Cottbus
Ostend
Brugge
Duisburg
Ghent
Antwerp
Düsseldorf
Kassel
Leipzig
Brussels
Maastricht
Cologne
Erfurt
Dresden
BELGIUM
Liège
Aachen
Bonn
GERMANY
Chemnitz
Mons
Namur
Koblenz
Wiesbaden
Frankfurt
LUXEMBOURG
Mainz
Offenbach
Arlon
Luxembourg
Würzburg
Mannheim
Saarbrücken
Nuremberg
Karlsruhe
Regensburg
Stuttgart
Ulm
Augsburg
Linz
St. Pölten
Vienna
Freiburg
Munich
Wels
Basel
Salzburg
Eisenstadt
St. Gall
Bregenz
Bad Ischl
Zurich
Neuchâtel
Bern
Lucerne
Vaduz
LIECHTENSTEIN
Innsbruck
AUSTRIA
Fohnsdorf
SWITZERLAND
Chur
Lienz
Graz
Lausanne
Geneva
Sion
Villach
Klagenfurt
Bellinzona

EASTERN EUROPE

Eastern Europe extends from the dune-lined Baltic coast in the north, through part of the North European Plain in Poland and a series of uplands in the south, to the Adriatic Sea in the southwest, and the Black Sea, outlet of the Danube River, in the southeast. An important plain in the region is the Great Alföld in Hungary. The north is cold and dry, but the south has a subtropical climate.

The region is culturally complex. It contains several language groups, including Slavic, Germanic, Finno-Ugric, and Romance languages. Religions, mainly Roman Catholicism, Orthodox Christianity, and Islam, also characterize the people.

Agriculture was the chief activity in the past. Under communism, however, great efforts were made to industrialize the region. This has caused extensive damage to the environment.

Eastern Europe extends from the cool Baltic Sea region in the north to the Mediterranean lands in the south. Until 1989, Eastern Europe formed a buffer zone of communist states between Western Europe and the Soviet Union. By 2001 some were considering joining the European Union.

THE POLITICAL AND CULTURAL WORLD

Eastern Europe contains 12 countries. Of these, Bosnia and Herzegovina, Croatia, Macedonia, Slovenia, and Yugoslavia (now consisting only of Serbia and Montenegro) made up Yugoslavia between 1918 and 1991. The Czech Republic and Slovakia came into being on January 1, 1993, when Czechoslovakia was divided into two parts.

This group of formerly communist countries has faced many problems since the collapse of their ideology in the late 1980s and early 1990s. Rivalries between ethnic groups have resurfaced, causing civil war in Yugoslavia, most recently in Kosovo. The countries have also faced many problems as they seek to reestablish free-enterprise economies.

Major changes occurred in Eastern Europe in the 1980s and 1990s. Those countries under communist rule emerged as struggling new democracies. Both Yugoslavia and Czechoslovakia refused to remain artificial unions of diverse nations, and they divided, in Yugoslavia's case with great violence and bloodshed. All the region's nations face economic hardship.

■ national capital
● other town

Albania
Area 11,100 sq mi (28,748 sq km)
Population 3,490,435

Bosnia and Herzegovina
Area 19,741 sq mi (51,129 sq km)
Population 3,835,777

Bulgaria
Area 42,855 sq mi (110,994 sq km)
Population 8,194,772

Area 21,829 sq mi (56,538 sq km)
Population 4,282,216
 Croatia

Area 30,450 sq mi (78,865 sq km)
Population 10,272,179
 Czech Republic

Area 35,919 sq mi (93,031 sq km)
Population 10,138,844
 Hungary

Area 9,928 sq mi (25, 713 sq km)
Population 2,041,467
 Macedonia

Area 120,728 sq mi (312,683 sq km)
Population 38,646,023
 Poland

Area 91,699 sq mi (237,500 sq km)
Population 22,411,121
 Romania

Area 18,933 sq mi (49,035 sq km)
Population 5,407,956
 Slovakia

Area 7,819 sq mi (20,251 sq km)
Population 1,927,593
 Slovenia

Area 39,518 sq mi (102,350 sq km)
Population 10,662,087
 Yugoslavia

RUSSIA AND ITS NEIGHBORS

The region covers about one-sixth of the world's land area. It straddles two continents, including the eastern parts of Europe and the northern part of Asia. It contains Russia, which stretches from the Baltic Sea to the Bering Sea, a distance of about 6,000 miles (9,650 km). Russia is also divided between Europe and Asia. The boundary runs down the Ural Mountains, through the Caspian Sea, and along the crest of the Caucasus Mountains.

The region consists of the 15 republics that made up the Soviet Union, together with land-locked Mongolia. In the west is part of the North European Plain, which extends from northern France to the Ural Mountains. East of the Urals is Siberia, a vast landscape of plains and plateaus, with uplands in the east. The far east contains the Kamchatka Peninsula, which has active volcanoes and forms part of the Pacific "ring of fire." In the southwest is the Caucasus Mountain range between the Black and Caspian seas. Further south are two bleak deserts, the Kara Kum and the Kyzyl Kum. On the region's southern flanks are the Pamirs and the Altai Mountains, which extend into Mongolia. Mongolia contains part of the cold Gobi Desert.

The former Soviet government recognized the existence of almost 100 nationalities within its borders. Slavs, including Belarusians, Russians, and Ukrainians, form the largest group. Like most people in the western part of the region, including Latvians and Lithuanians, their languages belong to the Indo-European family.

During the Cold War, the threat of the Soviet Union's military strength was pitted against that of the West. But economic crises in the late 1980s, caused partly by the high expenditure on defense, led to the collapse of communism and the breakup of the country. The newly independent Baltic states restored links with the neighboring Nordic and western European countries. But general political unrest and corruption has troubled Russia throughout the 1990s.

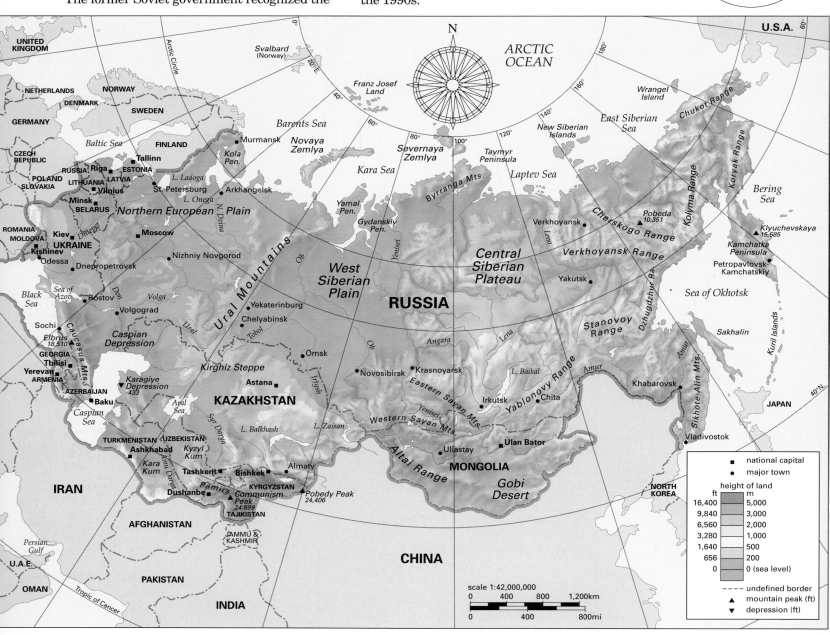

THE POLITICAL AND CULTURAL WORLD

Dramatic changes occurred in the late 1980s, when the leaders of the Soviet Union introduced new policies that involved radical political changes and the introduction of free market trading and private ownership. Estonia, Latvia, and Lithuania, former republics of the Soviet Union, became independent nations in 1991, and at the end of that year, the Soviet Union was formally abolished. The remaining 12 republics became independent states, though they retained contact through a loose structure called the Commonwealth of Independent States (C.I.S.). Mongolia followed the Soviet Union in abandoning communism in 1992.

In May 2000, Russia imposed direct rule on the independent Islamic republic of Chechnya. This followed nearly a decade of fighting during which thousands of people were killed.

The newly independent countries in the region include Estonia, Latvia, and Lithuania in the northeast, and Belarus and Ukraine in the west. Moldova lies south of Ukraine. Between the Black Sea and the Caspian Sea lie Georgia, Azerbaijan, and Armenia.

- national capital
- other town

Russia
Area 6,592,786 sq mi (17,075,200 sq km)
Population 146,001,176
Capital Moscow

Estonia
Area 17,462 sq mi (45,226 sq km)
Population 1,431,471
Capital Tallinn

Latvia
Area 24,938 sq mi (64,589 sq km)
Population 2,404,926
Capital Riga

Tajikistan
Area 55,251 sq mi (143,100 sq km)
Population 6,440,732
Capital Dushanbe

Armenia
Area 11,506 sq mi (29,800 sq km)
Population 3,344,336
Capital Yerevan

Georgia
Area 26,911 sq mi (69,700 sq km)
Population 5,019,538
Capital Tbilisi

Lithuania
Area 25,174 sq mi (65,200 sq km)
Population 3,620,756
Capital Vilnius

Turkmenistan
Area 188,457 sq mi (488,100 sq km)
Population 4,518,268
Capital Ashkhabad

Azerbaijan
Area 33,437 sq mi (86,600 sq km)
Population 7,748,163
Capital Baku

Kazakhstan
Area 1,049,158 sq mi (2,717,300 sq km)
Population 16,733,227
Capital Astana

Moldova
Area 13,067 sq mi (33,843 sq km)
Population 4,430,654
Capital Kishinev

Ukraine
Area 233,090 sq mi (603,700 sq km)
Population 49,153,027
Capital Kiev

Belarus
Area 80,155 sq mi (207,600 sq km)
Population 10,366,719
Capital Minsk

Kyrgyzstan
Area 76,641 sq mi (198,500 sq km)
Population 4,685,230
Capital Bishkek

Mongolia
Area 604,251 sq mi (1,565,000 sq km)
Population 2,650,952
Capital Ulan Bator

Uzbekistan
Area 172,742 sq mi (447,400 sq km)
Population 24,775,519
Capital Tashkent

SOUTHWEST ASIA

Southwest Asia, also known as the Middle East, contains some of the world's hottest and driest deserts. The two major rivers, the Tigris and Euphrates, rise in the mountains of Turkey and flow across the deserts of Syria and Iraq. The mountains of Turkey are part of a long chain of folded mountains that extends across the northern part of the region to the Hindu Kush in Afghanistan.

Southwest Asia contains several oil-rich nations, but most of the region is economically underdeveloped. It is the home of three religions —Judaism, Christianity, and Islam—but religion has divided people and has been the cause of both international and civil wars. Politically, it is an unstable region, whose conflicts periodically involve the world community.

Southwest Asia is the meeting place of three continents. Here early peoples began to plant crops, build cities, and found civilizations. Today the region is important economically and strategically because of its large reserves and production of oil and natural gas.

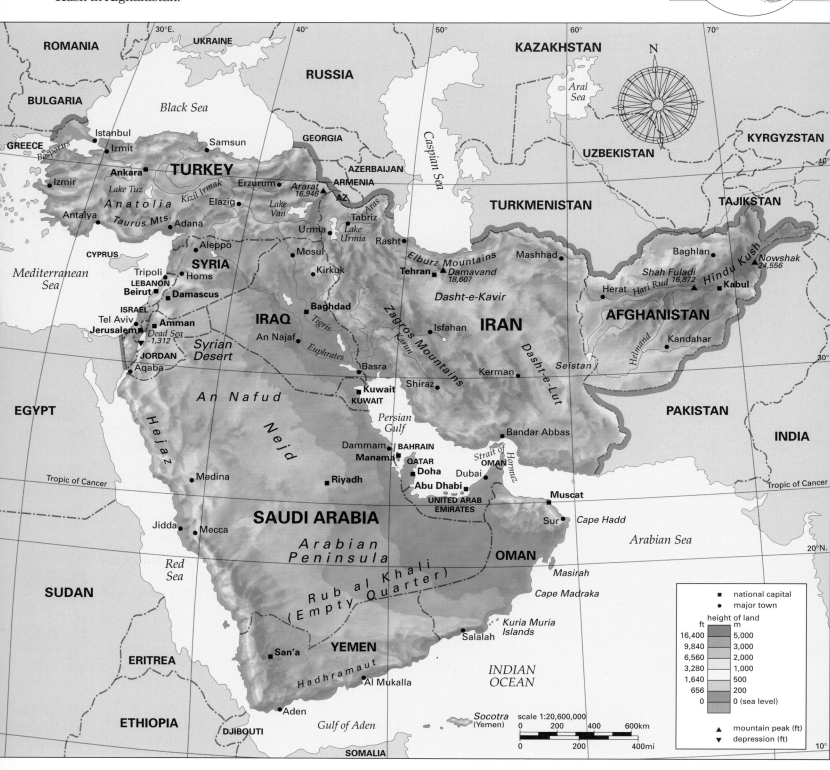

THE POLITICAL AND CULTURAL WORLD

Islam, spread throughout the area by Arabs from the seventh century A.D. on, is the dominant religion in Southwest Asia. Israel, the only country in which Muslims are not a majority, has been in conflict with Arab nations since it was created as a homeland for Jews in 1948.

Other conflicts have arisen because of rivalries between ethnic, cultural, and religious groups, as in Lebanon, and the aspirations of minorities, such as the Kurds, who would like to establish their own country in parts of Iraq, Iran, and Turkey. Territorial disputes have led to war between Iraq and Iran (1980–1988) and Iraq's invasion of Kuwait (1990–1991). Islamic forces gained control of Afghanistan in 1992 and established an interim government. Fighting continued and the conservative Islamic group called the Taliban seized power in Afghanistan in the late 1990s.

Afghanistan
Area 251,826 sq mi
(652,225 sq km)
Population 25,838,797
Capital Kabul

Bahrain
Area 267 sq mi
(691 sq km)
Population 634,137
Capital Manama

COUNTRIES IN THE REGION

Afghanistan, Bahrain, Iran, Iraq, Israel, Jordan, Kuwait, Lebanon, Oman, Qatar, Saudi Arabia, Syria, Turkey, United Arab Emirates (U.A.E.), Yemen

LANGUAGE

Countries with one official language (Arabic) Bahrain, Iraq, Jordan, Kuwait, Lebanon, Oman, Qatar, Saudi Arabia, Syria, U.A.E., Yemen; (Farsi) Iran; (Turkish) Turkey
Countries with two official languages (Arabic, Hebrew) Israel; (Dari, Pashtu) Afghanistan

RELIGION

Countries with one major religion (M) Afghanistan, Bahrain, Iran, Iraq, Jordan, Kuwait, Oman, Qatar, Saudi Arabia, Syria, Turkey, U.A.E., Yemen
Countries with more than one major religion (C, J, M) Israel; (C, D, M and other) Lebanon

Key: C-various Christian, D-Druze, J-Jewish, M-Muslim

STYLES OF GOVERNMENT

Republics Afghanistan, Iran, Iraq, Israel, Lebanon, Syria, Turkey, U.A.E., Yemen
Monarchies Bahrain, Jordan, Kuwait, Oman, Qatar, Saudi Arabia
Federal state U.A.E.
Multiparty states Afghanistan, Israel, Lebanon, Turkey
One-party states Iran, Iraq, Syria
States without parties Bahrain, Jordan, Kuwait, Oman, Qatar, Saudi Arabia, U.A.E., Yemen

Iran
Area 634,561 sq mi
(1,643,503 sq km)
Population 65,619,636
Capital Tehran

Iraq
Area 169,236 sq mi
(438,317 sq km)
Population 22,675,617
Capital Baghdad

Israel
Area 7,992 sq mi
(20,700 sq km)
Population 5,842,454
Capital Jerusalem

ECONOMIC INDICATORS

	U.A.E.	S.Arabia	Jordan
GDP (US$ billions)	45.1	145.8	7.9
GNP per capita (US$)	21,600	10,870	3,430
Annual rate of growth of GDP, 1980–1990	-4.5%	-1.7%	4.3%
Manufacturing as % of GDP	8.6%	8.7%	16.2%
Central government spending as % of GNP	11.8%	n/a	31.6%
Merchandise exports (US$ billions)	28.0	58.2	1.5
Merchandise imports (US$ billions)	30.3	27.8	4.3
Aid received as % of GNP *	–	–	7.2%

* The United Arab Emirates and Saudi Arabia are aid donors.

WELFARE INDICATORS

	U.A.E	S.Arabia	Jordan
Infant mortality rate (per 1,000 live births)			
1965	103	148	114
2000	16	23	26
Daily food supply available (calories per capita)	3,361	2,746	2,734
Population per physician (1993-4)	715	636	825
Teacher-pupil ratio (primary school, 1995)	1 : 17	1 : 13.3	1 : 21.5

Jordan
Area 34,443 sq mi
(89,206 sq km)
Population 4,998,564
Capital Amman

Kuwait
Area 6,880 sq mi
(17,818 sq km)
Population 1,973,572
Capital Kuwait

Lebanon
Area 3,950 sq mi
(10,230 sq km)
Population 3,578,036
Capital Beirut

Oman
Area 82,031 sq mi
(212,460 sq km)
Population 2,533,389
Capital Muscat

national capital
other town

Qatar
Area 4,402 sq mi
(11,400 sq km)
Population 744,483
Capital Doha

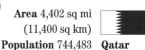

Saudi Arabia
Area 864,871 sq mi
(2,240,000 sq km)
Population 22,023,506
Capital Riyadh

Syria
Area 71,499 sq mi
(185,180 sq km)
Population 16,305,659
Capital Damascus

Turkey
Area 300, 949 sq mi
(779,452 sq km)
Population 65,666,677
Capital Ankara

Yemen
Area 203,851 sq mi
(527,970 sq km)
Population 17,479,206
Capital San'a

United Arab Emirates (U.A.E.)
Area 30,000 sq mi
(77,700 sq km)
Population 2,369,153
Capital Abu Dhabi

Southwest Asia has been unstable since 1945. Israel has fought four wars against its Arab foes, while the Palestinians in Israel continue their protests against Israeli rule. The Iran-Iraq war was the longest in the twentieth century, while the expulsion of Iraqi forces from Kuwait in 1991 involved many world powers.

NORTHERN AFRICA

The northern part of Africa consists largely of a low plateau broken by shallow basins and rugged volcanic highlands. The main land feature in the far northwest is the Atlas Mountain range. The other main highlands are in Ethiopia, though there are also mountain peaks in Algeria, Niger, Chad, and Sudan. Running through these highlands is a section of the Rift Valley, the world's longest geological depression, which runs from Syria, in Southwest Asia, to Mozambique, in Southern Africa.

South of the Mediterranean coastlands and the Atlas Mountains lies the Sahara, the world's largest desert. Only two major rivers, the Nile and the Niger, flow across North Africa throughout the year. But North Africa is not completely arid. South of the Sahara is a dry grassland region called the Sahel, which merges into tropical grassland, or savanna, and forest.

North Africa contains two main groups of people: Arabs and Berbers in the north and black Africans in the lands south of the Sahara. Nomadism is the traditional way of life in the Sahara, though it is now under threat. Most of the people are Muslims, though Christianity, introduced between the fourth and sixth centuries A.D., survived the spread of Islam in the unreachable highlands of Ethiopia. All the countries of the region except Ethiopia were colonized by the French, British, Italians, and Spanish between 1830 and 1914. (Ethiopia was only briefly conquered and ruled by Italy from 1935 to 1941.) Arabic is the official language in the northern states, though some people speak Berber dialects. By contrast, many languages are spoken in the lands south of the Sahara. The former colonial language is used in many countries as an official language or for business and trade.

Northern Africa is part of the ancient landmass of Gondwanaland, which separated between 200 and 100 million years ago. About 70 million years ago, Africa consisted of two land plates: North Africa was tilted downward, while Southern Africa was tilted upward. This divided Africa into a high plateau in the south and a low plateau in the north, which was flooded by the sea. New rocks were formed on the seabed. These rocks now contain water, oil, and natural gas.

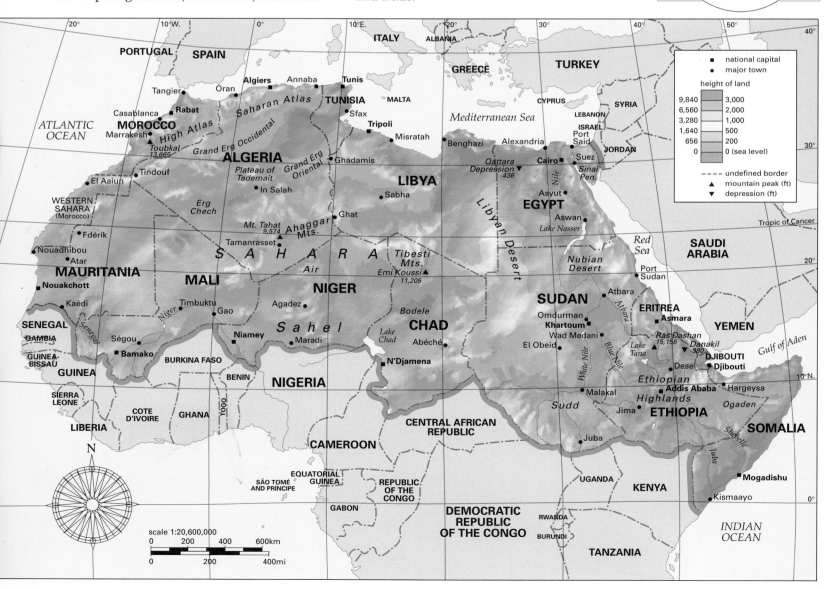

THE POLITICAL AND CULTURAL WORLD

Like many other parts of the developing world, Northern Africa has faced many problems since the countries of the region became independent from colonial rule.

Egypt was in the front line of the Arab-Israeli wars until it agreed to a peace treaty with Israel in 1979. To the south, Chad, Sudan, Ethiopia, and Somalia have suffered bitter civil wars, while Libya has fought with Chad over their disputed border.

Western Sahara (formerly Spanish Sahara), a thinly populated desert territory, was annexed by Morocco in 1991 in the face of opposition from native inhabitants.

Area 919,597 sq mi
(2,381,741 sq km)
Population 31,193,917

Algeria

Area 495,756 sq mi
(1,284,000 sq km)
Population 8,424,504

Chad

Area 8,958 sq mi
(23,200 sq km)
Population 451,442

Djibouti

Area 385,230 sq mi
(997,739 sq km)
Population 68,359,979

Egypt

Area 46,842 sq mi
(121,320 sq km)
Population 4,135,933

Eritrea

COUNTRIES IN THE REGION

Algeria, Chad, Djibouti, Egypt, Eritrea, Ethiopia, Libya, Mali, Mauritania, Morocco, Niger, Somalia, Sudan, Tunisia

MEMBERSHIP OF INTERNATIONAL ORGANIZATIONS

Arab League Algeria, Djibouti, Egypt, Libya, Mauritania, Morocco, Somalia, Sudan, Tunisia
Organization of African Unity (OAU) All countries in the region
Organization of Petroleum Exporting Countries (OPEC) Algeria, Libya

LANGUAGE

Countries with one official language (Amharic) Ethiopia; **(Arabic)** Algeria, Egypt, Libya, Morocco, Sudan, Tunisia; **(French)** Mali, Niger
Countries with two official languages (Arabic, French) Chad, Djibouti, Mauritania; **(Arabic, Somali)** Somalia
Country with more than two official languages (Afar, Amharic, Arabic, Tigre and Kunama, Tigrinya) Eritrea

RELIGION

Countries with one major religion (M) Algeria, Djibouti, Libya, Mauritania, Morocco, Niger, Somalia, Tunisia
Countries with more than one major religion (M, C) Egypt, Eritrea; **(M, EO, I)** Ethiopia; **(M, I, C)** Chad, Mali, Sudan

Key: C–Various Christian, EO–Ethiopian Orthodox, I–Indigenous religions, M– Muslim

Area 435,187 sq mi
(1,127,127 sq km)
Population 64,117,452

Ethiopia

Area 678,383 sq mi
(1,757,000 sq km)
Population 5,115,450

Libya

Area 478,842 sq mi
(1,240,192 sq km)
Population 10,685,948

Mali

Area 397,956 sq mi
(1,030,700 sq km)
Population 2,667,859

Mauritania

SYTLES OF GOVERNMENT

Republics All countries in the region except Morocco
Monarchy Morocco
Transitional governments Eritrea, Sudan
Multiparty states Algeria, Chad, Djibouti, Egypt, Ethiopia, Mali, Mauritania, Morocco, Tunisia
One-party states Eritrea, Libya, Somalia,
State without parties Niger
Military influence Algeria, Libya, Mauritania, Sudan
State without effective government (since 1991) Somalia

ECONOMIC INDICATORS

	Algeria	Egypt	Ethiopia
GDP (US$ billions)	45.9	75.5	6.3
GNP per capita (US$)	4,600	2,940	510
Annual rate of growth of GDP, 1990–1997	0.8%	4.0%	4.9%
Manufacturing as % of GDP	8%	24%	6.7%
Central government spending as % of GNP	n/a	37.4	18.1
Merchandise exports (US$ billions)	13.8	5.5	0.5
Merchandise imports (US$ billions)	8.1	14.2	1.0
Aid received as % of GNP	0.9%	2.2%	10.0%
Total external debt as % of GDP	69.0%	39.0%	149.0%

WELFARE INDICATORS

	Algeria	Egypt	Ethiopia
Infant mortality rate (per 1,000 live births)			
1965	154	145	165
2000	44	51	115
Daily food supply available (calories per capita)			
	3,020	3,289	1,845

Area 187,542 sq mi
(485,730 sq km)
Population 30,122,350

Morocco

Area 458,076 sq mi
(1,186,408 sq km)
Population 10,075,511

Niger

Area 246,201 sq mi
(637,657 sq km)
Population 7,253,137

Somalia

Area 966,759 sq mi
(2,503,890 sq km)
Population 35,079,814

Sudan

Area 59,664 sq mi
(154,530 sq km)
Population 9,593,402

Tunisia

- ■ national capital
- • other town

The boundaries of Northern Africa were drawn by the European colonial powers. The boundaries they mandated for many countries have caused friction in recent years. For example, the world's ninth largest country, Sudan, is divided into two cultural regions: the Arab north and the black African south. Tension between the ethnic regions has led to civil war.

CENTRAL AFRICA

Central Africa is made up of 26 countries, stretching from Cape Verde, an island nation in the Atlantic Ocean west of Senegal, to the Seychelles, another island nation, east of Kenya in the Indian Ocean.

West Africa, which extends from Senegal to Nigeria, consists of coastal plains that rise inland to low plateaus. Cameroon has some volcanic highlands, but the Congo basin is a shallow depression in the central plateaus. Beyond the Congo basin are mountains that overlook the Rift Valley, which contains Lakes Tanganyika, Edward, and Albert. East of the Rift Valley lie the high plateaus of East Africa. This region contains Africa's largest lake, Victoria, the source of the White Nile. The ancient volcanic mountain, Kilimanjaro, is Africa's highest peak. Such volcanoes were formed while earth movements were fracturing the continent, creating the Rift Valley.

Central Africa straddles the Equator, and the climate is generally hot and humid, though temperatures are much lower in the highlands. The world's second largest rain forest (after the Amazon basin) occupies parts of the Congo basin. Central Africa also contains large areas of savanna, home of much wildlife, especially in the national parks on the plateaus of East Africa.

Most of the people are black Africans, who are divided into many ethnic groups. Each group has its own language, art, customs, and traditional religion, though Islam has made inroads into northern West Africa and also East Africa. Christianity was introduced by European missionaries during the colonial period in the nineteenth and twentieth centuries.

Subsistence farming is the main activity, and manufacturing is generally limited to producing basic items such as cement, clothes, and processed food and drink for the home market.

Central Africa is part of the vast plateau of extremely old rocks that make up the African plateau. In places, the ancient rocks are overlaid by young sedimentary rocks and elsewhere by volcanic rocks. The volcanic rocks in East Africa reached the surface 35 to 25 million years ago through cracks formed when the plateaus were stretched by earth movements. These movements tore open the Rift Valley, which runs north-south through eastern Africa. The ancient rocks of Africa are rich in minerals.

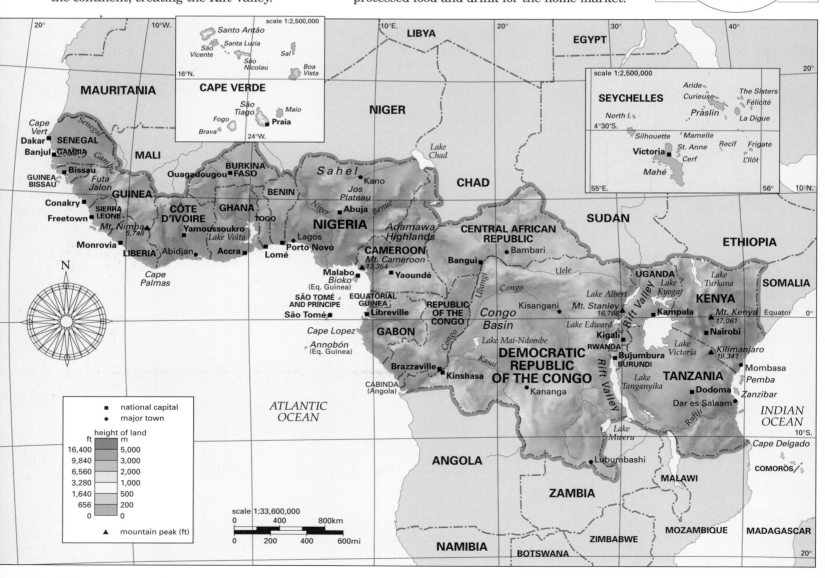

40 national capital
- major town

height of land
ft	m
16,400	5,000
9,840	3,000
6,560	2,000
3,280	1,000
1,640	500
656	200
0	0

▲ mountain peak (ft)

scale 1:33,600,000

THE POLITICAL AND CULTURAL WORLD

The European colonizers drew Africa's boundaries with little regard for existing ethnic groups. As a result, the nations of Central Africa contain many cultural groups.

Nigeria, for example, has over 200 ethnic groups. As no local language is used enough for it to be the official language, Nigeria, like most countries in the region, has adopted its former colonial language (English) for official purposes.

In 1962 Rwanda became an independent republic. Interethnic clashes between Hutu and Tutsi led to civil war in 1990. The war culminated, in April 1994, in a genocide halted only by international intervention. Civil strife continues into the 2000s.

COUNTRIES IN THE REGION

Benin, Burkina Faso, Burundi, Cameroon, Cape Verde, Central African Republic, Democratic Republic of the Congo, Côte d'Ivoire, Equatorial Guinea, Gabon, Gambia, Ghana, Guinea, Guinea-Bissau, Kenya, Liberia, Nigeria, Rwanda, São Tomé and Príncipe, Senegal, Seychelles, Sierra Leone, Tanzania, Togo, Uganda

Cabinda is a coastal enclave of Angola (see Southern Africa)

LANGUAGE

Countries with one official language (E) Gambia, Ghana, Liberia, Nigeria, Sierra Leone, Uganda; (F) Benin, Burkina Faso, Central African Republic, Congo, Congo (DR), Côte d'Ivoire, Gabon, Guinea, Senegal, Togo ; (P) Cape Verde, Guinea-Bissau, São Tomé and Príncipe; (S) Equatorial Guinea
Countries with two official languages (E, F) Cameroon; (E, Sw) Kenya, Tanzania; (F, K) Burundi; (F, R) Rwanda
Country with three official languages (C, E, F) Seychelles

Key: C–Creole, E–English, F–French, K–Kirundi, P–Portuguese, R–Rwandan, S–Spanish, Sw–Swahili

Numerous indigenous languages are spoken in the region.

Many countries in the region have been subject to one-party or military governments and are in transition toward civilian rule.

In 1997, Zaire's dictator, General Mobutu, was overthrown by a popular rebellion and the country was renamed the Democratic Republic of the Congo. Civil war continued until a cease-fire in 1999, but some fighting still goes on.

RELIGION

Countries with one major religion (M) Gambia; (RC) Cape Verde, Equatorial Guinea
Countries with two major religions (P, RC) São Tomé and Príncipe, Seychelles; (M, C) Nigeria
Countries with three or more major religions (I, M, RC) Benin, Burkina Faso, Côte d'Ivoire, Gabon, Guinea, Guinea-Bissau, Liberia, Senegal; (C, I, M, P, RC) Democratic Republic of the Congo, Kenya; (I, M, P, RC) Cameroon, Burundi, Central African Republic, Republic of the Congo, Ghana, Rwanda, Sierra Leone, Tanzania, Togo, Uganda

Key: C–Various Christian, I–Indigenous religions, M–Muslim, P–Protestant, RC–Roman Catholic

MEMBERSHIP OF INTERNATIONAL ORGANIZATIONS

Economic Community of West African States (ECOWAS) Benin, Burkina Faso, Cape Verde, Côte d'Ivoire, Gambia, Ghana, Guinea, Guinea-Bissau, Liberia, Nigeria, Senegal, Sierra Leone, Togo
Organization of African Unity (OAU) All countries in the region

STYLES OF GOVERNMENT

Republics All countries in the region
Transitional governments Democratic Republic of the Congo, Nigeria, Togo
Multiparty states All countries in the region except Uganda
One-party state Uganda
Military influence Burundi, Côte d'Ivoire, Democratic Republic of the Congo, Equatorial Guinea, Guinea, Guinea-Bissau, Sierra Leone, Togo

□ national capital
• other town

Benin **Area** 43,475 sq mi (112,600 sq km) **Population** 6,395,919

Burkina Faso **Area** 105,869 sq mi (274,200 sq km) **Population** 11,946,065

Burundi **Area** 10,026 sq mi (25,967 sq km) **Population** 6,054,714

Cameroon **Area** 178,963 sq mi (463,511 sq km) **Population** 15,421,937

Cape Verde **Area** 1,557 sq mi (4,033 sq km) **Population** 401,343

Central African Republic **Area** 240,324 sq mi (622,436 sq km) **Population** 3,512,751

Côte d'Ivoire **Area** 123,847 sq mi (320,763 sq km) **Population** 15,980,950

Democratic Republic of the Congo **Area** 905,448 sq mi (2,345,095 sq km) **Population** 51,964,999

Area 10,830 sq mi (28,051 sq km) **Population** 474,214

Equatorial Guinea

Area 103,347 sq mi (267,667 sq km) **Population** 1,208,436

Gabon

Area 4,127 sq mi (10,689 sq km) **Population** 1,367,124

Gambia

Area 92,098 sq mi (238,533 sq km) **Population** 19,533,560

Ghana

Area 94,926 sq mi (245,857 sq km) **Population** 7,466,200

Guinea

Area 13,948 sq mi (36,125 sq km) **Population** 1,285,715

Guinea-Bissau

Kenya **Area** 220,625 sq mi (571,416 sq km) **Population** 30,339,770

Liberia **Area** 38,250 sq mi (99,067 sq km) **Population** 3,164,156

Nigeria **Area** 356,669 sq mi (923,768 sq km) **Population** 123,337,822

Republic of the Congo **Area** 132,047 sq mi (342,000 sq km) **Population** 2,830,961

R
Rwanda **Area** 10,169 sq mi (26,338 sq km) **Population** 7,229,129

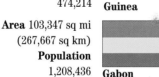
São Tomé and Príncipe **Area** 386 sq mi (1,001 sq km) **Population** 159,883

Senegal **Area** 75,955 sq mi (196,722 sq km) **Population** 9,987,494

Seychelles **Area** 175 sq mi (453 sq km) **Population** 79,326

Sierra Leone **Area** 27,699 sq mi (71,740 sq km) **Population** 5,232,624

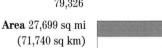
Tanzania **Area** 342,082 sq mi (885,987 sq km) **Population** 35,306,126

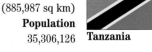
Togo **Area** 21,925 sq mi (56,785 sq km) **Population** 5,018,502

Uganda **Area** 91,134 sq mi (236,040 sq km) **Population** 23,317,560

SOUTHERN AFRICA

Southern Africa consists of ten mainland countries and three island nations – Madagascar, the Comoros, and Mauritius. The mainland is a high, saucer-shaped plateau bordered by mostly narrow coastal plains. The Drakensberg contains the highest peaks. The region also contains the most southerly part of the Rift Valley, enclosing Lake Malawi.

Forests and savanna are found in the north, but the south is dry grassland, merging into the Kalahari, a semidesert, and the Namib Desert, one of the driest places on the earth.

Colonization, involving the introduction of commercial farming, the exploitation of natural resources and the setting up of manufacturing industries, has made a great impact on the black African cultures of Southern Africa.

Nowhere has the impact been greater than in South Africa. Its history of racial conflict became an international political issue. Talks between the various ethnic groups in the early 1990s led to the adoption of a democratic constitution permitting all adults to vote. South Africa's first ever multiracial elections took place in 1994.

Southern Africa is a region of ancient, often mineral-rich rocks, which once formed part of the supercontinent of Gondwanaland. Younger rocks occur around the central plateau, which have been folded and faulted, notably in the extreme southwest. Apart from the Atlas Mountains, these ranges are Africa's only recently formed fold mountains.

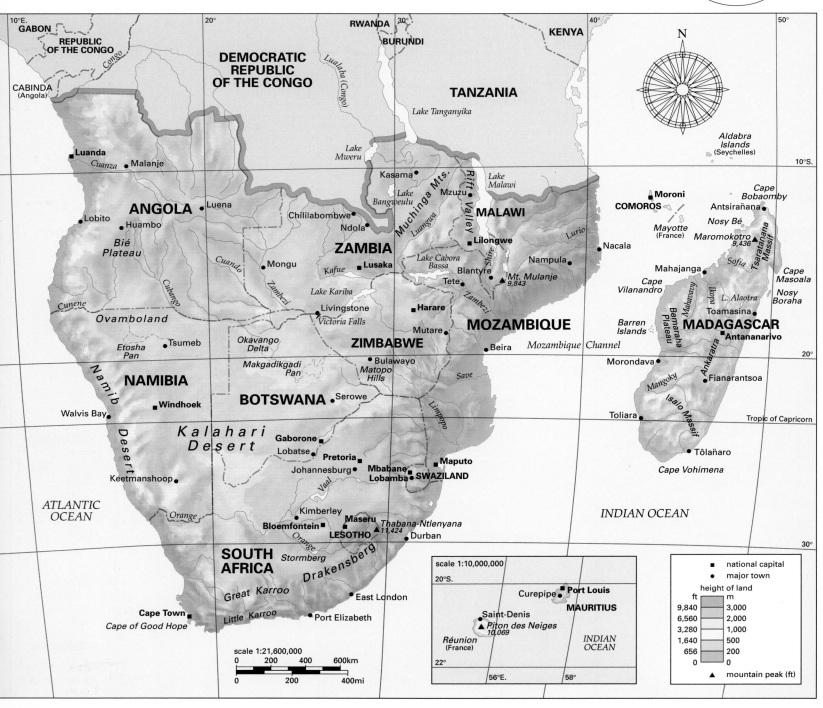

THE POLITICAL AND CULTURAL WORLD

D escendants of the region's earliest people, the Khoi-San (Hottentots and Bushmen), now make up extremely small groups. Most people are black Africans, who speak one of the many Bantu languages, including Tswana and Zulu.

The other main groups are the descendants of European settlers, including the Afrikaaners (descendants of early Dutch settlers in South Africa) and the British. Relationships between European settlers and black Africans have brought political strife to the region. In several countries, including Angola, Namibia, Mozambique, and Zimbabwe, independence was achieved only after long colonial conflicts.

COUNTRIES IN THE REGION

Angola (including Cabinda), Botswana, Comoros, Lesotho, Madagascar, Malawi, Mauritius, Mozambique, Namibia, South Africa, Swaziland, Zambia, Zimbabwe

MEMBERSHIP OF INTERNATIONAL ORGANIZATIONS

Organization of African Unity (OAU)
All countries in the region
Southern Africa Development Community (SADC)
Angola, Botswana, Lesotho, Malawi, Mozambique, Swaziland, Zambia, Zimbabwe

STYLES OF GOVERNMENT

Republics Angola, Botswana, Comoros, Madagascar, Malawi, Mozambique, Namibia, South Africa, Zambia, Zimbabwe
Monarchies Lesotho, Swaziland
Federal state Comoros
Multiparty states Angola, Botswana, Lesotho, Madagascar, Malawi, Mauritius, Mozambique, Namibia, South Africa, Zambia, Zimbabwe
One-party states Comoros, Swaziland
Military influence Comoros

LANGUAGE

Countries with one official language (E) Botswana, Mauritius, Zambia, Zimbabwe; (M) Madagascar; (P) Angola, Mozambique
Countries with two official languages (A, F) Comoros; (Af, E) South Africa, Namibia; (C, E) Malawi; (E, Se) Lesotho; (E, Si) Swaziland
Other significant languages in the region include Comorian (the majority language of the Comoros), ChiSona, Kimbundu, Lunda, Makua, Setwana, Si Ndebele, Tombuka, Umbundu and numerous other indigenous languages.

Key: A–Arabic, Af–Afrikaans, C–Chichewa, E–English, F–French, M–Malagasy, P–Portuguese, Se–Sesotho, Si–siSwati

RELIGION

Countries with one major religion (C) Lesotho, Namibia; (M) Comoros
Countries with two major religions (C, I) Angola, Botswana, Malawi, Swaziland, Zambia, Zimbabwe
Countries with three major religions (C, I, M) Madagascar, Mozambique
Country with more than three major religions (C, DR, H, I, M, RC) South Africa

Key: C–Various Christian, DR–Dutch Reformed, H–Hindu, I–Indigenous religions, M–Muslim, RC–Roman Catholic

Angola — **Area** 481,355 sq mi (1,246,700 sq km) **Population** 10,145,267

Botswana — **Area** 224,608 sq mi (581,730 sq km) **Population** 1,576,470

Comoros — **Area** 719 sq mi (1,862 sq km) **Population** 578,400

Lesotho — **Area** 11,720 sq mi (30,355 sq km) **Population** 2,143,141

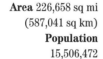
Madagascar — **Area** 226,658 sq mi (587,041 sq km) **Population** 15,506,472

Malawi — **Area** 45,745 sq mi (118,480 sq km) **Population** 10,385,849

Mauritius — **Area** 788 sq mi (2,040 sq km) **Population** 1,179,368

Mozambique — **Area** 308,643 sq mi (799,379 sq km) **Population** 19,104,696

Namibia — **Area** 317,818 sq mi (823,144 sq km) **Population** 1,771,327

South Africa — **Area** 473,291 sq mi (1,225,815 sq km) **Population** 43,421,021

Swaziland — **Area** 6,704 sq mi (17,364 sq km) **Population** 1,083,289

Zambia — **Area** 290,586 sq mi (752,614 sq km) **Population** 9,582,418

Zimbabwe — **Area** 150,873 sq mi (390,759 sq km) **Population** 11,342,521

■ national capital
• other town

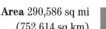

In the last 30 years, Southern Africa has been one of the world's most unstable regions. Civil wars occurred in Angola and Mozambique after independence, and a long armed struggle took place in South Africa, with the African National Congress leading the fight against apartheid.

INDIAN SUBCONTINENT

The region is a pendant-shaped landmass, extending from the world's highest mountain ranges in the north to the islands of Sri Lanka and the Maldives in the south.

The climate ranges from polar conditions on the mountains to hot tropical weather on the plains. The influence of monsoon winds, which bring rain between June and September, are felt throughout much of the region.

Over the centuries, many waves of migrants have settled in the subcontinent. Today the region has many languages and religions, reflecting its complex past. Cultural rivalries and religious differences sometimes cause conflict and violence. Despite such pressures and the poverty in which many people live, India remains the world's most heavily populated parliamentary democracy.

The Indian subcontinent was once part of the ancient continent of Gondwanaland. Plate movements propelled the landmass north until it collided with Eurasia, thrusting up the rocks on the intervening seabed into high fold mountains, the Himalayas, with the world's highest peak.

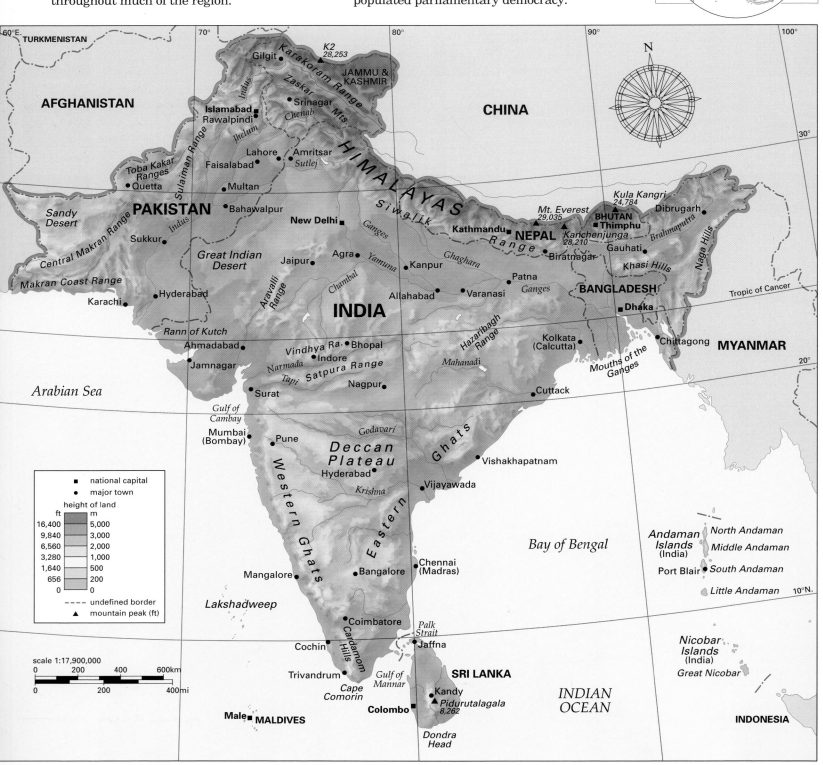

THE POLITICAL AND CULTURAL WORLD

In the mid-nineteenth century, most of the Indian subcontinent, apart from the remote mountain kingdoms of Bhutan and Nepal, was under British rule. But when British India became independent in 1947, the region split into two countries: the mainly Hindu India and Islamic Pakistan. Pakistan consisted of two parts: West and East Pakistan. After a civil war, East Pakistan broke away from West Pakistan in 1971 and proclaimed its independence as Bangladesh.

Tensions between India and the Islamic Republic of Pakistan continue, and the boundary between the two countries in the Jammu and Kashmir region in the northwest is still disputed.

COUNTRIES IN THE REGION

Bangladesh, Bhutan, India, Maldives, Nepal, Pakistan, Sri Lanka

Island territories
Andaman Islands, Nicobar Islands, Lakshadweep (India)

MEMBERSHIP OF INTERNATIONAL ORGANIZATIONS

Colombo Plan Bangladesh, Bhutan, India, Maldives, Nepal, Pakistan, Sri Lanka
South Asia Association for Regional Cooperation Committee (SAARC) All countries of the region

LANGUAGE

Countries with one official language (Bengali) Bangladesh; (Divehi) Maldives; (Nepali) Nepal; (Sinhalese) Sri Lanka; (Urdu) Pakistan
Country with two official languages (English, Hindi) India
Country with three official languages (Dzongkha, English, Lhotsam) Bhutan

India has 14 officially recognized languages. As well as Hindi and Urdu, the most significant languages in the region include Gujarati, Malayalam, Marathi, Punjabi, Tamil and Telugu. There are hundreds of local languages and dialects.

RELIGION

Countries with one major religion (M) Maldives, Pakistan
Countries with two major religions (B, H) Bhutan; (H, M) Bangladesh
Countries with three or more major religions (B, H, M) Nepal; (B, C, H, M) Sri Lanka; (B, C, H, J, M, S) India

Key: B–Buddhist, C–Various Christian, H–Hindu, J–Jain, M–Muslim, S–Sikh

ECONOMIC INDICATORS

	Bangladesh	India	Pakistan
GDP (US$ billions)	32.8	378.6	64.5
GNP per capita (US$)	1,050	1,650	1,590
Annual rate of growth of GDP, 1990–1997	4.7%	6.0%	4.2%
Manufacturing as % of GDP	9.4%	20	16.8%
Central government spending as % of GDP	10%	16.4%	23.2%
Merchandise exports (US$ billions)	4.8	35.4	8.3
Merchandise imports (US$ billions)	6.6	45.7	10.7
Aid received as % of GNP	3.9%	0.6%	1.4%
Total external debt as % of GNP	43%	23%	53%

WELFARE INDICATORS

	Bangladesh	India	Pakistan
Infant mortality rate (per 1,000 live births)			
1965	144	150	149
2000	79	72	74
Daily food supply available (calories per capita)	2,086	2,496	n/a

Pakistan
Area 307,375 sq mi (796,095 sq km)
Population 141,533,775
Capital Islamabad
Currency 1 Pakistan rupee (PRe) = 100 paisa

Bangladesh
Area 55,598 sq mi (143,998 sq km)
Population 129,194,224
Capital Dhaka
Currency 1 Bangladesh taka (Tk) = 100 poisha

Area 18,147 sq mi (47,000 sq km)
Population 2,005,222
Capital Thimphu
Currency 1 ngultrum (Nu) = 100 chetrum
Bhutan

India
Area 1,269,348 sq mi (3,287,590 sq km)
Population 1,014,003,817
Capital New Delhi
Currency I Indian rupee (Re) = 100 paise

Maldives
Area 116 sq mi (300 sq km)
Population 301,475
Capital Male
Currency 1 Maldivian rufiyaa (Rf) = 100 laari

Nepal
Area 56,827 sq mi (147,181 sq km)
Population 24,702,119
Capital Kathmandu
Currency 1 Nepalese rupee (NRe) = 100 paisa

Sri Lanka
Area 25,332 sq mi (65,610 sq km)
Population 19,144,875
Capital Colombo
Currency 1 Sri Lankan rupee (SLRe) = 100 cents

India is a nonaligned state and did not take sides in the Cold War. It possesses nuclear weapons. One family dominated Indian politics for many years. The country was led by the Nehru-Gandhi family from its independence in 1947 until prime minister Rajiv Gandhi was assassinated in May 1991.

■ national capital
• other town

CHINA AND TAIWAN

China is the world's third largest country in area and the largest in population. It contains great mountain ranges, high plateaus, deserts, grasslands, and fertile valleys.

The climate in the southwest Plateau of Tibet is very harsh. The deserts in the northwest have an arid climate with temperatures that may soar to 100°F (38°C) in summer and plunge to −29°F (−34°C) during winter nights. Most people live in the east, where the climate ranges from temperate to subtropical.

About 93 percent of the people in China belong to the Han group, a name that comes from the Han dynasty (206 B.C.–A.D. 220). The other 7 percent belong to minority groups.

Civilization in China dates back around 5,000 years. The Chinese empire became weak in the nineteenth century, and in 1912, the country became a republic. A communist regime has ruled since 1949, though from the late 1980s, the government began to introduce free enterprise economic policies.

China's gross domestic product quadrupled between 1978 and 1998 and, by 1997, China had become the world's second largest economy after the United States.

China is bordered by Mongolia and Russia to the north and the Indian subcontinent and Southeast Asia in the south. It shares Everest, the world's highest mountain, with Nepal. It also has deep basins, one reaching 505 ft (154 m) below sea level. The great plains of China are drained by the great Huang and Chang rivers.

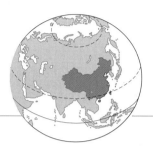

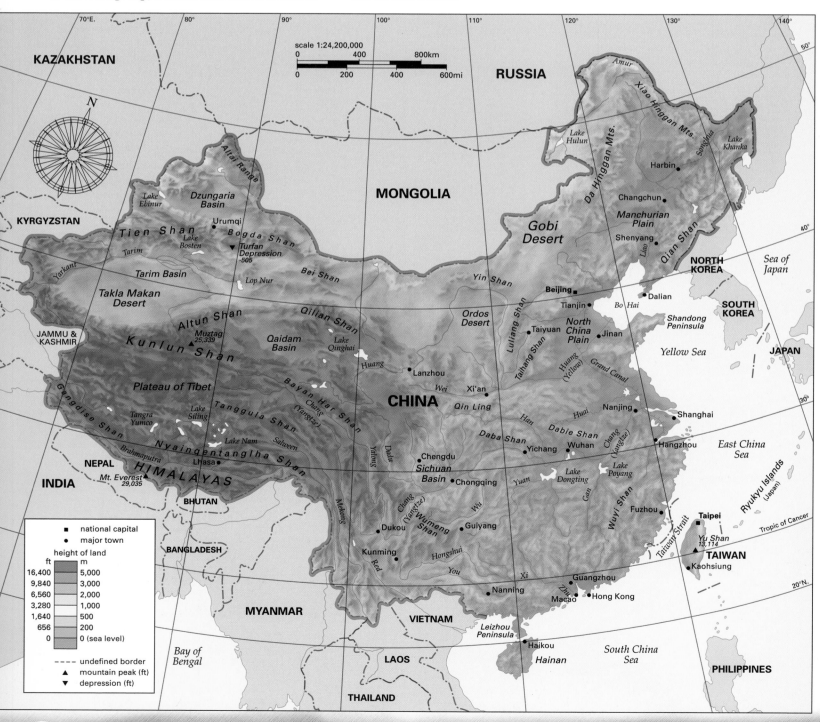

THE POLITICAL AND CULTURAL WORLD

The region includes Hong Kong, an extremely prosperous center for trade and finance on the southeast coast of China. Hong Kong was returned to communist China from British rule in 1997.

Near Hong Kong is the even smaller region of Macao, which Portugal returned to China in 1999, with an autonomous status similar to that of Hong Kong.

The independent island state of Taiwan lies off the southeast coast of China. Taiwan claims to be the sole legitimate Republic of China (its official name), a reflection of the fact that in 1949 it became the last refuge of China's nationalist government after its defeat by the communists on the mainland. Today, the island is discovering an identity of its own while maintaining close relations with China.

Since the death of China's communist leader Mao Zedong (1949–1976), China's leadership has tried to make friendlier relations with other countries, notably Russia and the United States. China was opened to foreign investment and free enterprise, and this led in the late 1980s to demands for political reform. Demonstrators for such changes were brutally suppressed.

COUNTRIES IN THE REGION

The People's Republic of China, Taiwan

Island territories Hainan (China)
Disputed borders China/India, China/Russia

LANGUAGE

Countries with one official language (Mandarin Chinese) China, Taiwan
Other significant languages in the region include Cantonese, Manchu, Miao, Mongol, Portuguese (in Macao), Tibetan, Uighur, and Yi. There are also numerous local languages and dialects.

RELIGION

China Although religion is officially discouraged, many people practice a combination of Confucianist, Taoist, and traditional folk belief. There are smaller groups of Buddhists, Muslims, and Christians.
In Hong Kong and Macao, separate from China for most of the past century until 1997 and 1999 respectively, religious practice is more widespread; in the former the figures are: Buddhist-Confucianist-Taoist (92%), Christian (1.1%), Muslim (0.1%); in the latter, Buddhist (45.1%), nonreligious (43.8%), Roman Catholic (7.4%), Protestant (1.3%)
Taiwan Confucianist-Taoist-traditional (48.5%), Buddhist (43%), Christian (7.4%), Muslim (0.5%)

STYLES OF GOVERNMENT

Republics China, Taiwan
Federal state China
Multiparty state Taiwan
One-party state China
One-chamber assembly China, Taiwan

ECONOMIC INDICATORS

	Taiwan	China
GDP (US$ billions)	357	902
GDP per capita (US$)	16,100	3,800
Annual rate of growth of GDP, 1990–1996	5.5%	11.6%
Manufacturing as % of GDP	n/a	38%
Central government spending as % of GDP	n/a	8.3%
Merchandise exports (US$ billions)	121.6	182.7
Merchandise imports (US$ billions)	101.7	136.4
Aid received as % of GNP	0%	0.3%
Total external debt as % of GDP	9.8%	16.6%

WELFARE INDICATORS

	Taiwan	China
Infant mortality rate (per 1,000 live births)		
1965	n/a	52.6
2000	7.06	41
Daily food supply available (calories per capita, 1995)	3,054	2,741
Population per physician (1995)	873	628
Teacher-pupil ratio (primary school, 1996)	1 : 20.6	1 : 24.3

China
Area 3,705,845 sq mi (9,598,073 sq km)
Population 1,269,394,378
Capital Beijing
Currency 1 yuan (Y) = 10 jiao = 100 fen

Taiwan
Area 13,892 sq mi (35,980 sq km)
Population 22,191,087
Capital Taipei
Currency 1 new Taiwan dollar (NT$) = 100 cents

- ■ national capital
- ■ provincial, municipal or regional capital
- • other town
- province
- municipality
- autonomous region
- special administrative region

Locales are given in present-day Pinyin spelling.

SOUTHEAST ASIA

Southeast Asia includes a peninsula and a vast archipelago, comprising over 20,000 islands. The region contains two zones where volcanic eruptions and earthquakes are caused by collisions between the huge plates that form the earth's crust. One zone runs east-west through southern Indonesia and the other from eastern Indonesia to the Philippines.

The region is humid and tropical. The south has rainfall throughout the year, but the north has a monsoon climate, with most rain coming in the summer months (June through August).

Small groups of Negritos, descendants of the earliest inhabitants, live in remote areas, but most Southeast Asians are of Malay or Chinese descent. The diversity of cultures shows how many outside influences have affected the region. Of the region's ten countries, only Thailand remained free. Wars in Europe marred the area's chances for independence, and the postcolonial years have been marked by civil wars and political instability. Agriculture is the main activity. Industry has been developing rapidly in some areas, including Manila and Singapore.

Southeast Asia lies between the eastern end of the Himalayas and northern Australia. Most of the region lies on the southeastern edge of the huge Eurasian plate and is bordered by deep ocean trenches. As the plates descend into the mantle, their edges melt, forming the molten rock that fuels Southeast Asia's volcanoes.

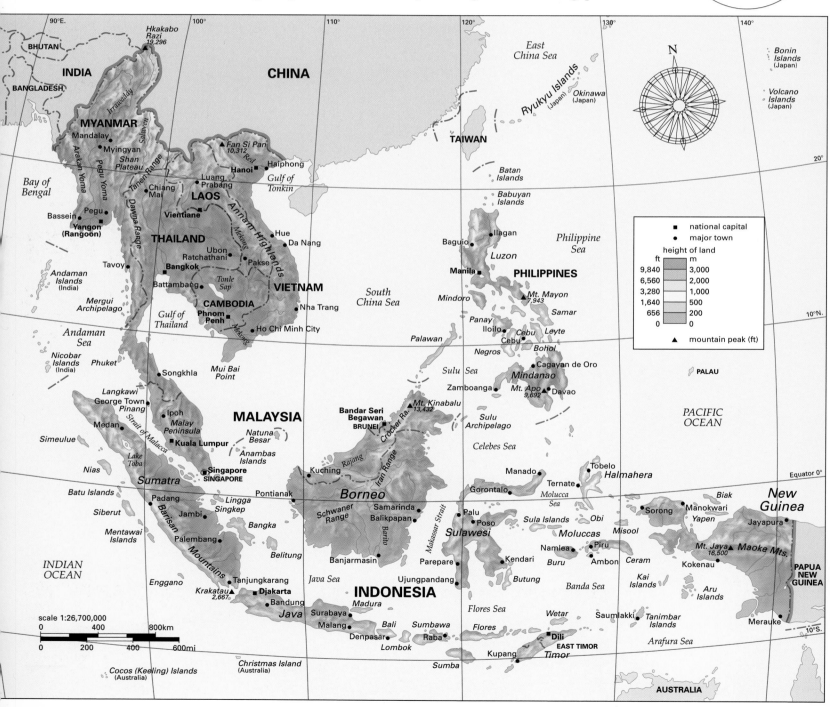

THE POLITICAL AND CULTURAL WORLD

After the defeat of Japan in 1945, communist forces began a long struggle for power in Southeast Asia. The British defeated them in Malaya, but after a long struggle in Vietnam, involving first France and then the United States, the communists emerged victorious in 1975.

In Myanmar (formerly Burma), Indonesia, and Thailand, army rulers have suppressed political parties, while Brunei's sultan has allowed no opposition to his government. The only countries with elements of parliamentary democracy are Cambodia, Malaysia, Singapore, and the Philippines.

Brunei, Cambodia, Indonesia, Laos, Malaysia, Myanmar, Philippines, Singapore, Thailand, Vietnam
Disputed borders Cambodia/Thailand, Cambodia/Vietnam, Indonesia/Malaysia, Vietnam/China

LANGUAGE

Countries with one official language (Bahasa Indonesia) Indonesia; (Bahasa Malaysia) Malaysia; (Burmese) Myanmar; (Khmer) Cambodia; (Lao) Laos; (Thai) Thailand; (Vietnamese) Vietnam
Countries with two official languages (English, Malay) Brunei; (English, Filipino) Philippines
Country with four official languages (Bahasa Malaysia, Chinese, English, Tamil) Singapore

RELIGION

Country with one major religion (B) Cambodia
Countries with two major religions (B, I) Laos; (B, M) Thailand
Countries with three or more major religions (B, C, T) Vietnam; (B, C, H, M) Indonesia; (B, C, I, M) Myanmar Brunei; (B, M, P, RC) Philippines; (B, C, H, M, T) Singapore, Malaysia

Key: B-Buddhist, C-various Christian, H-Hindu, I-Indigenous religions, M-Muslim; P-Protestant, RC-Roman Catholic, T-Taoist

ECONOMIC INDICATORS

	Singapore	Thailand	Indonesia
GDP (US$ billions)	96.3	157.2	214.6
GNP per capita (US$)	29,000	6,590	3,450
Annual rate of growth of GDP, 1990–1997	8.5%	7.4%	7.5%
Manufacturing as % of GDP	24.3%	28.4%	25.6%
Central government spending as % of GNP	15.9%	15.8%	14.7%
Merchandise exports (US$ billions)	125.8	56.7	56.3
Merchandise imports (US$ billions)	124.6	55.1	46.2
Aid received as % of GNP	–	0.5%	0.5%
Total external debt as % of GNP	–	62.6%	65.3%
Industrial production growth rate, 1999	14%	12.6%	1.5%

WELFARE INDICATORS

	Singapore	Thailand	Indonesia
Infant mortality rate (per 1,000 live births)			
1965	26	145	128
2000	5	29	48
Daily food supply available (calories per capita, 1995)	3,121	2,296	2,732
Population per physician (1993–4)	709	4,416	7,028
Teacher-pupil ratio (primary school, 1995)	1 : 25.3	1 : 19.3	1 : 22.3

national capital
• other town

While the region has a volatile recent political history, the people continue to follow their traditional religious beliefs. The main religions are Buddhism, chiefly on the mainland peninsula; Islam, in Indonesia; and Christianity, in the Philippines. All these religious influences come from outside the region.

East Timor's people voted for independence from Indonesia in 1999. The first free elections were held in 2001.

Area 2,228 sq mi (5,770 sq km)
Population 336,376
Capital Bandar Seri Begawan
 Brunei

Area 69,900 sq mi (181,040 sq km)
Population 12,212,306
Capital Phnom Penh
 Cambodia

Area 741,101 sq mi (1,919,440 sq km)
Population 224,784,210
Capital Djakarta
 Indonesia

Area 91,430 sq mi (236,800 sq km)
Population 5,497,459
Capital Vientiane
 Laos

Area 127,317 sq mi (329,750 sq km)
Population 21,793,293
Capital Kuala Lumpur
 Malaysia

Area 198,457 sq mi (514,000 sq km)
Population 61,230,874
Capital Bangkok
 Thailand

Area 127,244 sq mi (329,560 sq km)
Population 78,773,873
Capital Hanoi
 Vietnam

Area 250 sq mi (648 sq km)
Population 4,151,264
Capital Singapore
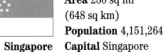 **Singapore**

Area 261,971 sq mi (678,500 sq km)
Population 41,734,853
Capital Yangon
Myanmar

Area 115,831 sq mi (300,000 sq km)
Population 81,159,644
Capital Manila
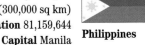 **Philippines**

JAPAN AND KOREA

Rugged mountains interspersed with lowlands dominate the landscapes of Japan and Korea. The Korean mountains are old and stable, but most of Japan's highest peaks are volcanic. Japan lies in an unstable zone. Earthquakes and tsunamis (powerful sea waves triggered by earth movements) are constant threats. The region has a monsoon climate, with hot, wet summers and cold winters.

Until fairly recent times, Japan and Korea were cut off from the rest of the world. But from the late 1860s, Japan began to modernize and become a world power. Its defeat in World War II proved a challenge. With help from the United States, it has become a major industrial power. Korea, which had been occupied by Japan from 1910 to 1945, is now split into free-enterprise South Korea and the communist North.

Japan and Korea occupy a frontier zone between Eurasia and the Pacific Ocean. Japan forms part of the Pacific "ring of fire," a zone of crustal instability that encircles the Pacific Ocean. Japan has 60 active volcanoes and has over a thousand earthquakes every year.

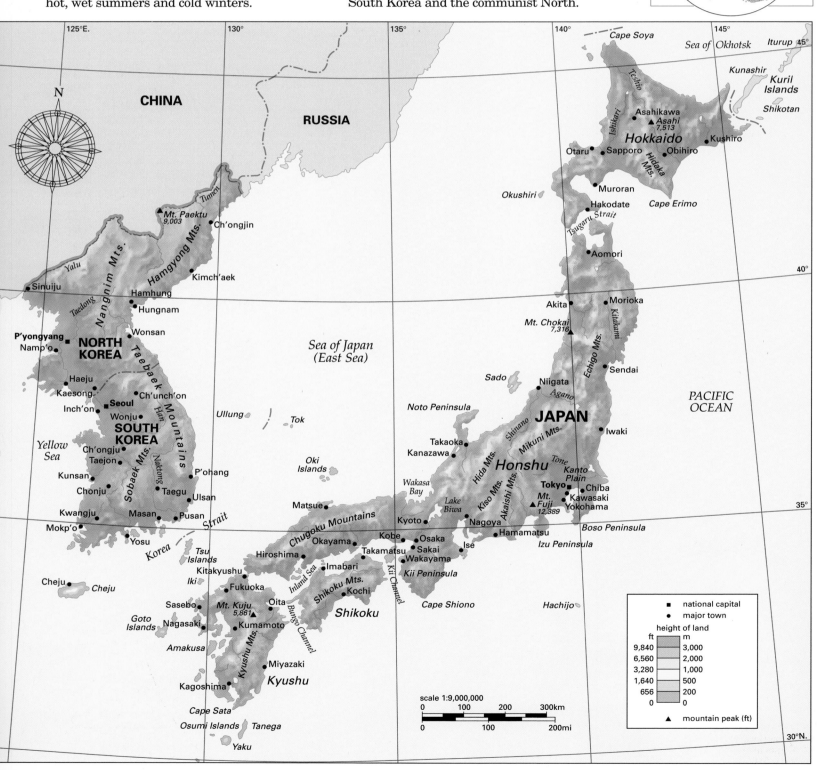

THE POLITICAL AND CULTURAL WORLD

Before World War II, Japan was a military dictatorship. After the war, the Allied forces occupied the country from 1945 to 1952. During this time a new constitution was adopted in which power was vested in a prime minister and cabinet, who were answerable to the Diet (parliament). The emperor was subsequently given a symbolic role in the country's leadership.

Korea was split into two parts in 1945. Separate governments for North and South Korea were set up in 1947. This action triggered the Korean War (1948–1953). In recent years, talks have been held about reunification, but little progress has been made.

COUNTRIES IN THE REGION

Japan, North Korea, South Korea
Island territories Ryukyu Islands (including Okinawa) (see map on page 128)
Disputed territories Japan/Russia (Kuril Islands and south Sakhalin)

MEMBERSHIP OF INTERNATIONAL ORGANIZATIONS

Colombo Plan Japan
Organization for Economic Cooperation and Development (OECD) Japan

LANGUAGE

Countries with one official language (Japanese) Japan; (Korean) North Korea, South Korea

RELIGION

Japan Most Japanese are adherents both of Shinto (93.1%) and Buddhism (73.9%); Christian (1.4%)
North Korea Nonreligious or atheist (67.9%), traditional beliefs (15.6%), Ch'ondogyo (13.9%), Buddhist (1.7%), Christian (0.9%)
South Korea Nonreligious or atheist (57.4%), Christian (20.7%), Buddhist (19.9%), Confucianist (1.2%), Ch'ondogyo (0.1%), others (0.7%)

STYLES OF GOVERNMENT

Republics North Korea, South Korea
Monarchy Japan
Multiparty states Japan, South Korea
One-party state North Korea
One-chamber assembly North Korea, South Korea
Two-chamber assembly Japan

ECONOMIC INDICATORS

	Japan	S. Korea
GDP (US$ billions)	4,201.6	438.2
GNP per capita (US$)	23,400	13,500
Annual rate of growth of GDP, 1990–1997	1.5%	7.2%
Manufacturing as % of GDP	24.3%	25.7%
Merchandise exports (US$ billions)	409.2	138.5
Merchandise imports (US$ billions)	307.6	141.8
Aid given as % of GNP	0.2%	n/a

WELFARE INDICATORS

	Japan	S. Korea
Infant mortality rate (per 1,000 live births)		
1965	18	62
2000	4	10
Daily food supply available (calories per capita, 1995)	2,887	3,268
Population per physician (1995)	546	784
Teacher-pupil ratio (primary school, 1995)	1 : 19.5	1 : 27.5

North Korea
Area 46,541 sq mi (120,540 sq km)
Population 21,687,550
Capital P'yongyang
Currency 1 won (Wn) = 100 chon

South Korea
Area 38,023 sq mi (98,480 sq km)
Population 47,470,969
Capital Seoul
Currency 1 won (W) = 100 chun

Area 145,883 sq mi (377,835 sq km)
Population 126,549,976
Capital Tokyo
Currency 1 yen ¥ = 100 sen
Japan

■ national capital
• other town

Japan is a constitutional monarchy. An emperor is the ceremonial head of state. The country is divided into 47 prefectures. South Korea is a republic, divided into nine provinces and five cities with the rank of province. North Korea is a communist state, divided into nine provinces and four city areas.

AUSTRALIA AND ITS NEIGHBORS

Australia is an ancient landmass that once formed part of the supercontinent of Gondwanaland. Australia is a stable continent, and its scenery is the result of constant erosion and deposition rather than great land movements.

Australia is the world's sixth largest country and its smallest continent. Most of the land is flat—plains or level plateaus make up nine-tenths of Australia. Papua New Guinea is more mountainous but has large lowlands.

The climate ranges from tropical in the north to Mediterranean in the south, though the interior is semiarid or desert. The southeast and Tasmania have a mild temperate climate.

Australia's Aboriginal people arrived from Southeast Asia at least 40,000 years ago. A nomadic people, they developed complex cultural and religious traditions. Most Australians today are of European descent, especially from Britain. Recent arrivals include Asians. Australia is a leading exporter of agricultural products, although the most important part of the economy is manufacturing.

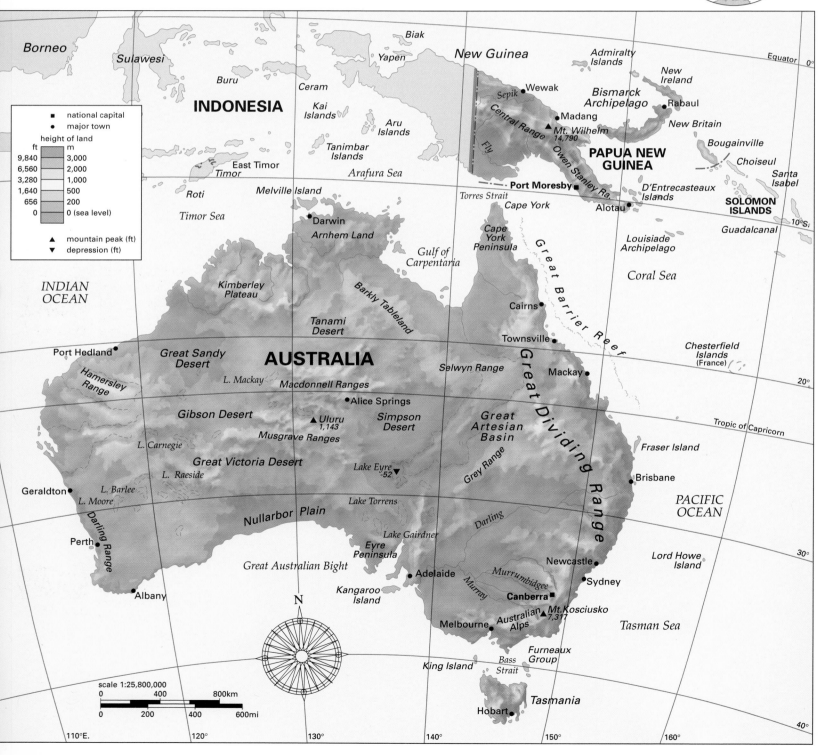

THE POLITICAL AND CULTURAL WORLD

In 1901, the former British colonies of New South Wales, Queensland, South Australia, Tasmania, Victoria, and Western Australia became states and federated to become the independent Commonwealth of Australia. Northern Territory was transferred from South Australia as a territory in 1911.

Today Australia remains a constitutional monarchy – its head of state is the British monarch, who is represented by a governor-general. Papua New Guinea, which was under Australian control during the colonial period, is another constitutional monarchy. Both countries are members of the British Commonwealth. In 1999 Australian voters rejected a republic, opting for the continuation of the British monarchy.

COUNTRIES IN THE REGION

Australia, Papua New Guinea

Island territories
Ashmore and Cartier Islands, Christmas Island, Cocos Islands, Coral Sea Islands, Norfolk Island, Heard Island and the McDonald Islands (Australia)

MEMBERSHIP OF INTERNATIONAL ORGANIZATIONS

Colombo Plan Australia, Papua New Guinea
Organization for Economic Cooperation and Development (OECD) Australia
South Pacific Forum Australia, Papua New Guinea

LANGUAGE

Countries with one official language
(English) Australia, Papua New Guinea

RELIGION

Papua New Guinea Various Christian, Indigenous religions, Roman Catholic

Australia Anglican, Jewish, Muslim, Nonreligious, Orthodox, Protestant, Roman Catholic

STYLES OF GOVERNMENT

Monarchies Australia, Papua New Guinea
Federal state Australia
Multiparty states Australia, Papua New Guinea

ECONOMIC INDICATORS

	Australia
GDP (US$ billions)	394
GNP per capita (US$)	20,170
Annual rate of growth of GDP, 1990–1997	3.6%
Manufacturing as % of GDP	13.5%
Central government spending as % of GNP	27.4%
Merchandise exports (US$ billions)	64.9
Merchandise imports (US$ billions)	63.0
Aid given as % of GNP	0.30%

WELFARE INDICATORS

	Australia
Infant mortality rate (per 1,000 live births)	
1965	19
2000	5.04
Daily food supply available (calories per capita)	3,068
Population per physician (1995)	400
Teacher-pupil ratio (primary school, 1995)	1 : 17

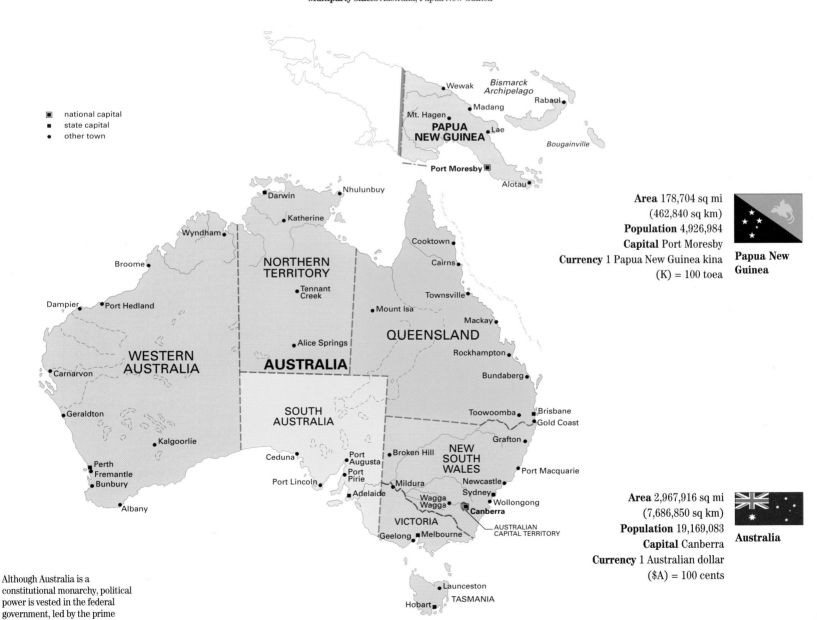

- ■ national capital
- ▪ state capital
- ● other town

Area 178,704 sq mi (462,840 sq km)
Population 4,926,984
Capital Port Moresby
Currency 1 Papua New Guinea kina (K) = 100 toea

Papua New Guinea

Area 2,967,916 sq mi (7,686,850 sq km)
Population 19,169,083
Capital Canberra
Currency 1 Australian dollar ($A) = 100 cents

Australia

Although Australia is a constitutional monarchy, political power is vested in the federal government, led by the prime minister. Each state also has its own parliament to deal with such matters as education and public welfare.

NEW ZEALAND AND ITS NEIGHBORS

New Zealand lies in the southwestern Pacific Ocean, 994 miles (1,600 km) southeast of Australia. It is in an unstable zone, characterized by earthquakes and volcanic eruptions. Glacial action has carved scenic fjords into the southwest coast of South Island.

New Zealand is an island nation with snow-capped mountains, fertile green plains, forested hills, and volcanic regions famous for their bubbling hot springs and explosive geysers. The climate varies from subtropical in North Island to wet temperate on South Island. The Southern Alps on South Island have a severe mountain climate.

The Maoris, a Polynesian people, settled in New Zealand (called Aotearoa, or "Land of the Long White Cloud") about A.D. 750. Dutch sailors reached the islands in 1642, but Europeans did not settle there until the early 1800s. Most New Zealanders are descendants of British immigrants. The country's economy was founded on farming and foreign trade.

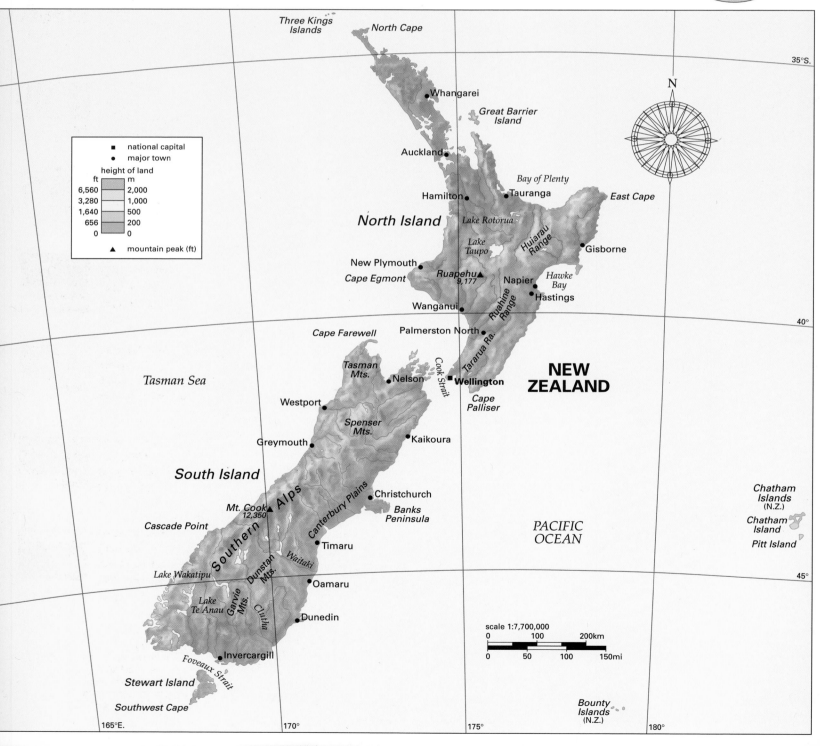

Legend

- ■ national capital
- ● major town

height of land

ft	m
6,560	2,000
3,280	1,000
1,640	500
656	200
0	0

▲ mountain peak (ft)

scale 1:7,700,000

0   100   200km
0   50   100   150mi

THE POLITICAL AND CULTURAL WORLD

With its Maori population, New Zealand is regarded as part of Polynesia, which also includes the independent island nations of Tonga, Tuvalu, and Samoa, as well as the American state of Hawaii.

Micronesia lies mainly in the North Pacific and includes Kiribati, Nauru, the Marshall Islands, Palau and the Federated States of Micronesia. Kiribati contains both Polynesians and Micronesians. Melanesia includes Papua New Guinea, the Solomon Islands, Vanuatu, and Fiji.

Fiji
Area 7,054 sq mi (18,270 sq km)
Population 832,494
Capital Suva

Kiribati
Area 277 sq mi (717 sq km)
Population 91,985
Capital Tarawa

Marshall Islands
Area 70 sq mi (181.3 sq km)
Population 68,126
Capital Majuro

Micronesia
Area 271 sq mi (702 sq km)
Population 133,144
Capital Palikir

COUNTRIES IN THE REGION

Federated States of Micronesia, Fiji, Kiribati, Marshall Islands, Nauru, New Zealand, Palau, Samoa, Solomon Islands, Tonga, Tuvalu, Vanuatu

Island territories Cook Islands, Niue, Tokelau (N.Z.)

LANGUAGE

Countries with one official language Federated States of Micronesia, Fiji, Kiribati, New Zealand, Solomon Islands (E); Nauru (N)
Countries with two official languages Marshall Islands (E, Ma); Palau (P, E); Tonga (E, To); Samoa (E, Sa)
Country with three or more official languages Vanuatu (B, E, F)
Country with no official language Tuvalu

Key: B-Bislama, E-English, F-French, Ma-Marshallese, N-Nauruan, P-Palauan, Sa-Samoan, To-Tongan

Other significant languages in the region include French and a great variety of indigenous Melanesian and Polynesian languages.

RELIGION

Countries with one major religion Marshall Islands, Tuvalu (P)
Countries with two major religions Kiribati, Nauru, Samoa, Tonga (P, RC); Palau, Vanuatu (C, I)
Countries with three or more major religions Fiji (C, H, M); Solomon Islands (A, I, P, RC); New Zealand (A, N, P, RC)

Key: A-Anglican, C-various Christian, H-Hindu, I-Indigenous religions, J-Jewish, M-Muslim, N-nonreligious, O-Orthodox, P-Protestant, RC-Roman Catholic

ECONOMIC INDICATORS

	New Zealand
GDP (US$ billions)	64.9
GNP per capita (US$)	16,600
Annual rate of growth of GDP, 1990–1997	3.4%
Manufacturing as % of GDP	19.3%
Central government spending as % of GNP	32.9%
Merchandise exports (US$ billions)	13.9
Merchandise imports (US$ billions)	13.5
Development aid donated as % of GNP	0.21%

WELFARE INDICATORS

	New Zealand
Infant mortality rate (per 1,000 live births)	
1965	20
2000	6.39
Daily food supply available (calories per capita)	3,379
Population per physician (1995)	318
Teacher-pupil ratio (primary school, 1995)	1 : 19.5

New Zealand
Area 103,738 sq mi (268,680 sq km)
Population 3,819,762
Capital Wellington

Palau
Area 177 sq mi (458 sq km)
Population 18,766
Capital Koror

Samoa
Area 1,104 sq mi (2,860 sq km)
Population 179,466
Capital Apia

Solomon Islands
Area 10,985 sq mi (28,450 sq km)
Population 466,194
Capital Honiara

Tonga
Area 289 sq mi (748 sq km)
Population 102,321
Capital Nuku'alofa

Tuvalu
Area 10 sq mi (26 sq km)
Population 10,838
Capital Funafuti

Vanuatu
Area 5,699 sq mi (14,760 sq km)
Population 189,618
Capital Port-Vila

Nauru
Area 8 sq mi (21 sq km)
Population 11,845
Capital Yaren

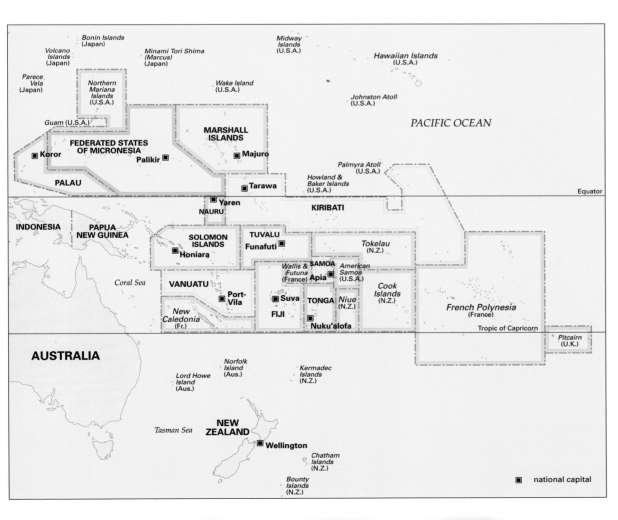

Oceania contains thousands of islands scattered across the Pacific Ocean. Some are mountainous and volcanic, while others are made up of coral that has accumulated on the tops of submerged volcanoes.

ANTARCTICA

Antarctica is the coldest place on earth. It is a mountainous and mostly ice-covered continent surrounding the South Pole. It is also the driest continent, though it holds almost nine-tenths of the planet's ice. Much of the region is poorly mapped because it is difficult to reach and has a very harsh climate. But research on Antarctica has helped in the understanding of the way the southern continents have reached their present positions. Its climate influences weather systems all over the world. The ice sheet over Antarctica holds a record of recent climatic change and of pollution, including the presence of greenhouse gases. The ice sheet comprises so much of the world's ice and snow, that were it to melt, the world mean sea level would rise by 200 ft (60 m).

Antarctica has no permanent population although scientists carry out research there. In 1982, scientists located a hole in the ozone layer of the atmosphere over Antarctica. The ozone layer screens out 90 percent of the sun's ultraviolet radiation. Damage to it has been attributed to chlorofluorocarbons, chemicals used as propellants in some aerosol spray cans. These chemicals are also used in industry and in the coolant system of refrigerators.

The ozone hole is seasonal, developing only in the Antarctic winter and spring, and its size also changes. An increase in ultraviolet radiation would decrease the yield of farmers' crops, change climates around the world, and also lead to an increase in the number of cases of skin cancer.

Antarctica was once part of the ancient supercontinent of Gondwanaland, which also comprised Australia, New Zealand, and the southwest Pacific islands. About 500 million years ago, it was near the equator and had a warm, wet climate. Coal deposits give evidence of this. As Gondwanaland broke up, the part that became Antarctica drifted toward the South Pole and remained there, while the other continents drifted away to the warmer north.

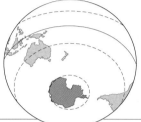

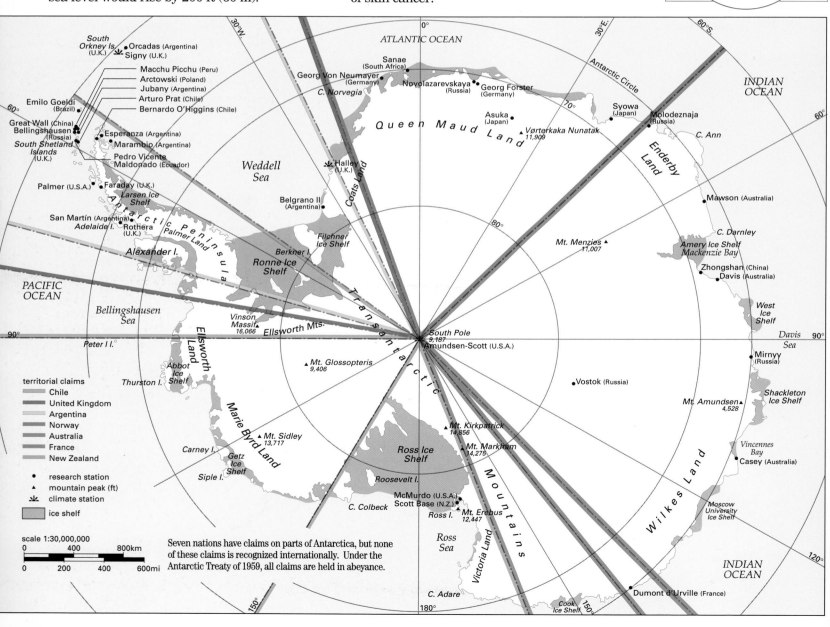

Seven nations have claims on parts of Antarctica, but none of these claims is recognized internationally. Under the Antarctic Treaty of 1959, all claims are held in abeyance.

THE POLITICAL AND CULTURAL WORLD

Despite claims to parts of Antarctica by various nations, people from any part of the world can go anywhere in Antarctica, providing their purpose is peaceful, because under international agreement, Antarctica is a demilitarized, nuclear-free zone.

Under recent agreements, restrictions have been placed on the development of the continent. Under the 1991 Environmental Protocol, for example, mining was banned for a period of 50 years. Some campaigning conservationists would like to go further and declare that Antarctica should become a world park, dedicated to science and the preservation of this fragile wilderness. Early this century several sledge expeditions set out to reach the South Pole at the heart of the interior. A Norwegian, Roald Amundsen (1872–1928), was the first to arrive on December 14, 1911. He was followed a month later by Robert F. Scott (1868–1912), and a team of British explorers, who perished in a blizzard on the return journey. In 1929 the American Richard E. Byrd (1888–1957) became the first man to fly over the South Pole.

LAND

Area of exposed rock 18,650 sq mi (48,310 sq km)
Highest point Vinson Massif 16,066 ft (4,897 m)
Height of surface at South Pole 9,187 ft (2,800 m)
Maximum thickness of ice 15,669 ft (4,776 m)

World's lowest recorded temperature, –128°F (–89.2°C) Vostok, Antarctica

HABITATS

The long chain of the Transantarctic Mountains runs across the whole of Antarctica, passing close to the South Pole and dividing the continent into two unequal parts: Lesser Antarctica and the massive semicircle of Greater Antarctica. From Lesser Antarctica the mountainous Antarctic Peninsula snakes northeast toward the southern tip of South America to the west of the Weddell Sea. The Ross Sea is a smaller gulf south of New Zealand. The southern end of both these seas is covered by permanent ice shelves.

The hostile conditions in Antarctica, combined with long months of darkness, limit plant life to lichens, mosses, algae, and molds in the few ice-free areas. There are no land mammals in Antarctica, but whales and seals feed on masses of tiny, shrimplike krill, while porpoises and dolphins are attracted by shoals of fish, especially Atlantic perch. With no land predators, the Antarctic coast is a haven for birds. Emperor penguins, Antarctic petrels, and South Polar skuas breed here and nowhere else, and more than 40 other species of birds live in Antarctica.

CLIMATE

Temperatures in Antarctica rarely rise above 32°F (0°C) in summer, and they plummet in winter from -40 to -94°F (-40 to -70°C). Strong winds sweep outward from the plateau at 43 mph (70 km/h), with gusts reaching 118 mph (190 km/h). The wind chill factor makes conditions even worse. On the Antarctic Peninsula, milder winds from neighboring oceans raise summer temperatures slightly. High atmospheric pressure, giving clear winter skies, dominates the interior of the continent.

The winds blow loose snow across the surface, creating blinding blizzards. Yet Antarctica has little precipitation. With about 2 in. (50 mm) of snow a year, it is classified as a desert. Only trace amounts of precipitation are recorded at climate stations in the region. By the end of March, the sun sets on Antarctica, and the continent is in freezing darkness for six months. Although the summer is very short, the land receives more sunlight than equatorial regions do throughout the year. However, the ice sheet reflects most of the sun's energy back into the atmosphere.

CLIMATE

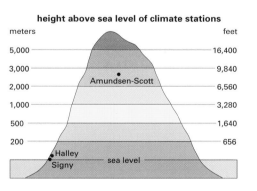

height above sea level of climate stations

Signy

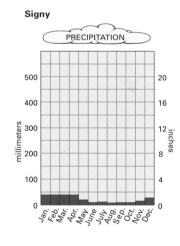

PRECIPITATION

Halley

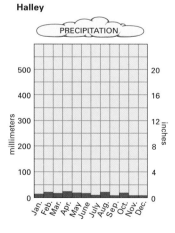

PRECIPITATION

Amundsen-Scott

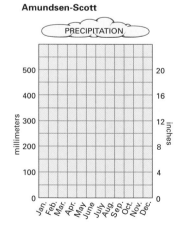

PRECIPITATION

Signy

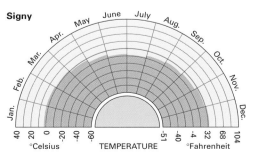

Halley

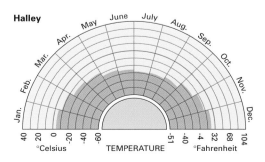

Amundsen-Scott

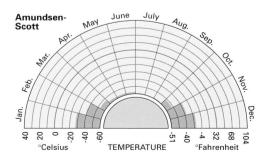

GLOSSARY

acid rain   Rain that has become more acid by combining with waste gases discharged into the atmosphere.

Arctic   The region lying north of latitude 66 32N, where for a time in summer the sun never sets and in winter it never rises.

arid dry   Arid areas generally have less than 10 in. (250 mm) of rain a year.

atoll   A coral reef enclosing a lagoon.

bauxite   The ore that is smelted to make the metal aluminum.

biome   A major global unit in ecology, with its own plants and animals, e.g. savanna grassland.

bituminous coal   Black coal with less carbon than anthracite but more than lignite.

cash crop   A crop grown for sale rather than subsistence.

cereal   A food crop and member of the grass family.

colony   A territory under the control of another country.

Commonwealth   A loose association of countries that are former members of the British empire.

communism   A social, political, and economic system based on the communal ownership of property.

coniferous forest   One of cone-bearing, usually evergreen trees.

conservation   The management and protection of natural resources.

constitutional monarchy   A form of government with a hereditary monarch and a constitution.

consumer goods   Goods bought for people's needs, rather than for manufacturing uses.

continental climate   A climate with a wide daily and seasonal variation of temperature and low rainfall, usually occurring in the interior of continents.

continental drift   The complex process by which the continents move their positions relative to each other on the plates of the earth's crust. Also known as plate tectonics.

coral reef   An underwater ridge or mound composed mostly of dead and living coral.

deciduous   Shedding leaves annually.

deforestation   Cutting down and clearing of forested land.

delta   A usually triangular deposit of sand and soil at the mouth of a river.

democracy   A form of government in which decisions are made by the people or those elected by them.

dependency   A territory subject to the laws of another country but not formally part of it.

desert   An arid area with less than 10 in. (250 mm) of rain a year.

desertification   The creation of desert by overgrazing, soil erosion, or climate change.

dictator   A ruler with absolute power.

empire   A political organization of countries and territories in which one dominates the rest.

endemic species   A species that is native to a specific area.

erosion   The process by which exposed land is broken down into small pieces or worn away by water, wind, or ice.

evergreen   Having green leaves throughout the year.

exports   Goods and services sold to other countries.

fault   A fracture in the earth's crust.

federalism   A form of constitutional government in which power is shared between a central, or federal, government and state or provincial governments.

ferroalloy metals   Metals blended with iron in the manufacture of steel.

fjord   A steep-sided inlet formed when a U-shaped valley is drowned by the sea.

fossil fuel   A fuel such as oil, coal, peat, or natural gas, formed from ancient organic remains.

global warming   An increase in the earth's average temperature, which some scientists believe will result from the greenhouse effect.

greenhouse effect   The process in which radiation from the sun passes through the atmosphere, is reflected off the surface of the earth, and is then trapped by gases in the atmosphere. The buildup of carbon dioxide and other gases increases the effect.

Gross Domestic Product (GDP)   The total value of a country's annual output of goods and services.

Gross National Product (GNP)   A country's GDP plus income from abroad.

habitat   The native environment in which a plant or animal lives.

hardwood   The wood from trees other than conifers, which produce softwood. Hardwoods are generally stronger and more resistant to rot.

ice age   A geological period during which glaciers covered large parts of the earth.

imports   Goods and services bought from other countries.

indigenous people   The original inhabitants of a region.

international dollar (Int $)   Standardized international dollar values are used to measure purchasing power parity. Using a standardized unit provides the best available starting point for comparisons of economic strength and well-being between countries without being influenced by currency exchange rates.

lava   Molten rock from a volcano; also its solid form when cooled.

lignite   A dark brownish coal that is softer than anthracite.

llanos   Tropical grasslands in South America.

maritime climate   A moist climate generally found in areas near the sea.

Mediterranean climate   One with warm, wet winters and hot, dry summers.

military regime   A government controlled by the armed forces.

monarchy   A form of rule where there is a hereditary head of state.

monsoon   Tropical wind systems that reverse direction with the seasons; also, the rain brought by these winds.

multiparty system   A system of rule in which parties compete for votes in elections.

nomad   A member of a group of people who migrate seasonally in search of food, water, or grazing for their animals.

official language   The language used by governments, schools, courts, and other official institutions in countries where there is no single common language.

one-party system   A system of rule where there is no competition at elections, and all but the government party is banned.

pampas   Temperate grasslands in South America.

peat   A thick layer of partly decomposed plant remains found in wetlands. High acidity, low temperatures, and low nutrient and oxygen levels prevent total decomposition.

per capita   For each person.

permafrost   A permanently frozen layer of soil beneath the topsoil.

plateau   A large area of level, high land.

polar regions   Regions extending from the poles to the lines of latitude known as the Arctic and Antarctic circles. At these high latitudes the sun does not set in midsummer.

polder   Low-lying land reclaimed from the sea by the building of dikes, particularly in the Netherlands.

prairie   The flat grassland in the interior of North America, used for cereal crops.

precipitation   Moisture reaching the earth from the atmosphere in the form of mist, dew, rain, sleet, snow, and hail.

province   An administrative division of a country.

purchasing power parity (PPP)   A way of measuring GDP based on standardized international dollar values (Int $). Using Int $ values means that the PPP is less prone to fluctuations in exchange rates that may distort the comparisons between countries.

radioactivity   The radiation emitted from atomic nuclei. This is greatest when the atom is split, as in a nuclear reactor.

rain forest   Forest where there is abundant rainfall all year. Tropical rain forests are rich in plant and animal species, and growth is lush and very rapid.

republic   A form of government with a head of state that is elected or nominated.

rift valley   A long valley formed when a block of land between two faults subsides.

Romance languages   Family of languages derived from Latin.

savanna   A habitat of open grassland with scattered trees in tropical and subtropical areas.

scrub vegetation   Area of low trees and shrubs with tough evergreen leaves, found where there is drought in summer.

sediment   Material, such as gravel, sand, or silt, that has been deposited by water, ice, or wind.

semiarid   Having little rainfall. Semiarid areas have enough moisture to support a little more vegetation than a desert can.

softwood   The wood from coniferous trees.

soil erosion   The removal of the topsoil from land, mainly by the action of wind and rain.

steppe   An open grassy plain with few trees or shrubs. It has low, sporadic rainfall, and wide ranges of annual temperature.

subsistence   The minimum level of providing for one's needs, such as food and shelter.

subtropical zone   Either of the two zones between the tropical and temperate zones. The subtropical zones have marked seasonal changes of temperature but are never very cold.

sustainable development   Use of the earth's resources to improve people's lives without diminishing the ability of the earth to support life today and in the future.

taiga   The coniferous, evergreen forests of subarctic lands, covering large areas of northern North America and Eurasia.

temperate zone   Either of the two zones in the middle latitudes. Such zones lie between the warm tropics and cold polar regions.

tropics   The area between the Tropic of Cancer and the Tropic of Capricorn. The lines mark latitudes farthest from the equator where the sun is still found directly overhead at midday in midsummer.

tundra   Level, treeless land lying in the very cold northern parts of Europe, Asia, and North America.

wetland   Land having wet and spongy soil, such as a swamp, bog, or marsh.

Gazetteer and Index

This gazetteer and index lists places, features, such as rivers or mountains, and subjects found in the atlas. Page references given in **bold** type refer to a map entry. Page references in *italic* type refer to a flag entry. Page numbers in regular type refer to text entries. Where applicable, the first number (in **bold** type) includes coordinates giving the latitude (distance north or south of 0°, the Equator) and longitude (distance east or west of 0°, the Greenwich Meridian).

Abbreviations:
b. bay, *c.* country, *d.* district, *des.* desert, *est.* estuary, *f.* feature, *i.* island, *isls.* islands, *l.* lake, *mt.* mountain, *mts.* mountains, *p.* province, *pen.* peninsula, *r.* river, *s.* state, *str.* strait

Aachen (Germany) **31**
Aare (*r.*) (Switzerland), **30**, 47.37N 8.13E
Abadan (Iran) **37**
Abbot Ice Shelf (Antarctica), **56**, 73.00S 92.00W
Abéché (Chad), **38**, 13.49N 20.49E; **39**
Aberdeen, **22** (Scotland, United Kingdom), 57.08N 2.07W; **23**
Aberystwyth (Wales, United Kingdom), **22**, 52.25N 4.06W; **23**
Abidjan (Côte d'Ivoire), **40**, 2.19N 4.01W; **41**
Aboriginal Australians 52
Abu Dhabi (United Arab Emirates), **36**, 24.27N 54.23E; **37**
Abuja (Nigeria), **40**, 9.12N 7.11E; **41**
Acapulco (Mexico), **16**, 16.51N 99.56W
Accra (Ghana), **40**, 5.33N 0.15W; **41**
Achill (*i.*) (Ireland), **22**, 53.57N 10.00W; **23**
Acid rain 8
Acklins Island (Bahamas), **16**, 22.30N 74.10W
Aconcagua (*mt.*) (Argentina), **18**, 32.37S 70.00W; **4**, **6**, **10**
Adamawa Highlands, **40**, 7.05N 12.00E
Adana (Turkey), **36**, 37.00N 35.19E; **37**
Adare, Cape (Antarctica), **56**, 71.17S 170.14E
Adda (*r.*) (Italy), **28**, 45.08N 9.55E
Addis Ababa (Ethiopia), **38**, 9.03N 38.42E; **39**
Adelaide (South Australia), **52**, 34.56S 138.36E; **53**
Adelaide Island (Antarctica), **56**, 67.15S 68.30W
Aden (Yemen), **36** 12.50N 45.00E; **37**
Aden, Gulf of, **36**, 13.00N 47.00E
Adige (*r.*) (Italy), **28**, 45.10N 12.20E
Admiralty Islands (Papua New Guinea), **52**, 2.00S 147.20E
Adour (*r.*) (France), **24**, 43.32N 1.32W
Adriatic Sea **28**, **32**, 32
Aegean Sea **28**
Afar language 39
Afghanistan (*c.*), **36**, 33.00N 65.30E; **5**, **34**, 36, *37*, **44**
Africa **7**, **11**
see also Central Africa; Northern Africa; Southern Africa
Afrikaaners 43
Afrikaans language 43
Agadez (Niger), **38**, 17.00N 7.56E; **39**
Agano (*r.*) (Japan), **50**, 37.58N 139.02E
Agra (India), **44**, 27.09N 78.00E; **45**
Agriculture **10–11**, 10
Ahaggar (*mts.*) (Algeria), **38**, 24.00N 5.50E; **5**, **7**, **11**
Ahmadabad (India), **44**, 23.03N 72.40E; **45**
Ahvaz (Iran) **37**
Air (*mts.*) (Niger), **38**, 20.00N 8.30E
Aix-en-Provence (Provence-Alpes-Côte-d'Azur, France) **25**
Ajaccio (Corsica, France), **24**, 41.55N 8.43E; **25**
Akaishi Mountains (Japan), **50**, 35.20N 138.10E
Akita (Japan), **50**, 39.44N 140.05E; **51**
Akranes (Iceland) **21**
Aksau (Xinjiang, China) **47**
Aktyubinsk (Kazakhstan) **35**
Akureyri (Iceland), **20**, 65.41N 18.04W; **21**
Alabama (*s.*) (United States) **15**
Åland (*isls.*) (Finland), **20**, 60.00N 20.00W; 20, **21**, 21
Alaotra, Lake (Madagascar), **42**, 17.30S 48.30E
Alaska (*s.*) (United States), **14**, 66.00N 153.00W; 14, **15**, 15
Alaska Current **7**
Alaska, Gulf of **4**, **6**, **10**
Alaska Peninsula (United States), **14**, 56.00N 160.00W
Alaska Range (*mts.*) (United States), **14**, 62.10N 152.00W
Albacete (Spain), **26**, 39.00N 1.52W; **27**
Albania (*c.*), **32**, 41.00N 20.00E; **5**, *33*
Albanian language 29, 33
Albany (New York, United States) **15**
Albany (*r.*) (Canada), **12**, 52.10N 82.00W
Albany (Western Australia) **52**, 34.57S 117.54E; **53**
Alberta (*p.*) (Canada) **13**
Albert, Lake (Uganda/Democratic Republic of the Congo), **40**, 1.45N 31.00E; 40
Ålborg (Denmark), **20**, 57.03N 9.56E; **21**
Aldabra Islands (Seychelles), **42**, 9.00S 47.00E
Aleppo (Syria), **36**, 36.14N 37.10E; **37**
Alessandria (Italy) **29**
Ålesund (Norway), **20**, 62.28N 6.11E; **21**
Aleutian Is. (United States), **14**, 52.00N 170.00W; **4**, **6**, **10**
Alexander Archipelago (United States), **14**, 56.30N 134.30W
Alexander Island (Antarctica), **56**, 71.00S 70.00W
Alexandria (Egypt), **38**, 31.13N 29.55E; **39**
Algeria (*c.*), **38**, 25.00N 3.00E; **5**
Algiers (Algeria), **38**, 36.50N 3.00E; **39**
Al Hillah (Iraq) **37**
Al Hillah (Saudi Arabia) **37**
Aliakmon (*r.*) (Greece), **28**, 40.30N 22.38E
Alicante (Spain), **26**, 38.21N 0.29W; **27**
Alice Springs (Northern Territory, Australia), **52**, 23.42S 133.52E; **53**
Al Jaghbub (Libya) **39**
Al Jawf (Libya) **39**
Al Jawf (Saudi Arabia) **37**
Allahabad (India), **44**, 25.27N 81.50E; **45**
Allegheny Mountains (United States), **14**, 40.00N 80.00W
Aller (*r.*) (Germany), **30**, 52.57N 9.11E
Allier (*r.*) (France), **24**, 46.58N 3.30E
Almaty (Kazakhstan), **34**, 43.19N 76.55E; **35**
Almería (Spain), **26**, 36.50N 2.26W; **27**
Al Mukalla (Yemen), **36**, 14.34N 49.09E; **37**
Alotau (Papua New Guinea), **52**, 10.20S 150.23E; **53**
Alps (*mts.*), **30**, 46.00N 6.50E; **5**, **7**, 30
Al Qaysumah (Saudi Arabia) **37**
Al Qunfudhah (Saudi Arabia) **37**
Alsace (*d.*) (France) **25**
Alsatian language 25
Altai (*mts.*) (Mongolia), **34**, 46.30N 93.30E; **5**, **7**, 34
Altay (Xinjiang, China) **47**
Altun Shan (*mts.*) (China), **46**, 38.10N 87.50E
Aluminum 10
Al Wajh (Saudi Arabia) **37**
Amakusa (*i.*) (Japan), **50**, 32.30N 130.00E; **51**
Amazon basin 8
Amazon (*r.*), **18**, 2.00S 50.00W; **4**, **6**, **10**
Ambalantota (Sri Lanka) **45**
Ambon (Indonesia), **48**, 3.50S 128.10E; **49**
American Samoa (*isls.*) (United States) 15, **55**
Amery Ice Shelf (Antarctica), **56**, 69.30S 72.00E
Amharic language 39
Amiens (Picardy, France), **24**, 49.54N 2.18E; **25**
Amman (Jordan), **36**, 31.57N 35.56E; **37**
Amritsar (India), **44**, 31.35N 74.56E
Amsterdam (Netherlands), **30**, 52.22N 4.54E; **31**
Amu Darya (*r.*) (Turkmenistan/Uzbekistan), **34**, 43.50N 59.00E; **5**, **7**
Amundsen, Mount (Antarctica), **56**, 67.14S 100.00E
Amundsen-Scott (Antarctica), **56**, 90.00S 0.00
Amur (*r.*) (Russia/China), **46**, 53.17N 140.00E; **5**, **7**
Anadyr (Russia) **35**
Anambas Islands (Indonesia), **48**, 3.00N 106.10E; **49**
Anatolia (*f.*) (Turkey), **36**, 38.00N 35.00E
Anchorage (Alaska, United States), **14**, 61.10N 150.00W; **15**
Ancona (Italy) **29**
Andaman Islands (India), **44**, 12.00N 93.00E; **5**, **7**, 45
Andaman Sea **48**
Andes (*mts.*), **18**, 15.00S 72.00W; **4**, **6**, **10**
Andoany (Madagascar) **43**
Andorra (*c.*), **24**, 42.30N 1.32E; **5**, *25*
Andorra la Vella (Andorra), **24**, 42.30N 1.31E; **25**
Andros (*i.*) (Bahamas), **16**, 24.30N 78.00W
Andros (*i.*) (Greece), **28**, 37.50N 24.50E; **29**
Aneto Peak (Spain), **26**, 42.38N 0.40W
Angara (*r.*) (Russia), **34**, 59.00N 100.00E
Angerman (*r.*) (Sweden), **20**, 63.00N 17.43E
Angers (Pays de la Loire, France), **24**, 47.29N 0.32W; **25**
Anglesey (*i.*) (Wales, United Kingdom), **22**, 53.16N 4.25W; **23**
Angoche (Mozambique) **43**
Angola (*c.*), **42**, 11.45S 18.00E; **5**, 42, *43*
Anguilla (*i.*) (United Kingdom), **17**, 18.14N 63.05W; 17
Anhui (*d.*) (China) **47**
Ankara (Turkey), **36**, 39.55N 32.50E; **37**
Ankaratra (*mts.*) (Madagascar), **42**
Annaba (Algeria), **38**, 36.55N 7.47E; **39**
An Nafud (*des.*) (Saudi Arabia), **36**, 28.40N 41.30E
An Najaf (Iraq), **36**, 31.59N 44.19E; **37**
Annam Highlands (Loas/Vietnam), **48**, 17.40N 105.30E
Annamite Range (*mts.*), **48**, 17.40N 105.30E
Annapolis (Maryland, United States) **15**
Ann, Cape (Antarctica) **56** 66.13S 51.10E
Annecy (Rhône-Alpes, France) **25**
Annobón (*i.*) (Equatorial Guinea), **40**, 1.25S 5.36E; **41**
Anshan (Liaoning, China) **47**
Antalya (Turkey), **36**, 36.53N 30.42E; **37**
Antananarivo (Madagascar), **42**, 18.55S 47.31E; **43**
Antarctica 6, **7**, **56**
Antarctic Circle **7**, **56**
Antarctic Peninsula (Antarctica), **56**, 69.30S 65.00W; **6**
Antigua and Barbuda (*c.*), **17**, 17.30N 61.49W; **4**, *17*
Antilles (*isls.*), **16**, 17.00N 70.00W; 16
Antofagasta (Chile), **18**, 23.40S 70.23W; **19**
Antrim (*mts.*), (Northern Ireland, United Kingdom), **22**, 55.00N 6.10W
Antsirabe (Madagascar) **43**
Antsiranana (Madagascar), **42**, 12.19S 49.17E; **43**
Antwerp (Belgium), **30**, 51.13N 3.14E; **31**
Aomori (Japan), **50**, 40.50N 140.43E; **51**
Aotearoa *see* New Zealand, 54
Apennines (*mts.*) (Italy), **28**, 42.00N 13.30E; 29
Apia (Samoa) **55**
Apo (*mt.*) (Philippines), **48**, 6.58N 125.17E
Appalachian Mountains (Canada/United States), **14**, 39.30N 80.00W; **4**, **6**, **10**
Aqaba (Jordan), **36**, 29.32N 35.00E; **37**
Aquitaine (*d.*) (France) **25**
Arabian Peninsula, **36**, 21.20N 46.44E; **5**, **7**
Arabian Sea **5**, **7**, **36**, **44**
Arabic language 25, 37, 38, 39, 43
Arab League 39
Arabs 38
Arad (Romania) **33**
Arafura Sea **48**, **52**
Araguaia (*r.*) (Brazil), **18**, 5.30S 48.05W
Arakan Yoma (*mts.*) (Myanmar), **48**, 20.00N 94.00E
Aral Sea (Kazakhstan/Uzbekistan), **34**, 44.00N 60.00E; **5**, **7**, **36**
Aralsk (Kazakhstan) **35**
Aran Is. (Ireland), **22**, 53.07N 9.38W; **23**
Ararat (*mt.*) (Turkey), **36**, 39.45N 44.15E
Aras (*r.*), **36**, 40.00N 48.28E
Aravalli Range (*mts.*) (India), **44**, 25.30N 74.00E
Arawak language 19
Arbil (Iraq) **37**
Arctic **6–7**
Arctic Circle **5**, **7**, **14**, **20**, **34**
Arctic Ocean **5**, **7**, **14**, **20**, **34**
Arctowski (Antarctica), **56**, 62.09S 58.28W
Ardennes (*f.*) (France), **24**, 49.40N 5.00E
Arequipa (Peru), **18**, 17.58S 63.14W; **19**
Argentina (*c.*), **18**, 35.00S 65.00W; **4**, *19*
Argos (Greece) **29**
Århus (Denmark), **20**, 56.09N 10.13E; **21**
Arica (Chile), **18**, 18.30S 70.20W; **19**
Arid regions 6
Aride (*i.*), **40**, 4.13S 55.40E
Arizona (*s.*) (United States) **15**
Arkansas (*s.*) (United States) **15**
Arkansas (*r.*) (United States), **14**, 33.50N 91.00W
Arkhangelsk (Russia), **34**, 64.32N 40.40E; **35**
Arlon (Belgium) **31**
Armenia (*c.*), **34**, 40.00N 45.00E; **5**, 34, *35*
Armenian language 35
Arnhem (Netherlands) **31**
Arnhem Land (*f.*) (Australia), **52**, 13.10S 134.30E
Arno (*r.*) (Italy), **28**, 43.43N 10.17E
Arran (*i.*) (Scotland, United Kingdom), **22**, 55.35N 5.14W; **23**
Aru Islands (Indonesia), **48**, 6.00S 134.30E; **52**
Arua (Uganda) **41**
Aruba (*i.*) (Netherlands), **17**, 12.30N 70.00W; 17
Asahikawa (Japan), **50**, 43.46N 142.23E; **51**
Asahi (*mt.*) (Japan), **50**, 43.42N 142.54E
Ascension (*i*) (United Kingdom) **5**, **7**, 23
Ash 8
Ashkhabad (Turkmenistan), **34**, 37.58N 58.24E; **35**
Ashmore and Cartier Islands (Australia) **53**
Ash Sharawrah (Saudi Arabia) **37**
Asia **7**
see also Southeast Asia; Southwest Asia
Asmara (Eritrea), **38**, 15.20N 38.58E; **39**
Assab (Eritrea) **39**
As Sulaymaniyah (Iraq) **37**
Astana (Kazakhstan), **34**, 51.10N 71.28E; **35**
Astrakhan (Russia) **35**
Asuka (Antarctica), **56**, 71.32S 24.08E
Asunción (Paraguay) **18**, 25.15S 57.40W; **19**
Aswan (Egypt), **38**, 24.05N 32.56E; **39**
Asyut (Egypt), **38**, 27.14N 31.07E; **39**
Atacama Desert (Chile), **18**, 21.00S 69.00W; **4**, **6**, **10**
Atar (Mauritania), **38**, 20.32N 13.08W; **39**
Atbara (Sudan), **38**, 17.42N 34.00E; **39**
Atbara (*r.*), **38**, 17.47N 34.00E
Athabasca, Lake (Canada), **12**, 59.07N 110.00W
Athabasca (*r.*) (Canada), **12**, 58.40N 110.50W
Athens (Greece), **28**, 37.59N 23.42E; **29**, 29
Atlanta (Georgia, United States), **14**, 33.45N 84.23W; **15**
Atlantic Ocean **4**, **6**, **10**, 18
Atlantic ridge 20
Atlas Mountains *see* High Atlas; Saharan Atlas
At Ta'if (Saudi Arabia) **37**
Atyrau (Kazakhstan) **35**
Auckland (New Zealand), **54**, 36.55S 174.45E
Augsburg (Germany) **31**
Augusta (Maine, United States) **15**
Aurangabad (India) **45**
Austin (Texas, United States) **15**
Australia (*c.*), **52**, 27.00S 135.00E; **5**, **7**, 52, *53*
Australian Alps (Australia), **52**, 36.30S 148.30E

Australian Capital Territory (*d.*) (Australia) **53**
Austria (*c.*), **30**, 47.30N 14.00E; **5**, 30, *31*
Auvergne (*d.*) (France) **25**
Auxerre (Burgundy, France) **25**
Aveiro (Portugal) **27**
Avignon (Provence-Alpes-Côte-d'Azur, France), **24**, 43.56N 4.48E; **25**
Avila (Spain) **27**
Ayers Rock *see* Uluru
Azerbaijan (*c.*), **34**, 40.10N 47.50E; **5**, 34, *35*
Azeril language 35
Azores (*isls.*) (Portugal) **5**, **7**, **26, 27**
Azov, Sea of (Ukraine/Russia), **34**

Babuyan Islands (Philippines), **48**, 19.20N 121.30E; **49**
Bacău (Romania) **33**
Back (*r.*) (Canada), **12**, 66.37N 96.00W
Bacolod (Philippines) **49**
Badajoz (Spain), **26**, 38.53N 6.58W; **27**
Bad Ischl (Austria) **31**
Baffin Bay, **12**, 72.00N 63.00W; **4**, **6**, **10**
Baffin Island (Canada), **12**, 68.05N 70.00W; **4**, **6**, **10**
Baghdad (Iraq), **36**, 33.20N 44.26E; **37**
Baghlan (Afghanistan), **36**, 36.11N 68.44E; **37**
Baguio (Philippines), **48**, 16.25N 120.37E; **49**
Bahamas (*c.*), **16**, 23.30N 75.00W; **4**, **6**, **10**, 16, *17*
Bahasa Indonesia language 49
Bahasa Malaysia language 49
Bahawalpur (Pakistan), **44**, 29.24N 71.36E; **45**
Bahía Blanca (Argentina), **18**, 38.45S 62.15W; **19**
Bahrain (*c.*), **36**, 26.00N 50.35E; **5**, 36, *37*
Baicheng (Jilin, China) **47**
Baikal, Lake (Russia), **34**, 53.30N 108.00E; **5**, **7**
Baja California (*pen.*) (Mexico), **16**, 25.00N 112.00W
Baker Island (United States) 15, **55**
Baku (Azerbaijan), **34**, 40.22N 49.53E; **35**
Balaton, Lake (Hungary), **32**, 46.55N 17.50E
Balaton Füred (Hungary) **33**
Balearic Islands (Spain), **26**, 39.30N 2.30W; 26, **27**, 27
Bali (*i.*) (Indonesia), **48**, 8.30S 115.05E; **49**
Balikpapan (Indonesia), **48**, 1.15S 116.50E; **49**
Balkan Mountains, **32**, 42.50N 24.30E
Balkhash, Lake (Kazakhstan), **34**, 46.40N 75.00E; **5**, **7**
Balsas (*r.*) (Mexico), **16**, 18.10N 102.05W
Baltic Sea **5**, **7**, **20**, **30**, 32, **34**, 34
Baltimore (Maryland, United States), **14**, 39.17N 76.37W; **15**
Bamako (Mali), **38**, 12.40N 7.59W; **39**
Bambari (Central African Republic), **40**, 5.45N 20.40E
Banda Aceh (Indonesia) **49**
Bandar Abbas (Iran), **36**, 27.10N 56.15E; **37**
Bandar Seri Begawan (Brunei), **48**, 4.56N 114.58E; **49**
Banda Sea **48**
Bandung (Indonesia), **48**, 6.57S 107.34E; **49**
Bangalore (India), **44**, 12.58N 77.35E; **45**
Bangassou (Central African Republic) **41**
Bangka (*i.*) (Indonesia), **48**, 2.20S 106.10E; **49**
Bangkok (Thailand), **48**, 13.45N 100.35E; **49**
Bangladesh (*c.*), **44**, 24.00N 90.00E; **5**, 44, *45*
Bangui (Central African Republic), **40**, 4.23N 18.37E; **41**
Bangweulu, Lake (Zambia), **42**, 11.15S 29.45E
Banja Luka (Bosnia and Herzegovina), **32**, 44.47N 17.11E; **33**
Banjarmasin (Indonesia), **48**, 3.22S 114.36E; **49**
Banjul (Gambia), **40**, 13.28N 16.39W; **41**
Banks Island (Canada), **12**, 73.00N 122.00W
Banks Peninsula (New Zealand), **54**, 43.45S 173.10E
Banská Bystrica (Slovakia) **33**
Baotou (Inner Mongolia, China) **47**
Barbados (*c.*), **17**, 13.20N 59.40W; **4**, 16, *17*
Barcelona (Spain), **26**, 41.25N 2.10E
Barents Sea **5**, **7**, **34**
Bari (Italy), **28**, 41.08N 16.52E; **29**
Barisan Mountains (Indonesia), **48**, 3.30S 102.30E
Barito (*r.*) (Borneo), **48**, 3.35S 114.35E
Barkly Tableland (*f.*) (Australia), **52**, 19.00S 136.40E
Barlee, Lake (dry) (Australia), **52**, 29.30S 119.30E
Barnaul (Russia) **35**
Barra (*i.*) (Scotland, United Kingdom), **22**, 56.59N 7.28W
Barranquilla (Colombia), **18**, 11.00N 74.50W; **19**
Barren Islands (Madagascar), **42**, 18.55S 44.15E
Barrow (Alaska, United States), **14**, 71.16N 156.50W; **15**
Barrow (*r.*) (Ireland), **22**, 52.17N 7.00W
Basel (Switzerland) **30**, 47.33N 7.36 E; **31**
Bashkir language 35
Basque language 25, 27
Basra (Iraq), **36**, 30.33N 47.50E; **37**
Bassein (Myanmar), **48**, 16.45N 94.30E
Basseterre (St. Kitts-Nevis), **17**, 17.17N 62.43W
Bass Strait, **52**, 39.45S 146.00E
Bastia (Corsica, France), **24**, 42.41N 9.26E; **25**
Batan Islands (Philippines), **48**, 20.50N 121.55E; **49**
Baton Rouge (Louisiana, United States) **15**
Battambang (Cambodia), **48**, 13.06N 103.13E; **49**
Batticaloa (Sri Lanka) **45**
Batu Islands (Indonesia), **48**, 0.30S 98.20E; **49**
Baubau (Indonesia) **49**
Bauxite 10
Bavarian Alps (*mts.*) (Germany), **30**, 47.38N 11.30E
Bayan Har Shan (*mts.*) (China), **46**, 34.00N 97.20E
Baydhabo (Somalia) **39**
Bayonne (Aquitaine, France) **25**
Bear Island (Norway) 20
Beaufort Sea **4**, **6**, **10**
Béchar (Algeria) **39**
Beech 6, 8
Beijing (Peking) (China), **46**, 39.55N 116.25E; **47**
Beira (Mozambique), **42**, 19.49S 34.52E; **43**
Beirut (Lebanon), **36**, 33.52N 35.30E; **37**
Bei Shan (*mts.*) (China), **46**, 42.00N 96.00E
Beja (Portugal) **27**
Belarus (*c.*), **34**, 53.00N 27.00E; **5**, 34, *35*
Beledweyne (Somalia) **39**
Belém (Brazil), **18**, 1.27S 48.29W; **19**
Belfast (Northern Ireland, United Kingdom), **22**, 54.36N 5.57W; **23**
Belgium (*c.*), **30**, 51.00N 4.30E; **5**, 30, *31*
Belgrade (Yugoslavia), **32**, 44.49N 20.28E; **33**
Belgrano (Antarctica), **56**, 77.58S 38.48W
Belitung (*i.*) (Indonesia), **48**, 3.00S 108.00E; **49**
Belize (*c.*), **16**, 17.00N 88.30W; **4**, 16, *17*
Belle-Ile (*i.*) (France), **24**, 47.20N 3.10W
Bellingshausen (Antarctica), **56**, 62.12S 58.54W
Bellinzona (Switzerland) **31**
Belmopan (Belize), **16**, 17.25N 88.46W
Belo Horizonte (Brazil), **18**, 19.45S 43.53W; **19**
Bemaraha, Plateau of (Madagascar), **42**, 20.00S 45.15E
Bengal, Bay of, **44**, 13.00N 85.00E; **5**, **7**
Bengali language 23, 45
Benghazi (Libya), **38**, 32.07N 20.05E; **39**
Bengkulu (Indonesia) **49**
Benguela (Angola) **43**
Benguela Current **7**
Benin (*c.*), **40**, 9.00N 2.30E; **5**, 40, *41*
Ben Nevis (*mt.*) (Scotland, United Kingdom), **22**, 56.48N 5.00W
Benue (*r.*) (Cameroon/Nigeria), **40**, 7.52N 6.45E
Berbera (Somalia) **39**
Berbers 38
Bergen (Norway), **20**, 60.23N 5.20E; **21**
Bering Sea **5**, **7**, **14**, **34**, 34
Bering Strait, **14**, 65.30N 169.00W; 14
Berkner (*i.*) (Antarctica), **56**, 79.30S 49.30W
Berlin (Germany), **30**, 52.31N 13.24E; **31**
Bermuda (*i.*) (United Kingdom), **17**, 32.18N 65.00W; **4**, 17
Bern (Switzerland), **30**, 46.57N 7.26E; **31**
Bernardo O'Higgins, **56**, 63.19S 57.54W
Bernese Alps (*mts.*) (Switzerland), **30**, 46.30N 7.37E
Besançon (Franche-Comté, France), **24**, 47.14N 6.02E; **25**
Bhopal (India), **44**, 23.17N 77.28E; **45**
Bhubaneshwar (India) **45**
Bhutan (*c.*), **44**, 27.25N 90.00E; **5**, 44, *45*
Biak (*i.*) (Indonesia), **48**, 0.55S 136.00E; **49**, **52**
Bialystok (Poland), **32**, 53.09N 23.01E; **33**
Bié Plateau (Angola), **42**, 13.00S 16.00E
Bihać (Bosnia and Herzegovina) **33**
Bihor Mountains (Romania), **32**, 46.26N 22.43E
Bikaner (India) **45**
Bilbao (Spain), **26**, 43.15N 2.56W; **27**
Bilefeld (Germany) **31**
Billings (Montana, United States) **15**
Bilma (Niger) **39**
Bioko (*i.*) (Equatorial Guinea), **40**, 3.25N 8.45E; **41**
Biratnagar (Nepal), **44**, 26.18N 87.17E; **45**
Birjand (Iran) **37**
Birmingham (Alabama, United States) **15**
Birmingham (England, United Kingdom), **22**, 52.30N 1.55W; **23**
Biscay, Bay of, **24**, 45.00N 3.00W
Bishkek (Kyrgyzstan), **34**, 42.53N 74.46E; **35**
Bislama language 55
Bismarck (North Dakota, United States) **15**
Bismarck Archipelago (Papua New Guinea), **52**, 3.35S 147.00E; **5**, **7**, **53**
Bissau (Guinea-Bissau), **40**, 11.52N 15.39W; **41**
Bitterroot Range (*mts.*) (United States), **14**, 47.06N 115.00W
Biwa, Lake (Japan), **50**, 35.20N 136.10E
Black Forest (Germany), **30**, 48.00N 8.00E
Black Hills (United States), **14**, 44.17N 103.28W
Black Sea **5**, **7**, **28**, **32**, **34**, 34, **36**
Blagoveshchensk (Russia) **35**
Blanc, Mont, **24**, 45.50N 6.52E; **5**, **7**
Blantyre (Malawi), **42**, 15.46S 35.00E; **43**
Bloemfontein (South Africa), **42**, 29.07S 26.14E; **43**
Blue Ridge Mountains (United States), **14**, 36.30N 80.15W
Boa Vista (*i.*) (Cape Verde), **40**, 16.10N 22.50W
Bobaomby, Cape (Madagascar), **42**, 11.48S 49.19E
Bobotov Kuki (*mt.*) (Yugoslavia), **32**, 43.08N 19.03E
Bodele (*f.*) (Chad), **38**, 16.50N 17.10E
Bodo (Norway) **21**
Bogda Shan (*mts.*) (Xinjiang, China), **46**, 44.00N 92.00E
Bogotá (Colombia), **18**, 4.38N 74.05W; **19**
Bo Hai (*b.*), **46**, 38.30N 119.30E
Bohemian Forest, **30**, 49.20N 13.10E; **32**
Bohol (*i.*) (Philippines), **48**, 9.45S 124.10E
Boise (Idaho, United States) **15**
Bokna Fjord (Norway), **20**, 59.10N 5.35E
Bolivia (*c.*), **18**, 17.00S 65.00W; **4**, 18, *19*
Bolmen (*l.*) (Sweden), **20**, 56.55N 13.40E
Bologna (Italy), **28**, 44.30N 11.20E; **29**
Bolzano (Italy) **29**
Bombay *see* Mumbai
Bonaire (*i.*) (Netherlands Antilles), **17**, 12.15N 68.27W
Bonin Islands (Japan), **48**, 27.00N 142.00E; **55**
Bonn (Germany), **30**, 50.44N 7.05E; **31**
Boothia Peninsula (Canada), **12**, 70.30N 95.00W
Borås (Sweden) **21**
Borborema, Plateau of (Brazil) **18**, 8.00S 37.00W
Bordeaux (Aquitaine, France), **24**, 44.50N 0.34W; **25**
Borneo (*i.*) (Indonesia), **48**, 1.00N 114.00E; **5**, **7**, **49**, **52**
Bornholm (*i.*) (Denmark), **20**, 55.10N 15.00E; **21**
Bosnia and Herzegovina (*c.*), **32**, 44.20N 17.50E; **5**, **28**, 32, *33*
Bosnian language 33
Boso Peninsula (Japan), **50**, 35.20N 140.00E
Bosporus (*str.*), **32**, 41.07N 29.04E; **36**
Bosten, Lake (Xinjiang, China), **46**, 42.00N 87.00E
Boston (Massachusetts, United States), **14**, 42.21N 71.04W; **15**
Bothnia, Gulf of, **20**, 63.30N 20.30E
Botrange (*mt.*) (Belgium), **30**, 50.30N 6.04E
Botswana (*c.*), **42**, 21.00S 24.00E; **5**, 42, *43*
Bougainville (*i.*) (Papua New Guinea), **52**, 6.00S 155.00E; **53**
Boulougne (Nord-Pas-de-Calais, France) **25**
Bounty Islands (New Zealand), **54**, 48.20S 179.00E; **55**
Bourges (Centre, France) **25**
Brač (*i.*) (Croatia), **32**, 43.20N 16.38E
Bradford (England, United Kingdom) **23**
Brahmaputra (*r.*), **44**, 23.50N 89.45E
Brandon (Manitoba, Canada) **13**
Brasília (Brazil), **18**, 15.54S 47.50W; **19**
Braşov (Romania), **32**, 45.40N 25.35E; **33**
Bratislava (Slovakia), **32**, 48.10N 17.10E; **33**
Brava (*i.*) (Cape Verde) **40**, 15.00N 24.55W
Brazil (*c.*), **18**, 10.00S 52.00W; **4**, **17**, 18, *19*
Brazil Current **7**
Brazilian Highlands **4**, **6**, **10**
Brazil, Plateau of, **18**, 14.00S 45.00W
Brazzaville (Republic of the Congo), **40**, 4.14S 15.14E; **41**
Brecon Beacons (*mts.*) (Wales, United Kingdom), **22**, 51.53N 3.27W
Bregenz (Austria) **31**
Breidafjördhur (Iceland), **20**, 65.15N 23.00W
Bremen (Germany), **30**, 53.05N 8.49E; **31**
Bremerhaven (Germany) **31**
Brescia (Italy) **29**
Brest (Brittany, France), **24**, 48.24N 4.29W; **25**
Breton language 25
Bridgetown (Barbados), **17**, 13.06N 59.37W
Brighton (England, United Kingdom), **22**, 50.50N 0.09W; **23**
Brindisi (Italy) **29**
Brisbane (Queensland, Australia), **52**, 27.30S 153.00E; **53**
Bristol (England, United Kingdom), **22**, 51.26N 2.35W; **23**
Bristol Channel, **22**, 51.17N 3.20W
British Columbia (*p.*) (Canada) **13**
British Indian Ocean Territory (United Kingdom) **23**
British Isles **5**, **7**
Brittany (*d.*) (France) **25**
Brno (Czech Republic), **32**, 49.11N 16.39E; **33**
Broken Hill (New South Wales, Australia) **53**
Brooks Range (*mts.*) (Alaska, United States), **14**, 68.50N 152.00W
Broome (Western Australia) **53**
Brugge (Bruges) (Belgium), **30**, 51.13N 3.14E; **31**
Brunei (*c.*), **48**, 4.56N 114.58E; **5**, 48, *49*
Brunswick (Germany) **31**
Brussels (Belgium), **30**, 50.50N 4.23E; **31**
Bucharest (Romania), **32**, 44.25N 26.06E; **33**
Budapest (Hungary), **32**, 47.30N 19.03E; **33**
Buenos Aires (Argentina), **18**, 34.40S 58.30W; **19**
Buffalo (New York, United States) **15**
Bug (*r.*), **32**, 52.29N 21.11E
Bujumbura (Burundi), **40**, 3.22S 29.21E; **41**
Bukavu (Democratic Republic of the Congo) **41**
Bulawayo (Zimbabwe), **42**, 20.10S 28.43E; **43**
Bulgaria (*c.*), **32**, 42.30N 25.00E; **5**, 32, *33*
Bulgarian language 33
Bumba (Democratic Republic of the Congo) **41**
Bunbury (Western Australia) **53**
Bundaberg (Queensland, Australia) **53**
Bungo Channel (Japan), **50**, 32.52N 132.30E
Bunia (Democratic Republic of the Congo) **41**
Buraydah (Saudi Arabia) **37**
Burgas (Bulgaria), **32**, 42.30N 27.29E; **33**
Burgos (Spain), **26**, 42.21N 3.41W; **27**
Burgundy (*d.*) (France) **25**
Burkina Faso (*c.*), **40**, 12.15N 1.30W; **5**, 40, *41*
Burma *see* Myanmar
Burmese language 49
Burren (Ireland), **22**, 53.00N 9.00W
Buru (*i.*) (Indonesia), **48**, 3.30S 126.30E; **49**
Burundi (*c.*), **40**, 3.30S 30.00E; **5**, 40, *41*
Butte (Montana, United States) **15**
Butung (*i.*) (Indonesia), **48**, 5.00S 122.50E; **49**
Buzău (Romania) **33**
Byala (Bulgaria) **33**
Bydgoszcz (Poland) **32**, 53.16N 18.00E; **33**

Byelorusian language 35
Byrranga Mountains (Russia), **34**, 75.00N 100.00E

Cabinda (*d.*) (Angola), **40**, 5.34S 12.12E; **5**, **41**, 41
Cabora Bassa, Lake (Mozambique), **42**, 15.20S 32.50E
Čačak **33**
Cáceres (Spain) **27**
Cádiz (Spain), **26**, 36.32N 6.18W; **27**
Caen (Lower Normandy, France), **24**, 49.11N 0.22W; **25**
Cagayan de Oro (Philippines), **48**, 8.29N 124.40E
Cagliari (Italy), **28**, 39.14N 9.07E; **29**
Cairngorm Mountains (Scotland, United Kingdom), **22**, 57.04N 3.30W
Cairns (Queensland, Australia), **52**, 16.51S 145.43E; **53**
Cairo (Egypt), **38**, 30.03N 31.15E; **39**
Calais (Nord-Pas-de-Calais, France), **24**, 50.57N 1.52E; **25**
Calatayud (Spain) **27**
Calcutta *see* Kolkata
Calgary (Alberta, Canada), **12**, 51.00N 114.10W; **13**
Cali (Colombia), **18**, 3.24N 76.30W; **19**
California (*s.*) (United States) **15**
California Current **7**
California, Gulf of, **16**, 28.30N 111.00W
Caluula (Somalia) **39**
Camagüey (Cuba), **16**, 21.25N 77.55W
Camargue (*f.*) (France), **24**, 43.40N 4.35E
Cambay, Gulf of, **44**, 20.30N 72.00E
Cambodia (*c.*), **48**, 12.00N 105.00E; **5**, 48, *49*
Cambrian Mountains (Wales, United Kingdom), **22**, 52.33N 3.33W
Cambridge (England, United Kingdom) **23**
Cambridge Bay (*town*) (Nunavut, Canada) **13**
Cameroon (*c.*), **40**, 6.00N 12.30E; **5**, 40, *41*
Cameroon, Mount (Cameroon), **40**, 4.20N 9.05E; **5**, **7**
Campeche, Bay of, **16**, 20.58N 94.00W
Campo Grande (Brazil) **19**
Canada (*c.*), **12**, 55.00N 100.00W; **4**, 12, *13*
- agriculture and fisheries 12
- French 13
- industry 12
- population 8, 12, 13

Canadian (*r.*) (United States), **14**, 35.20N 95.40W
Canadian Shield (*f.*), **12**, 54.00N 82.00W; 12
Canaries Current **7**
Canary Islands (Spain), **5**, **7**, 26, 27
Canberra (Australian Capital Territory), **52**, 35.18S 149.08E; **53**
Cannes (Provence-Alpes-Côte-d'Azur, France) **25**
Cantabrian Mountains (Spain), **26**, 42.55N 5.10W; 26, 27
Canterbury Plains (New Zealand), **54**, 43.50S 171.40E
Cantonese language 47
Cap Corse (Corsica, France) **24**
Cap de la Hague (France), **24**, 49.44N 1.56W
Cape Breton Island (Canada), **12**, 46.00N 60.30W
Cape Cod (Massachusetts, United States), **14**, 42.08N 70.01W
Cape Town (South Africa), **42**, 33.56S 18.28E; **43**
Cape Verde Islands, **40**, 16.00N 24.00W; **5**, **7**, 40, *41*, 103
Cape Vert (Senegal), **40**, 14.45N 17.25W
Cape York Peninsula (Australia), **52**, 12.405S 142.20E
Capitán Arturo Prat (Antarctica), **56**, 62.30S 59.41W
Capri (*i.*) (Italy), **28**, 40.33N 14.13E; **29**, 29
Caracas (Venezuela), **18**, 10.35N 66.56W; **19**
Cardamom Hills (India), **44**, 9.30N 76.55E
Cardiff (Wales, United Kingdom), **22**, 51.28N 3.11W; **23**
Caribbean **4**, **6**, **10**, **16**, 16
Carib language 17, 19
Carnarvon (Western Australia) **53**
Carnegie, Lake (dry) (Australia), **52**, 26.05S 122.30E
Carney Island (Antarctica), **56**, 74.00S 121.00W
Carnic Alps (*mts.*) (Italy), **28**, 46.40N 12.48E
Caroline Islands *see* Federated States of Micronesia
Carpathian Mountains, **32**, 46.20N 25.40E; **5**, **7**
Carpentaria, Gulf of, **52**, 14.00S 139.00E
Carson City (Nevada, United States) **15**
Cartagena (Spain) **26**, 37.36N 0.59W; **27**
Casablanca (Morocco), **38**, 33.39N 7.35W; **39**
Cascade Point (New Zealand), **54**, 44.01S 168.22E
Cascade Range (*mts.*) (United States), **14**, 44.00N 121.30W; 14
Casey (Antarctica), **56**, 66.17S 110.32E
Caspian Depression (Russia/Kazakhstan), **34**, 47.00N 48.00E
Caspian Sea **5**, **7**, **34**, 34, **36**
Cassiar Mountains (Canada), **12**, 58.00N 129.00W
Castellón de la Plana (Spain), **26**, 39.59N 0.03W; **27**
Castelo Branco (Portugal) **27**
Castries (Santa Lucia), **17**, 14.01N 60.59W
Catalan language 25, 27, 29
Catania (Italy), **28**, 37.31N 15.05E; **29**
Caucasus Mountains, **34**, 43.00N 44.00E; **5**, **7**, 34
Cayenne (French Guiana), **18**, 4.55N 52.18W; **18**, **19**
Cayman Islands (United Kingdom), **16**, 19.00N 81.00W; 17
Cebu (Philippines), **48**, 10.15N 123.45E; **49**
Cebu (*i.*) (Philippines), **48**, 10.17N 123.56E
Ceduna (South Australia) **53**
Celebes Sea **48**
Central Africa 40
Central African Republic (*c.*), **40**, 6.30N 20.00E; **5**, **38**, 40, *41*
Central America **4**, **6**, **10**, **16**, 16
Central Europe 30
Central Makran Range (*mts.*) (Pakistan), **44**, 26.30N 65.00E
Central Range (*mts.*) (Papua New Guinea), **52**, 6.00S 144.00E
Central Siberian Plateau (Russia), **34**, 66.00N 108.00E; **5**, **7**, **11**
Centre (*d.*) (France) **25**
Cephalonia (*i.*) (Greece), **28**, 38.15N 20.33E; **29**
Ceram (*i.*) (Indonesia), **48**, 3.10S 129.30E; **49**
Cerf (*i.*) (Seychelles), **40**, 4.38S 55.30E
Ceské Budějovice (Czech Republic) **33**
Ceuta (Spain), **26**, 35.53N 5.19W; 27
Cévennes (*mts.*) (France), **24**, 44.00N 3.30E
Chad (*c.*), **38**, 13.00N 19.00E; **5**, 38, *39*
Chad, Lake, **38**, 13.30N 14.00E; **40**
Chaghcharan (Afghanistan) **37**
Chalcidice (*i.*) (Greece), **28**, 40.30N 23.40E
Chalon (Burgundy, France) **25**
Châlons-sur-Marne (Champagne-Ardenne, France) **25**
Chambal (*r.*) (India), **44**, 25.30N 77.00E
Champagne-Ardenne (*d.*) (France) **25**
Chandrigarth (India) **45**
Chang (Yangtze) (*r.*) (China), **46**, 31.40N 121.15E; 46
Changchun (Jilin, China), **46**, 43.50N 125.20E; **47**
Changsha (Hunan, China) **47**
Channel Islands (United Kingdom), **24**, 49.28N 2.13E; 23
Charente (*r.*) (France), **24**, 45.57N 1.05W
Charleston (South Carolina, United States) **15**
Charleston (West Virginia, United States) **15**
Charlotte (North Carolina, United States) **15**
Charlottetown (Prince Edward Island) (Canada) **13**
Chartres (Centre, France) **25**
Chatham Island (New Zealand), **54**, 44.00S 176.40W
Chatham Islands (New Zealand), **54**, 44.00S 176.40W; **55**
Chechnya 35
Cheju (South Korea), **50**, 33.31N 126.32E; **51**
Cheju (*i.*) (South Korea), **50**, 33.30N 126.35E; **51**
Chelyabinsk (Russia), **34**, 55.10N 61.25E; **35**
Chemnitz (Germany) **31**
Chenab (*r.*) (India/Pakistan), **44**, 32.00N 75.00W
Chengdu (Sichuan, China), **46**, 30.37N 104.06E; **47**
Chennai (Madras) (India), **44**, 13.05N 80.18E; **45**
Cherbourg (Lower Normandy, France) **25**
Cherskiy (Russia) **35**
Cherskogo Range (*mts.*) (Russia), **34**, 65.50N 143.00E
Chesterfield Islands (France), **52**, 19.30S 158.00E
Cheviot Hills (United Kingdom), **22**, 55.22N 2.24W
Cheyenne (Wyoming, United States) **15**
Chiang Mai (Thailand), **48**, 18.48N 98.59E; **49**
Chiba (Japan), **50**, 35.38N 140.07E; **51**
Chicago (Illinois, United States), **14**, 41.50N 87.45W; **15**
Chichewa language 43
Chiclayo (Peru), **18**, 6.47S 79.47W; **19**
Chile (*c.*), **18**, 26.00S 71.00W; **4**, 18, *19*
Chililabombwe (Zambia), **42**, 12.29S 27.53E
Chiloé Island (Chile), **18**, 43.00S 73.00W; **19**
Chiltern Hills (England, United Kingdom), **22**, 51.40N 0.53W
China (*c.*), **46**, 33.00N 105.00E; **5**, **34**, **44**, 46, *47*, **48**, **50**
- population 46

Chinese language 23, 49
Chingola (Zambia) **43**
Chios (*i.*) (Greece), **28**, 38.23N 26.04E; **29**
Chipata (Zambia) **43**
Chiredzi (Zimbabwe) **43**
Chirripó (*mt.*) (Costa Rica), **16**, 9.31N 83.30W
ChiSona language 43
Chita (Russia), **34**, 52.03N 113.35E; **35**
Chittagong (Bangladesh), **44**, 22.20N 91.48E; **45**
Chlorofluorocarbons (CFCs) 56
Choiseul (*i.*) (Solomon Islands), **52**, 7.00S 156.40E
Chokai (*mt.*) (Japan), **50**, 39.08N 140.04E
Ch'ongjin (North Korea), **50**, 41.55N 129.50E; **51**
Ch'ongju (South Korea), **50**, 36.39N 127.27E; **51**
Chongqing (China), **46**, 29.31N 106.35E; **47**
Chonju (South Korea), **50**, 36.39N 127.31E
Christchurch (New Zealand), **54**, 43.32S 172.37E
Christmas Island (Australia), **48**, 10.30S 105.40E; 53
Chronos Archipelago (Chile), **18**, 45.00S 73.00W
Chugoku Mountains (Japan), **50**, 35.00N 133.00E
Chukot Range (*mts.*) (Russia), **34**, 68.13N 179.55E; **34**
Chumphon (Thailand) **49**
Ch'unch'on (South Korea), **50**, 37.52N 127.43E; **51**
Chur (Switzerland) **31**
Churchill (Manitoba, Canada) **13**
Churchill (*r.*) (Canada), **12**, 58.47N 94.12W
Chuvash language 35
Cincinnati (Ohio, United States), **14**, 39.10N 84.30W
Citlaltépetl (*mt.*) (Mexico), **16**, 19.00N 97.20W; **4**, **6**, **10**
Ciudad Bolivár (Venezuela), **18**, 8.06N 1.59W; **18**, **19**
Ciudad Juárez (Mexico), **16**, 31.42N 106.29W
Ciudad Real (Spain) **27**
Ciudad Rodrigo (Spain) **27**
Clermont-Ferrand (Auvergne, France), **24**, 45.47N 3.05E; **25**
Clervaux (Luxembourg), **30**, 50.04N 6.01E
Cleveland (Ohio, United States), **14**, 41.30N 81.41W; **15**
Climate 4, 6
Climatic change 56
Clipperton Island (France), **16**, 10.17N 109.13W
Cluj-Napoca (Romania), **32**, 46.47N 23.37E; **33**
Clutha (*r.*) (New Zealand), **54**, 46.18S 169.05E
Clyde (*r.*) (Scotland, United Kingdom), **22**, 55.58N 4.53W
Coal 10, 56
Coast Mountains (Canada), **12**, 55.00N 129.00W; **4**, **6**
Coast Range (*mts.*) (United States), **14**, 40.00N 123.00W; **4**, **6**, **10**
Coats Land (Antarctica), **56**, 77.00S 28.00W; **7**
Cochin (India), **44**, 9.56N 76.15E
Coco (*r.*) (Honduras), **16**, 14.58N 83.15W
Cocos (*i.*) (Costa Rica), **18**, 5.32N 87.04W
Cocos Islands (Australia), **48**, 12.10S 96.55E; 53
Coimbatore (India), **44**, 11.00N 76.57E
Coimbra (Portugal), **26**, 40.12N 8.25W; **27**
Colbeck, Cape (Antarctica), **56**, 77.06S 157.48W
Cologne (Germany), **30**, 50.56N 6.59E; **31**
Colombia (*c.*), **18**, 5.00N 75.00W; **4**, **17**, 18, *19*
Colombo (Sri Lanka), **44**, 6.55N 79.52E; **45**
Colombo Plan 15, 23, 45, 51, 53
Colorado (*s.*) (United States) **15**
Colorado (*r.*) (Argentina), **18**, 39.50S 62.02W
Colorado (*r.*) (United States), **14**, 28.36N 95.58W
Colorado (*r.*) (United States), **14**, 31.45N 114.40W
Colorado Plateau (United States), **14**, 36.00N 112.00W
Columbia (*r.*) (United States), **14**, 46.15N 124.05W
Columbia (South Carolina, United States) **15**
Columbus (Ohio, United States) **15**
Communism Peak (Tajikistan), **34**, 38.39N 72.01E
Como, Lake (Italy), **28**, 46.05N 9.17E
Comorian language 43
Comorin, Cape (India), **44**, 8.04N 77.35E
Comoros (*c.*), **42**, 12.15S 44.00E; **5**, **7**, 42, *43*
Conakry (Guinea), **40**, 9.30N 13.43W; **41**
Concepción (Chile), **18**, 36.50S 73.03W; **19**
Conchos (*r.*) (Mexico), **16**, 29.34N 104.30W
Concord (New Hampshire, United States) **15**
Congo (*r.*), **40**, 6.04S 12.24E; **5**, **7**
Congo Basin, **40**, 0.30S 17.00E; 40
Congo, Democratic Republic of the, (*c.*), **40**, 2.00S 22.00E; **5**, **38**, 40, *41*
Congo, Republic of the (*c.*), **40**, 0.30N 16.00E; **5**, **38**, 40, *41*
Coniferous forest 6
Connecticut (*s.*) (United States) **15**
Constance, Lake, **30**, 47.40N 9.30E
Constanța (Romania), **32**, 44.10N 28.31E; **33**
Constantine (Algeria) **39**
Continental drift 4, 16, 18, 56
Cook Ice Shelf (Antarctica), **56**, 68.40S 152.30E
Cook Islands (New Zealand), **55**, 17.00S 160.00W
Cook, Mount (New Zealand), **54**, 43.45S 170.12E; **5**, **7**
Cook Strait, **54**, 41.15S 174.30E
Cooktown (Queensland, Australia) **53**
Copenhagen (Denmark), **20**, 55.40N 12.35E; **21**
Copper 10
Coral Harbour (Nunavut, Canada) **13**
Coral Sea **5**, **7**, **52**, **55**
Coral Sea Islands (Australia) 53
Cordillera Occidental (*mts.*), **18**, 5.00S 76.15W
Cordillera Oriental (*mts.*), **18**, 5.00S 74.30W
Córdoba (Argentina), **18**, 31.25S 64.11W; **19**
Córdoba (Spain), **26**, 37.53N 4.46W; **27**
Corfu (Greece), **28**, 39.37N 19.50E; **29**, **32**
Corfu (*i.*) (Greece), **28**, 39.37N 19.50E; **29**
Corinth (Greece) **29**
Cork (Ireland), **22**, 51.54N 8.28W; **23**
Corner Brook (Newfoundland, Canada) **13**
Corrib, Lough (Ireland), **22**, 53.26N 9.14W
Corrientes, Cape (Mexico), **16**, 20.37N 105.38W
Corse, Cape, **24**, 43.00N 9.25E
Corsica (*i.*) (France), **24**, 42.00N 9.10E; **25**, 25
Corsican language 25
Cosenza (Italy), **28**, 39.17N 16.14E; **29**
Costa Rica (*c.*), **16**, 10.00N 84.00W; **4**, 16, *17*
Côte d'Ivoire (*c.*), **40**, 7.00N 5.30W; **5**, **38**, 40, *41*
Cotopaxi (Ecuador) (*mt.*), **18**, 0.40S 78.30W
Cotswold Hills (England, United Kingdom), **22**, 51.50N 2.00W
Cottbus (Germany) **31**
Council of Europe 21, 23, 25
Coventry (England, United Kingdom), **22**, 52.38N 1.17W; **23**
Craiova (Romania), **32**, 44.18N 23.46E; **33**
Creole language 17, 41
Cres (*i.*) (Croatia), **32**, 44.50N 14.20E
Crete (*i.*) (Greece), **28**, 35.15N 25.00E; **29**, 29
Crete, Sea of **28**
Creuse (*r.*) (France), **24**, 47.00N 0.35E
Croatia (*c.*), **32**, 45.20N 16.30E; **5**, **28**, **30**, 32, *33*
Croatian language 33
Crocker Range (*mts.*) (Malaysia), **48**, 5.00N 115.30E
Cuando (*r.*), **42**, 18.30S 23.30E
Cuanza (*r.*) (Angola), **42**, 9.22S 13.09E
Cuba (*c.*), **16**, 22.00N 79.00W; **4**, **6**, **10**, 16, *17*

Cubango (*r.*) (Angola/Namibia), **42**, 18.30S 22.04E
Cúcuta (Colombia) **19**
Cuenca (Spain) **27**
Cuiabá (Brazil), **18**, 15.32S 56.05W; **19**
Cumbrian Mountains (England, United Kingdom), **22**, 54.32N 3.05W
Cunene (*r.*) (Angola/Namibia), **42**, 17.15S 11.50E
Curaçao (*i.*) (Netherlands Antilles), **17**, 12.15N 69.00W
Curepipe (Mauritius), **42**, 30.16S 57.36E
Curieuse (*i.*) (Seychelles), **40**, 4.15S 55.14E
Curitiba (Brazil) **19**
Cuttack (India), **44**, 20.26N 85.56E; **45**
Cuzco (Peru), **18**, 13.32S 72.10W; **19**
Cyclades (*isls.*) (Greece), **28**, 37.00N 25.00E; **29**
Cyprus (*c.*), **28**, 35.00N 33.00E; **5**, 28, *29*, **36**, **38**
Czech language 33
Czechoslovakia 33
Czech Republic (*c.*), **32**, 49.30N 15.30E; **5**, **30**, 32, *33*

Daba Shan (*mts.*) (China), **46**, 31.30N 110.00E
Dadu (*r.*) (China), **46**, 28.47N 104.40E
Da Hinggan Mountains (Inner Mongolia, China), **46**, 49.30N 122.00E
Dakar (Senegal), **40**, 14.38N 17.27W; **41**
Dal (*r.*) (Sweden), **20**, 60.38N 17.27E
Dalian (Liaoning, China), **46**, 38.53N 121.37E; **47**
Dallas (Texas, United States), **14**, 32.47N 96.48W; **15**
Dalmatia (*f.*), **32**, 43.30N 17.00E
Damascus (Syria), **36**, 33.30N 36.19E; **37**
Damavand (*mt.*) (Iran), **36**, 35.47N 52.04E
Dammam (Saudi Arabia), **36**, 26.25N 50.06E; **37**
Dampier (Western Australia) **53**
Danakil Depression (Ethiopia), **38**, 13.00N 41.00E
Da Nang (Vietnam), **48**, 16.04N 108.14E; **49**
Danish language 21
Danube (*r.*), **32**, 45.26N 29.38E; **5**, **7**, **30**, 32
Da Qaidam (Qinghai, China) **47**
Daravica (*mt.*) (Yugoslavia), **32**, 42.32N 20.08E
Dar es Salaam (Tanzania), **40**, 6.51S 39.18E; **41**
Dari language 37
Darling (*r.*) (Australia), **52**, 34.05S 141.57E; **5**, **7**
Darling Range (*mts.*) (Australia), **52**, 32.00S 116.30E
Darnley, Cape (Antarctica), **56**, 70.00S 68.00E
Dartmoor (*f.*) (England, United Kingdom), **22**, 50.33N 3.55W
Darwin (Northern Territory, Australia), **52**, 12.23S 130.44E; **53**
Dasht-e-Kavir (*des.*) (Iran), **36**, 34.40N 55.00E
Dasht-e-Lut (*des.*) (Iran), **36**, 31.30N 58.00E
Davao (Philippines), **48**, 7.05N 125.38E; **49**
Davis (Antarctica), **56**, 68.35S 77.58E
Davis Strait, **12**, 66.00N 58.00W
Dawna Range (*mts.*) (Myanmar/Thailand), **48**, 17.30N 98.00E
De Aar (South Africa) **43**
Dead Sea **36**
Death Valley (California, United States), **14**, 36.30N 117.00W; 14
Debre Markos (Ethiopia) **39**
Deccan Plateau (*f.*) (India), **44**, 18.00N 77.30E; **5**, **7**
Delaware (*s.*) (United States) **15**
Delgado, Cape (Mozambique), **40**, 10.45S 40.38E
Democratic Republic of the Congo the *see* Congo, Democratic Republic of the
Denmark (*c.*), **20**, 56.05N 10.00E; **5**, 20, *21*, **30**, *see also* Greenland
Denpasar (Indonesia), **48**, 8.40S 115.14E; **49**
D'Entrecasteaux Islands (Papua New Guinea), **52**, 9.30S 150.40E
Denver (Colorado, United States), **14**, 39.43N 105.01W; **15**
Derby (England, United Kingdom) **23**
Derg, Lough (Ireland), **22**, 52.57N 8.18W
Dese (Ethiopia), **38**, 11.05N 39.40E; **39**
Desert 4, **6–7**, 6
Desertification **8–9**, 8
Des Moines (Iowa, United States) **15**
Detroit (Michigan, United States), **14**, 42.20N 83.03W; **15**
Devon Island (Canada), **12**, 75.00N 86.00W
Dhaka (Bangladesh), **44**, 23.42N 90.22E; **45**
Diamonds 10
Dibrugarh (India), **44**, 27.29N 94.56E
Dickson (Russia) **35**
Dieppe (Upper Normandy, France) **25**
Dijon (Burgundy, France), **24**, 47.20N 5.02E; **25**
Dili (East Timor), **48**, 8.35S 125.35E; **49**
Dinaric Alps (*mts.*) (Croatia/Bosnia and Herzegovina), **32**, 44.00N 16.30E
Divehi language 45
Diyarbakir (Turkey) **37**
Djado (Niger) **39**
Djakarta (Indonesia), **48**, 6.08N 106.45E; **49**
Djanet (Algeria) **39**
Djibouti (*c.*), **38**, 12.00N 42.50E; **5**, **36**, 38, *39*
Djibouti (*city*) (Djibouti), **38**, 11.35N 43.11E; **39**
Dnepropetrovsk (Ukraine), **34**, 48.29N 35.00E; **35**
Dnieper (*r.*), **34**, 46.30N 32.25E
Dodecanese (*isls.*) (Greece), **28**, 36.00N 27.00E; **29**
Dodoma (Tanzania), **40**, 6.10S 35.40E; **41**
Doha (Qatar), **36**, 25.15N 51.34E; **37**
Dolomites (*mts.*) (Italy), **28**, 46.25N 11.50E
Dominica (*c.*), **17**, 15.30N 61.30W; **4**, 16, *17*
Dominican Republic (*c.*), **17**, 18.00N 70.00W; **4**, 16, *17*
Don (*r.*) (Russia), **34**, 47.06N 39.16E
Dondra Head (Sri Lanka), **44**, 5.55N 80.20E
Donegal Bay (Ireland), **22**, 54.32N 8.18W
Donetsk (Ukraine) **35**
Dongting, Lake (China), **46**, 29.40N 113.00E
Dordogne (*r.*) (France), **24**, 45.02N 0.35W
Dortmund (Germany) **31**
Douala (Cameroon) **41**
Doubs (*r.*) (France), **24**, 46.54N 5.02E
Douglas (United Kingdom), **22**, 54.09N 4.29W
Douro (*r.*) (Portugal), **26**, 41.10N 8.40W
Dover (Delaware, United States) **15**
Dover (England, United Kingdom), **22**, 51.08N 1.19E; **23**
Dover, Strait of, **22**, 51.00N 1.30E
Downs, North (*f.*) (England, United Kingdom), **22**, 51.18N 0.40W
Downs, South (*f.*) (England, United Kingdom), **22**, 50.54N 0.34W
Drakensberg (*mts.*) (South Africa), **42**, 30.00S 29.00E; **5**, **7**, 42
Drammen (Norway), **20**, 59.45N 10.15E; **21**
Drava (*r.*) (Hungary/Croatia), **32**, 45.34N 18.56E; **30**
Dresden (Germany), **30**, 51.03N 13.44E; **31**
Drina (*r.*) (Yugoslavia), **32**, 44.53N 19.20E
Drogheda (Ireland) **23**
Dryanovo (Bulgaria) **33**
Dubai (United Arab Emirates), **36**, 25.13N 55.17E; **37**
Dublin (Ireland), **22**, 53.21N 6.18W; **23**
Dubrovnik (Croatia), **32**, 42.40N 18.07E; **33**
Duero (*r.*) (Spain) **26**, 27
Duisburg (Germany) **31**
Dukou (China), **46**, 26.33N 101.44E
Dumfries (Scotland, United Kingdom), **22**, 55.04N 3.37W; **23**
Dumont d'Urville (Antarctica), **56**, 66.40S 140.01E
Dundalk (Ireland), **22**, 54.01N 6.25W; **23**
Dundee, **22** (Scotland, United Kingdom), 56.28N 3.00W; **23**
Dund-Us (Mongolia) **35**
Dunedin (New Zealand), **54**, 45.53S 170.31E
Dunstan Mountains (New Zealand), **54**, 44.45S 169.45E
Durance (*r.*) (France), **24**, 43.55N 4.44E
Durban (South Africa), **42**, 29.53S 31.00E; **43**
Durrës (Albania), **32**, 41.19N 19.27E; **33**
Dushanbe (Tajikistan), **34**, 38.38N 68.51E; **35**
Düsseldorf (Germany), **30**, 51.12N 6.47E; **31**
Dutch language 19, 31
Dvina, North (*r.*) (Russia), **34**, 64.40N 40.50E
Dzhugdzhur Range (Russia), **34**, 57.30N 138.00E
Dzonghka language 45
Dzungaria Basin (Xinjiang, China), **46**, 44.30N 83.07E

Earthquakes 4
East African Rift Valley *see* Rift Valley
East Australian Current **7**
East Cape (New Zealand), **54**, 37.42S 178.35E
East China Sea **5**, **7**, **46**, **48**
Easter Island (Chile) **19**
Eastern Europe 32–33
  agriculture and fisheries 32
East Frisian Islands (Germany), **30**, 53.45N 7.00E; **31**
East London (South Africa), **42**, 33.00S 27.54E; **43**
East Pakistan *see* Bangladesh
East Sea *see* Japan, Sea of
East Siberian Sea **5**, **7**, **34**
East Timor (*c.*), **48**, 9.00S 126.00E; **5**, **49**, **52**
Ebinur (*l.*) (Xinjiang, China), **46**, 45.00N 82.30E
Ebro (*r.*) (Spain), **26**, 40.43N 0.54W; 26
Echigo Mountains (Japan), **50**, 38.30N 140.30E
Economic Community of West African States (ECOWAS) 41
Ecuador (*c.*), **18**, 2.00S 78.00W; **4**, 18, *19*
Edessa (Greece) **29**
Edinburgh (Scotland, United Kingdom), **22**, 55.57N 3.13W; **23**
Edmonton (Alberta, Canada), **12**, 53.30N 113.30W; **13**
Edward, Lake (Uganda/Democratic Republic of the Congo), **40**, 0.30S 29.30E; 40
Edwards Plateau (United States), **14**, 31.20N 101.00W
Egadi Islands (Italy), **28**, 38.00N 12.10E; **29**, 29
Egmont, Cape (New Zealand), **54**, 39.16S 173.45E
Egypt (*c.*), **38**, 26.30N 29.30E; **5**, **36**, 38, *39*
Eifel (*f.*) (Germany), **30**, 50.10N 6.45E
Eindhoven (Netherlands), **30**, 51.26N 5.30E; **31**
Eisenstadt (Austria) **31**
El Aaiún (Western Sahara), **38**, 27.09N 13.12W; **39**
Elazig (Turkey), **36**, 38.41N 39.14E; **37**
Elba (*i.*) (Italy), **28**, 42.47N 10.17E; **29**, 29
Elbe (*r.*) (Germany), **30**, 53.33N 10.00E
Elbert, Mount (United States), **14**, 39.07N 106.27W
Elblag (Poland), **32**, 54.10N 19.25E
Elbrus (*mt.*) (Russia), **34**, 43.21N 42.29E
Elburz Mountains (Iran), **36**, 36.00N 52.00E
Elche (Spain) **27**
Eldoret (Kenya) **41**
Eleuthera (*i.*) (Bahamas), **16**, 25.00N 76.00W
El Fasher (Sudan) **39**
El Golea (Algeria) **39**
Ellesmere Island (Canada), **12**, 78.00N 82.00W; **4**, **6**, **10**, 12
Ellice Islands **5**, **7**
Ellsworth Land (Antarctica), **56**, 75.30S 80.00W; **6**
Ellsworth Mountains (Antarctica), **56**, 79.00S 85.00W
El Minya (Egypt) **39**
El Obeid (Sudan), **38**, 13.11N 30.10E; **39**
El Oued (Algeria) **39**
El Paso (Texas, United States), **14**, 45.00N 93.10W; **15**
El Salvador (*c.*), **16**, 13.30N 89.00W; **4**, 16, *17*
Emi Koussi (*mt.*) (Chad), **38**, 19.58N 18.30E
Emilo Goeldi (Antarctica), **56**, 61.00S 55.00W
Ems (*r.*) (Germany), **30**, 53.14N 7.25E
Endangered habitats and species **8–9**, 8
Ende (Indonesia) **49**
Enderby Land (Antarctica), **56**, 67.30S 53.00E; **7**
Energy resources **10–11**, 10
Enggano (*i.*) (Indonesia), **48**, 5.20S 102.15E; **49**
England (United Kingdom) **22**, **23**, 24
English Channel, **22**, 50.15N 1.00W; 22
English language 13, 15, 17, 23, 29, 41, 43, 45, 49, 53, 55
Enns (*r.*) (Austria), **30**, 48.14N 14.22E
Enschede (Netherlands) **31**
Enugu (Nigeria) **41**
Equator **5**, **7**, **18**, **40**, 40, **48**, **52**, **55**
Equatorial Countercurrent **7**
Equatorial Guinea (*c.*), **40**, 1.30N 10.30E; **5**, 40, *41*
Erebus, Mount (Antarctica), **56**, 77.32S 167.09E
Erfurt (Germany) **31**
Erg Chech (*des.*) (Algeria), **38**, 24.30N 2.30W
Erie, Lake (United States/Canada), **12**, 42.15N 81.00W; **14**
Erimo, Cape (Japan), **50**, 41.55N 143.13E
Eritrea (*c.*), **38**, 16.30N 38.00E; **5**, **36**, 38, *39*
Erosion 4, 8
Erzgebirge (*mts.*) (Germany/Czech Republic), **30**, 50.34N 13.00E
Erzurum (Turkey), **36**, 39.57N 41.17E; **37**
Esbjerg (Denmark), **20**, 55.28N 8.27E; **21**
Eskisehir (Turkey) **37**
Esla (*r.*) (Spain), **26**, 42.00N 5.40W
Esperanza (Antarctica), **56**, 63.16S 56.49W
Espoo (Finland) **21**
Essen (Germany), **30**, 51.27N 6.57E; **31**
Estonia (*c.*), **34**, 58.45N 25.30E; **5**, **20**, 34, *35*
Estonian language 35
Ethiopia (*c.*), **38**, 7.30N 40.00E; **5**, **36**, 38, *39*, **40**
Ethiopian Highlands (Ethiopia), **38**, 10.00N 38.45E; **5**, **7**, 38
Etna (*mt.*) (Italy), **28**, 37.43N 14.59E
Etosha Pan (*f.*) (Namibia), **42**, 18.50S 16.30E
Euboea (*i.*) (Greece), **28**, 38.30N 23.50E; **29**
Euphrates (*r.*) (Iraq), **36**, 31.00N 47.27E; **5**, **7**, 36
Europe **7**
  see also Central Europe; Eastern Europe
European Free Trade Association (EFTA) 21
European Union (EU) 13, 21, 23, 25, 31, 32
Everest, Mount (Nepal/China), **44**, 27.59N 86.56E; **5**, **7**
Évora (Portugal) **27**
Exmoor (*f.*) (England, United Kingdom), **22**, 51.08N 3.45W
Eyre, Lake (dry) (Australia), **52**, 28.30S 137.25E; **5**, **7**
Eyre Peninsula (Australia), **52**, 34.00S 135.45E

Faeroe Islands (Denmark), **20**, 62.00N 7.00W; 20, 21
Fairbanks (Alaska, United States), **14**, 64.50N 147.50W; **15**
Faisalabad (Pakistan), **44**, 31.25N 73.09E; **45**
Falkland Islands (United Kingdom), **18**, 58.00S 60.00W; **4**, **5**, **6**, **10**, **19**, 19, 23
Falster (*i.*) (Denmark), **20**, 54.48N 11.58E
Falun (Sweden) **21**
Fan Si Pan (*mt.*) (Vietnam), **48**, 22.30N 104.00E
Faraday (Antarctica), **56**, 65.15S 64.16W
Farah (Afghanistan) **37**
Farewell, Cape (Greenland), **12**, 60.00N 44.20W
Farewell, Cape (New Zealand), **54**, 40.29S 172.43E
Faro (Portugal), **26**, 37.01N 7.56W; **27**
Farsi language 37
Faxaflói (*b.*) (Iceland), **20**, 64.30N 22.50W
Faya-Largeau (Chad) **39**
Fdérik (Mauritania), **38**, 22.30N 12.30W; **39**
Federated States of Micronesia, **55**, 7.28N 151.1E; **5**, **7**, 55
Fehmarn (*i.*) (Germany), **30**, 54.30N 11.05E; **31**
Félicité (*i.*) (Seychelles), **40**, 4.19S 55.52E
Fens, The (*f.*) (England, United Kingdom), **22**, 52.30N 0.40E
Fernando de Noronha (*i.*) (Brazil), **18**, 3.50S 32.25W
Ferrara (Italy) **29**
Fianarantsoa (Madagascar), **42**, 21.26S 47.05E; **43**
Figueras (Spain) **27**
Fiji (*c.*), **55**, 18.08S 178.25E; **5**, **7**, 55
Filchner Ice Shelf (Antarctica), **56**, 79.00S 40.00W
Filipino language 49
Finisterre, Cape (Spain), **26**, 42.54N 9.16W
Finland (*c.*), **20**, 62.30N 26.00E; **5**, 20, *21*, **34**
Finland, Gulf of, **20**, 59.30N 24.00E
Finnish language 21
Fishing industry **10–11**, 10
Finsteraarhorn (*mt.*) (Switzerland), **30**, 46.32N 8.08S
Fjords 20, 54

Flemish language 25
Flensburg (Germany) **31**
Florence (Italy), **28**, 43.46N 11.15E; **29**
Flores (*i.*) (Indonesia), **48**, 8.40S 121.20E; **49**
Flores Sea **48**
Florida (*s.*) (United States) **15**
Fly (*r.*) (Papua New Guinea), **52**, 8.22S 142.23E
Foggia (Italy) **28**, 41.28N 15.33E; **29**
Fogo (*i.*) (Cape Verde), **40** , 15.04N 24.20W
Fohnsdorf (Austria) **31**
Fontur (Iceland), **20**, 66.23N 14.30W
Forest 6
coniferous 6
deciduous 6, 8
deforestation **8–9**, 8
rain 6, **8–9**, 8
Forestry **10–11**, 10
Formentera (*i.*) (Spain), **26**, 38.41N 1.30E; **27**
Fort Albany (Ontario, Canada), **12**, 52.15N 81.35W; **13**
Fortaleza (Brazil), **18**, 3.45S 38.45W; **19**
Forth, Firth of (*est.*) (Scotland, United Kingdom), **22**, 56.05N 3.00W
Fort Worth (Texas, United States) **15**
Fossil fuels 10
Foveaux Strait, **54**, 46.40S 168.00E
France (*c.*), **24**, 47.00N 2.00E; **5**, **22**, 24, *25*, **26**, **28**, **30**
agriculture and fisheries 24
dependencies 17
Franche-Comté (*d.*) (France) **25**
Francistown (Botswana) **43**
Franconian Jura (*mts.*) (Germany), **30**, 49.30N 11.10E
Frankfort (Kentucky, United States) **15**
Frankfurt (Germany), **30**, 50.07N 8.40E; **31**
Franz Josef Land (*isls.*) (Russia), **34**, 81.00N 50.00E; **5**, **7**, **35**
Fraser (*r.*) (Canada), **12**, 49.07N 123.11W
Fraser Island (Australia), **52**, 25.15S 153.10E
Fredericton (New Brunswisk, Canada) **13**
Freetown (Sierra Leone), **40**, 8.30N 13.17W; **41**
Freiburg (Germany) **31**
Fremantle (Western Australia) **53**
French Guiana (*d.*), **18**, 3.40N 53.00W; **4**, **19**, **25**
French language 13, 15, 17, 25, 30, 31, 39, 41, 43, 55
French Polynesia (*isls.*) (France), **55**, 20.00S 145.00W; 25
Frigate (*i.*) (Seychelles), **40**, 4.35S 55.56E
Fujian (*d.*) (China) **47**
Fuji, Mount (Japan), **50**, 35.23N 138.42E
Fukui (Japan) **51**
Fukuoka (Japan), **50**, 33.39N 130.21E; **51**
Fukushima (Japan) **51**
Funafuti (Tuvalu), **55**, 8.31S 179.13E
Furneaux Group (*isls.*) (Australia), **52**, 40.15S 148.15E
Fushun (Liaoning, China) **47**
Futa Jalon (*f.*) (Guinea), **40**, 11.30N 12.30W
Fuzhou (Fujian, China), **46**, 26.01N 119.20E; **47**
Fyn (*i.*) (Denmark), **20**, 55.20N 10.30E

Gabon (*c.*), **40**, 0.00 12.00E; **5**, 40, *41*
Gaborone (Botswana), **42**, 24.45S 25.55E; **43**
Gaelic language 23
Gairdner, Lake (Australia), **52**, 31.30S 136.00E
Galápagos Islands (Ecuador), **18**, 0.30S 90.30W; **4**, **6**, **10**, 19
Galaţi (Romania), **32**, 45.27N 27.59E; **33**
GaldhØpiggen (*mt.*), **20**, 61.38N 8.19E
Galician language 27
Gällivare (Sweden) **21**
Galway (Ireland), **22**, 53.17N 9.04W; **23**
Gambia (*c.*), **40**, 13.30N 15.00W; **5**, 40, *41*
Gambia (*r.*), **40**, 13.28N 15.55W
Gan (*r.*) (China), **46**, 27.30N 115.00E
Gandhinagar (India) **45**
Gangdise Shan (*mts.*) (Tibet, China) **46**, 32.00N 81.00E
Ganges (*r.*) (India/Bangladesh), **44**, 23.30N 90.25E; **5**, **7**
Ganges, Mouths of the (Bangladesh), **44**, 21.00N 90.00E
Gansu (*d.*) (China) **47**
Ganzhou (Jiangxi, China) **47**
Gao (Mali), **38**, 16.19N 0.09W **39**
Garda, Lake (Italy), **28**, 45.40N 10.40E; 29
Gargano Promontory (Italy), **28**, 41.49N 16.12E
Garonne (*r.*) (France), **24**, 45.02N 0.36W
Garoua (Cameroon) **41**
Garvie Mountains (New Zealand), **54**, 45.15S 169.00E
Gascony, Gulf of (France), **24**, 44.00N 2.40W
Gas, natural 10
Gate, Cape (Cyprus), **28**, 34.33N 33.03E
Gauhati (India), **44**, 26.05N 91.55E
Gävle (Sweden), **20**, 60.14N 17.10E; **21**
Gdansk (Poland), **32**, 54.22N 18.38E; **33**
Gdansk, Gulf of, **32**, 54.45N 19.15E
Gdynia (Poland) **33**
Geelong (Victoria, Australia) **53**
General B. O'Higgins (Antarctica) **56**
Geneva (Switzerland) **31**
Geneva, Lake (Switzerland/France), **30**, 46.25N 6.30E; **24**, **28**
Genil (*r.*) (Spain), **26** 37.30N 5.00W
Genoa (Italy), **28**, 44.24N 8.54E; **29**, 29
Georgetown (Guyana), **18**, 6.48N 58.08W; **18**, **19**
George Town (Malaysia), **48**, 5.30N 100.16E; **49**
Georg Forster (Antarctica), **56,** 70.05S 112.00E
Georgia (*c.*), **34**, 42.00N 43.30E; **5**, 34, *35*, **36**
Georgia (*s.*) (United States) **15**
Georgian language 35
Georg Von Neumayer (Antarctica), **56**, 70.37S 8.22W
Geraldton (Western Australia), **52**, 28.49S 114.36E; **53**
Gerlachovka (*mt.*) (Slovakia), **32**, 49.10N 20.10E
German language 15, 25, 29, 30, 31, 35
Germany (*c.*), **30**, 52.00N 10.00E; **5**, **20**, **24**, **28**, 30, *31*, **32**
Gerona (Spain) **27**
Getz Ice Shelf (Antarctica), **56**, 75.00S 129.00W
Ghadamis (Libya), **38**, 30.10N 9.30E; **39**
Ghaghara (*r.*) (India/Nepal), **44**, 25.45N 84.50E
Ghana (*c.*), **40**, 8.00N 1.00W; **5**, 40, *41*
Ghardaia (Algeria) **39**
Ghat (Libya), **38**, 24.59N 10.11E; **39**
Ghats, Eastern (*mts.*) (India), **44**, 16.30N 80.30E
Ghats, Western (*mts.*) (India), **44**, 15.30N 74.30E
Ghent (Belgium), **30**, 51.02N 3.42E; **31**
Gibraltar (United Kingdom), **26**, 36.07N 5.22W; 23, 26
Gibraltar, Strait of, **26**, 36.00N 5.25W; 26
Gibson Desert (Australia), **52**, 24.00S 125.00E
Gijón (Spain) **27**
Gilbert Islands **5**, **7**
Gilgit (Jammu and Kashmir), **44**, 35.54N 74.20E; **45**
Gisborne (New Zealand), **54**, 38.39S 178.01E
Gjøvik (Norway) **21**
Glaciers 4, 12, 20, 23, 54
Glåma (*r.*), **20**, 59.12N 10.57E
Glasgow (Scotland, United Kingdom), **22**, 55.52N 4.15W; **23**
Glittertind (*mt.*) (Norway), **20**, 61.39N 8.33E
Global warming 8
Glossopteris (*mt.*) (Antarctica), **56**, 84.44S 113.51W
Gloucester (England, United Kingdom) **23**
Goba (Ethiopia) **39**
Gobi (*des.*) (Mongolia/China), **46**, 43.30N 114.00E; **5**, **7**, **34**, 34
Godavari (*r.*) (India), **44**, 16.40N 82.15E
Godthåb (Greenland), **12**, 64.10N 51.40W; **13**
Goiânia (Brazil) **19**
Gold Coast (Queensland, Australia) **53**
Gonder (Ethiopia) **39**
Gondwanaland 18, 38, 42, 44, 52, 56
Good Hope, Cape of (South Africa), **42**, 34.20S 18.25E; **5**, **7**
Goose Bay (*town*) (Newfoundland, Canada), **12**, 53.15N 60.20W
Gorontalo (Indonesia), **48**, 0.33N 123.05E; **49**
Göta (*r.*) (Sweden), **20**, 57.42N 11.52E
Göteborg (Sweden), **20**, 57.43N 11.58E; **21**
Gotland (*i.*) (Sweden), **20**, 57.30N 18.33E; **21**
Goto Islands (Japan), **50**, 32.43N 128.36E; **51**
Göttingen (Germany) **31**
Gozo (*i.*) (Malta), **28**, 36.03N 14.16E; **29**
Gracias á Dios, Cape (Honduras), **16**, 15.00N 83.10W
Grafton (New South Wales, Australia) **53**
Grampian Mountains (Scotland, United Kingdom), **22**, 56.55N 4.00W
Granada (Spain), **26**, 37.10N 3.35W; 26, **27**
Gran Chaco (*f.*), **18**, 23.30S 60.00W
Grand Bahama (*i.*) (Bahamas), **16**, 26.35N 78.00W
Grand Canal (China), **46**, 39.10N 117.12E
Grand Canyon (United States), **14**, 36.10N 112.45W; 14
Grand Erg Occidental (*des.*) (Algeria), **38**, 30.10N 0.00
Grand Erg Oriental (*des.*) (Algeria), **38**, 30.00N 7.00E
Gran Paradiso (*mt.*) (Italy), **28**, 45.31N 7.15E
Grassland 6
desertification 8
Graz (Austria), **30**, 47.05N 15.27E; **31**
Great Abaco (*i.*) (Bahamas), **16**, 26.30N 77.00W
Great Alföld (*f.*) (Hungary), **32**, 47.20N 20.30E; 32
Great Artesian Basin (*f.*) (Australia), **52**, 26.30S 143.02E
Great Australian Bight (*b.*) (Australia), **52**, 33.10S 129.30E
Great Barrier Island (New Zealand), **54**, 36.15S 175.30E
Great Barrier Reef (*f.*), **52**, 16.30S 146.30E
Great Basin (United States), **14**, 40.35N 116.00W
Great Bear Lake (Canada), **12**, 66.00N 120.00W
Great Dividing Range (Australia), **52**, 29.00S 152.00E; **5**, **7**
Greater Antarctica 57
Greater Antilles (*isls.*), **16**, 17.00N 70.00W; **4**, **6**, **10**, 16
Great Inagua (*i.*) (Bahamas), **17**, 21.00N 73.20W
Great Indian Desert (India), **44**, 28.00N 72.00E; **5**, **7**
Great Karroo (*f.*) (South Africa), **42**, 32.50S 22.30E
Great Lakes **4**, **6**, **10**, 12, **14**
Great Nicobar (*i.*) (India), **44**, 7.00N 93.50E
Great Ouse (*r.*) (England, United Kingdom), **22**, 52.47N 0.23E
Great Plains (Canada) **4**, **6**, **10**, **12**
Great Plains (United States), **14**, 50.00N 110.00W; **4**, **6**, **10**
Great Rift Valley *see* Rift Valley
Great Salt Lake (United States), **14**, 41.10N 112.30W
Great Sandy Desert (Australia), **52**, 20.30S 123.35E; **5**, **7**
Great Slave Lake (Canada), **12**, 61.23N 115.38W
Great Victoria Desert (Australia), **52**, 29.00S 127.30E
Great Wall (Antarctica), **56**, 62.13S 58.58W
Greece (*c.*), **28**, 38.00N 22.30E; **5**, 28, *29*, **32**, **36**, **38**
climate 29
Greek language 29
Greenland (*i.*) (Denmark), **12**, 75.00N 40.00W; **5**, 6, **7**, 12, 20, 21
Greenock (Scotland, United Kingdom) **23**
Grenada (*c.*), **17**, 12.15N 61.45W; **4**, 16, *17*
Grenoble (Rhône-Alpes, France), **24**, 45.11N 5.43E; **25**
Greymouth (New Zealand), **54**, 42.29S 171.13E
Grey Range (Australia), **52**, 27.30S 143.59E
Grimsey (*i.*) (Iceland), **20**, 66.33N 18.00W
Groningen (Netherlands), **30**, 53.13N 6.35E; **31**
Grosser Arber (*mt.*) (Germany), **30**, 49.07N 13.07E
Grossglockner (*mt.*) (Austria), **30**, 47.05N 12.50E
Guadalajara (Mexico), **16**, 20.30N 103.20W
Guadalcanal (*i.*) (Solomon Islands), **52**, 9.32S 160.12E
Guadalquivir (*r.*) (Spain), **26**, 36.50N 6.20W; 26
Guadeloupe (*i.*) (France), **17**, 16.20N 61.40W; 17, 25
Guadiana (*r.*) (Spain/Portugal), **26**, 37.10N 7.36W
Guam (*i.*) (United States) **5**, 15, **55**
Guangdong (*d.*) (China) **47**
Guangxi (*d.*) (China) **47**
Guangzhou (Guangdong, China), **46**, 23.20N 113.30E; **47**
Guantánamo (Cuba), **17**, 20.09N 75.14W
Guarda (Portugal) **27**
Guatemala (*c.*), **16**, 15.40N 90.00W; 4, 16, *17*
Guatemala City (Guatemala), **16**, 14.38N 90.22W
Guayaquil (Ecuador), **18**, 2.13S 79.54W; **19**
Guiana Highlands, **18**, 4.00N 59.00W; **4**, **6**, **10**
Guilin (Guangxi, China) **47**
Guinea (*c.*), **40**, 10.30N 10.30W; **5**, **7**, **38**, 40, *41*
Guinea-Bissau (*c.*), **40**, 12.00N 15.30W; **5**, 40, *41*
Guinea Current **7**
Guiyang (Guizhou, China), **46**, 26.35N 106.40E; **47**
Guizhou (*d.*) (China) **47**
Gujarati language 23, 45
Gujranwala (Pakistan) **45**
Gulf Stream 6, **7**, 22
Gulu (Uganda) **41**
Guyana (*c.*), **18**, 5.00N 59.00W; **4**, **17**, 18, *19*
Gwalior (India) **45**
Gweru (Zimbabwe) **43**
Gyangze (Tibet, China) **47**
Gydanskiy Peninsula (Russia), **34**, 70.00N 78.30E
Györ (Hungary), **32**, 47.41N 17.40E; **33**

Haardt (*mts.*) (Germany), **30**, 49.21N 7.55E
Haarlem (Netherlands), **30**, 52.23N 4.38E; **31**
Habitats **6–7**, 6
endangered **8–9**, 8
Hachijo (*i.*) (Japan), **50**, 33.10N 139.45E
Hachinohe (Japan) **51**
Hadd, Cape (Oman), **36**, 22.32N 59.49E
Hadhramaut (*f.*) (Yemen), **36**, 16.30N 49.30E
Haeju (North Korea), **50**, 38.04N 125.40E; **51**
Hague, The (Netherlands), **30**, 52.05N 4.16E; **31**
Haikou (Hainan, China), **46**, 20.05N 110.25E; **47**
Ha'il (Saudi Arabia) **37**
Hailar (Inner Mongolia, China) **47**
Hainan (*i.*) (China), **46**, 18.30N 109.40E; **47**, **5**, **7**, 47
Haiphong (Vietnam), **48**, 20.58N 106.41E; **49**
Haiti (*c.*), **17**, 19.00N 73.00W; **4**, 16, *17*
Hakodate (Japan), **50**, 41.46N 140.44E; **51**
Halifax (Nova Scotia, Canada), **12**, 44.39N 63.36W; **13**
Hall Beach (*town*) (Nunavut, Canada) **13**
Halley (Antarctica), **56**, 75.31S 26.56W; **57**
Halmahera (*i.*) (Indonesia), **48**, 0.45N 128.00E; **49**
Hälsingborg (Sweden), **20**, 56.05N 12.45E
Haltiatunturi (*mt.*) (Finland) **20**, 69.17N 21.21E
Hamadan (Iran) **37**
Hamamatsu (Japan), **50**, 34.42N 137.42E; **51**
Hamburg (Germany), **30**, 53.33N 9.59E; **31**
Hamersley Range (Australia), **52**, 22.00S 118.00E
Hamgyong (*mts.*) (North Korea), **50**, 41.00 128.30E
Hamhung (North Korea), **50**, 39.54N 127.35E; **51**
Hamilton (New Zealand), **54**, 37.47S 175.17E
Hamilton (Ontario, Canada) **13**
Han 46
Han (*r.*) (China) **46**, 32.20N 111.30E
Han (*r.*) (South Korea), **50**, 37.30N 127.00E
Handan (Hebei, China) **47**
Hangzhou (Zhejiang, China), **46**, 30.10N 120.07E; **47**
Hannover (Germany), **30**, 52.24N 9.44E; **31**
Hanoi (Vietnam), **48**, 21.01N 105.52E; **49**
Happy Valley-Goose Bay (Newfoundland, Canada) **13**
Harare (Zimbabwe), **42**, 17.49S 31.04E; **43**
Harbin (Heilongjiang, China), **46**, 45.45N 126.41E **47**
Hardanger Fjord (Norway), **20**, 60.10N 6.00E
Hargeysa (Somalia), **38**, 9.31N 44.02E; **39**
Hari Rud (*r.*) (Afghanistan), **36**, 35.42N 61.12E
Harney Basin (United States), **14**, 43.15N 120.40W
Harris (*i.*) (Scotland, United Kingdom), **22**, 57.50N 6.55W
Harrisburg (Pennsylvania, United States) **15**
Hartford (Connecticut, United States) **15**

Harz (*mts.*) (Germany), **30**, 51.43N 10.40E
Hastings (New Zealand), **54**, 39.39S 176.52E
Hatteras, Cape (United States), **14**, 35.14N 75.31W
Haugesund (Norway) **21**
Hauki (*l.*) (Finland), **20**, 62.10N 28.30E
Havana (Cuba), **16**, 23.07N 82.25W
Havel (*r.*) (Germany), **30**, 52.53N 11.58E
Hawaii (*s.*) (*i.*) (United States), **14**, 21.00N 157.30W; 14, **55**, 55
Hawaiian Islands (United States), **14**, 21.00N 157.00W; **15**
Hawke Bay (New Zealand), **54**, 39.18S 177.15E
Hay River (*town*) (Northwest Territories, Canada), **12**, 60.51N 115.44W; **13**
Hazaribagh Range (India), **44**, 22.00N 83.00E
Heard Island (Australia) 53
Hebei (*d.*) (China) **47**
Hebrew language 37
Hebrides, Inner (*isls.*) (Scotland, United Kingdom), **22**, 57.00N 7.00W; **23**
Hebrides, Outer (*isls.*) (Scotland, United Kingdom), **22**, 58.00N 7.45W; **23**
Hefei (Anhui, China) **47**
Heilongjiang (*d.*) (China) **47**
Heimaey (*i.*) (Iceland), **20**, 63.25N 20.17W
Hejaz (*f.*) (Saudi Arabia), **36**, 25.00N 39.00E
Helena (Montana, United States) **15**
Helmand (*r.*) (Afghanistan), **36**, 31.10N 61.20E
Helsingborg (Sweden), **20**, 56.05N 12.45E; **21**
Helsinki (Finland), **20**, 60.08N 25.00E; **21**
Henan (*d.*) (China) **47**
Herat (Afghanistan), **36**, 34.21N 62.10E; **37**
Hidaka Mountains (Japan), **50**, 42.50N 143.00E
Hida Mountains (Japan), **50**, 36.35N 137.00E
High Atlas (*mts.*) (Morocco), **38**, 32.00N 5.50W; **5**, **7**, 38
Hildesheim (Germany) **31**
Hilo (Hawaii, United States) **15**
Himalayas (*mts.*), **44**, 29.00N 84.00E; **5**, **7**, 44, **46**
Hindi language 17, 45
Hindu Kush (*mts.*) (Afghanistan/ Pakistan), **36**, 36.40N 70.00E; 36
Hinney (*i.*) (Norway), **20**, 68.35N 15.50E
Hirosaki (Japan) **51**
Hiroshima (Japan), **50**, 34.30N 132.27E; **51**
Hispaniola (*i.*), **17**, 19.00N 71.00W; 16
Hkakabo Razi (*mt.*) (Myanmar), **48**, 28.17N 97.46E
Hobart (Tasmania, Australia), **52**, 42.54S 147.18E; **53**
Ho Chi Minh City (Vietnam), **48**, 10.46N 106.43E; **49**
Hodeida (Yemen) **37**
Hofn (Iceland), **20**, 64.16N 15.10W
Hofsjökull (*mt.*) (Iceland), **20**, 64.50N 19.00W
Hofuf (Saudi Arabia) **37**
Hohhot (Inner Mongolia, China) **47**
Hokkaido (*i.*) (Japan), **50**, 43.00N 144.00E; **5**, **7**, **51**
Holyhead (Wales, United Kingdom) **23**
Homs (Syria), **36**, 34.44N 36.43E; **37**
Honduras (*c.*), **16**, 14.30N 87.00W; **4**, 16, *17*
Hong Kong (China), **46**, 22.30N 114.10E; **47**, 47
Hongshui (*r.*) (China), **46**, 25.00N 106.00E
Honiara (Solomon Islands), **55**, 9.28S 159.52E
Honolulu (Hawaii, United States), **14**, 21.19N 157.50W; **15**
Honshu (*i.*) (Japan), **50**, 36.00N 138.00E; **5**, **7**, **51**
Hormuz, Strait of, **36**, 26.35N 56.20E
Hornavan (*l.*) (Sweden), **20**, 66.10N 17.30E
Horn, Cape, **18**, 55.47S 67.00W; **4**, **6**, **10**, 18
Hotan (Xinjiang, China) **47**
Hottentot 43
Houston (Texas, United States), **14**, 29.46N 95.22W; **15**
Howland Island (United States) 15, **55**
Hoy (*i.*) (Scotland, United Kingdom), **22**, 58.51N 3.17W
Hradec Králové (Czech Republic) **33**
Huai (*r.*) (China), **46**, 32.2N 116.00E
Huainan (Anhui, China) **47**
Huambo (Angola), **42**, 12.47S 15.44E; **43**
Huang (*r.*) (Yellow River) (China), **46**, 37.55N 118.46E; **5**, **7**, 46
Huascarán (*mt.*) (Peru), **18**, 9.20S 77.36W; **4**, **6**, **10**
Hubei (*d.*) (China) **47**
Hudson (*r.*) (United States), **14**, 40.42N 74.02W
Hudson Bay (Canada), **12**, 58.00N 86.00W; **4**, **6**, **10**
Hudson Strait (Canada), **12**, 62.00N 70.00W
Hue (Vietnam), **48**, 16.28N 107.35E; **49**
Huelva (Spain), **26**, 37.15N 6.56W; **27**
Huiarau Range (New Zealand), **54**, 38.20S 177.15E
Hulun (*l.*) (Inner Mongolia, China), **46**, 49.00N 117.30E
Humboldt Current **7**
Húnaflói (*b.*) (Iceland), **20**, 65.40N 19.00W
Hunan (*d.*) (China) **47**
Hungarian language 33
Hungary (*c.*), **32**, 47.20N 19.00E; **5**, **28**, **30**, 32, *33*
Hungnam (North Korea), **50**, 39.49N 127.40E; **51**
Hunsrück (*mts.*) (Germany), **30**, 49.45N 7.00E
Huron, Lake (United States/Canada), **12**, 44.30N 82.15W
Hutu 41
Hvannadalshnúkur (*mt.*) (Iceland), **20**, 64.02N 16.35W
Hvar (*i.*) (Croatia), **32**, 43.10N 16.45E
Hwange (Zimbabwe) **43**
Hyderabad (India), **44**, 17.22N 78.26E; **45**
Hyderabad (Pakistan), **44**, 25.23N 68.24E; **45**
Hydroelectric power 10, 20

Iași (Romania), **32**, 47.09N 27.38E; **33**
Ibiza (Spain), **26**, 38.55N 1.30E
Ibiza (*i.*) (Spain), **26**, 39.00N 1.23E; **27**
Iceland (*c.*), **20**, 64.45N 18.00W; **5**, **7**, **12**, 20, *21*
Icelandic language 21
Idaho (*s.*) (United States) **15**
Idhi (*mt.*) (Greece), **28**, 35.13N 24.45E
Iguaçu Falls (Argentina/Brazil), **18**, 25.35S 54.22W
Ijssel (*r.*) (Netherlands), **30**, 52.34N 5.50E
Ijsselmeer (*l.*) (Netherlands), **30**, 52.45N 5.20E
Iki (*i.*) (Japan), **50**, 33.50N 129.38E; **51**
Ikopa (*r.*) (Madagascar), **42**, 16.29S 46.43E
Ilagan (Philippines), **48**, 17.07N 121.53E
Ile-de-France (*d.*) (France) **25**
Ile de Ré (*i.*) (France) **24**
Ile d'Oléron (*i.*) (France) **24**
Illinois (*s.*) (United States) **15**
Iloilo (Philippines), **48**, 10.45N 122.33E; **49**
Ilorin (Nigeria) **41**
Imabari (Japan), **50**, 34.04N 132.59E
Imperatriz (Brazil) **19**
Inari, Lake (Finland), **20**, 69.00N 28.00E
Inca 18
Inch'on (South Korea), **50**, 37.28N 126.38E; **51**
Indal (*r.*) (Sweden), **20**, 62.30N 17.20E
India (*c.*), **44**, 24.00N 78.00E; **5**, **34**, **36**, 44, *45*, **46**, **48**
Indiana (*s.*) (United States) **15**
Indianapolis (Indiana, United States), **14**, 39.45N 86.10W; **15**
Indian Ocean **5**, **7**, **36**, **38**, **40**, **44**, **48**, **52**, **56**
Indian subcontinent 44–45
Indonesia (*c.*), **48**, 6.00S 118.00E; **5**, **44**, 48, *49*, **52**, **55**
Indore (India), **44**, 22.42N 75.54E
Indre (*r.*) (France), **24**, 47.16N 0.19E
Indus (*r.*), **44**, 24.00N 67.33E; **5**, **7**
Inhambane (Mozambique) **43**
Inland Sea (Japan), **50**
Inn (*r.*) (Austria), **30**, 48.35N 13.28E
Inner Mongolia 47
Innsbruck (Austria), **30**, 47.16N 11.24E; **31**
In Salah (Algeria), **38**, 27.13N 2.28E; **39**
Inuit 12, 13
Inuvik (Northwest Territories, Canada), **12**, 68.16N 133.40W
Invercargill (New Zealand), **54**, 46.25S 168.21E
Inverness (Scotland, United Kingdom), **22**, 57.27N 4.15W; **23**
Ioánnina (Greece) **29**
Ionian Islands (Greece), **28**, 38.45N 19.40E; **29**, 29
Ionian Sea **28**
Iowa (*s.*) (United States) **15**
Ipoh (Malaysia), **48**, 4.36N 101.02E; **49**
Ipswich (England, United Kingdom), **22**, 52.04N 1.09E; **23**
Iqaluit (*town*) (Nunavut, Canada), **12**, 63.44N 68.31W
Iquitos (Peru), **18**, 3.51S 73.13W; **19**
Iráklion (Greece), **28**, 35.20N 25.08E; **29**
Iran (*c.*), **36**, 32.00N 54.30E; **5**, **34**, 36, *37*
Iran Range (*mts.*) (Indonesia), **48**, 3.20N 115.00E
Iraq (*c.*), **36**, 33.00N 44.00E; **5**, 36, *37*
Ireland (*c.*), **22**, 53.00N 7.00W; **5**, 22, *23*
Irish language 23
Irish Sea **22**
Irkutsk (Russia), **34**, 52.18N 104.15E; **35**
Iron 10
Irrawaddy (*r.*) (Myanmar), **48**, 17.45N 95.25E
Irtysh (*r.*), **34**, 61.00N 68.40E; **5**, **7**
Irvine (Scotland, United Kingdom), **22**, 55.37N 4.40W; **23**
Isafjördhur (Iceland), **20**, 66.05N 23.06W; **21**
Isalo Massif (*mts.*) (Madagascar), **42**, 23.50S 45.00E
Isar (*r.*) (Germany), **30**, 48.49N 12.58E
Ischia (*i.*) (Italy), **28**, 40.43N 13.54E; **29**, 29
Ise (Japan), **50**, 34.29N 136.41E
Isère (*r.*) (France), **24**, 44.59N 4.51E
Isfahan (Iran), **36**, 32.42N 51.40E; **37**
Ishikari (*r.*) (Japan), **50**, 43.15N 141.20E
Ishinomaki (Japan) **51**
Isla de la Juventud (*i.*) (Cuba) **16**
Islamabad (Pakistan), **44**, 33.40N 73.08E; **45**
Islay (*i.*) (Scotland, United Kingdom), **22**, 55.45N 6.20W; **23**
Israel (*c.*), **36**, 32.0N 34.50E; **5**, 36, *37*, **38**
Istanbul (Turkey), **36**, 41.02N 28.58E; **37**
Istria (*pen.*) (Croatia), **32**, 45.12N 13.55E
Italian language 15, 23, 25, 29, 31
Italy (*c.*), **28**, 44.30N 11.00E; **5**, **24**, 28, *29*, **30**, **32**, **38**
climate 29
Iturup (*i.*) (Russia), **50**, 44.54N 147.30E
Ivory Coast *see* Côte d'Ivoire
Izhevsk (Russia) **35**
Izmir (Turkey), **36**, 38.24N 27.09E; **37**
Izmit (Turkey), **36**, 40.48N 29.55E; **37**
Izu Peninsula (Japan), **50**, 34.55N 139.00E

Jabalpur (India) **45**
Jackson (Mississippi, United States) **15**
Jacksonville (Florida, United States), **14**, 30.20N 81.40W; **15**
Jacmel (Haiti), **17**, 18.14N 72.32W
Jaffna (Sri Lanka), **44**, 9.38N 80.02E; **45**
Jaipur (India), **44**, 26.53N 75.50E; **45**
Jakobshavn (Greenland) **13**
Jakobstad (Finland), **20**, 63.40N 22.42E; **21**
Jamaica (*c.*), **16**, 18.00N 77.00W; **4**, 16, *17*
Jambi (Indonesia), **48**, 1.36S 103.39E; **49**
Jammu (Jammu and Kashmir), **44**, 34.00N 78.30E; **45**
Jammu & Kashmir (*d.*) **34**
Jamnagar (India), **44**, 22.28N 70.06E; **45**
Jan Mayen Islands (Norway) 21
Japan (*c.*), **50**, 38.00N 137.00E; **5**, **34**, **46**, 50, *51*
agriculture and fisheries 10
Japanese language 51
Japan, Sea of **5**, **7**, **46**, **50**
Japurá (*r.*) (Colombia/Brazil), **18**, 3.00S 64.50W
Jarvis Island (United States) 15
Java (*i.*) (Indonesia), **48**, 7.30S 111.00E; **5**, **7**, **49**
Java Sea **48**
Jaya, Mount (Indonesia), **48**, 4.00S 137.15E
Jayapura (Indonesia), **48**, 2.28S 140.38E; **49**
Jefferson City (Missouri, United States) **15**
Jerez de la Frontera (Spain) **27**
Jerusalem, **36**, 31.47N 35.13E; **37**
Jews 37
Jhelum (*r.*) (Pakistan), **44**, 31.00N 72.00E
Jiangsu (*d.*) (China) **47**
Jiangxi (*d.*) (China) **47**
Jidda (Saudi Arabia), **36**, 21.30N 39.10E; **37**
Jilin (Jilin, China) **47**
Jilin (*d.*) (China) **47**
Jima (Ethiopia), **38**, 7.39N 36.47E; **39**
Jinan (Shandong, China), **46**, 36.50N 117.00E; **47**
Jivaro language 17
Jodhpur (India) **45**
Joetsu (Japan) **51**
Johannesburg (South Africa), **42**, 26.11S 28.04E; **43**
John o'Groats (Scotland, United Kingdom) **22**, 58.49N 3.02W
Johnston Atoll (*i.*) (United States) **55**, 17.10N 169.08W; 15
Jönköping (Sweden), **20**, 57.47N 14.11E; **21**
Jordan (*c.*), **36**, 31.00N 36.00E; **5**, 36, *37*, **38**
Jos Plateau (Nigeria), **40**, 10.00N 9.00E
Jotunheimen (*mts.*) (Norway), **20**, 61.38N 8.18E
Juan Fernandez Islands (Chile), **18**, 34.20S 80.00W; 19
Juba (Sudan), **38**, 4.50N 31.35E; **39**
Juba (*r.*) (Ethiopia/Somalia), **38** 0.20S 42.53E
Jubany (Antarctica) **56**, 62.14S 58.38W
Júcar (*r.*) (Spain), **26**, 39.10N 0.15W
Juneau (Alaska, United States), **14**, 58.26N 134.30W; **15**
Jura (*i.*) (Scotland, United Kingdom), **22**, 55.58N 5.55W; **23**
Jura (*mts.*) (France/Switzerland), **24**, 46.50N 5.50E; **30**
Juruá (*r.*) (Brazil), **18**, 2.33S 65.50W
Jutland (*pen.*) (Denmark), **20**, 56.12N 9.20E
Juventud, Isla de la (Cuba), **16**, 21.40N 82.40W
Jyväskylä (Finland), **20**, 62.14N 25.44E; **21**

K2 (*mt.*) (Jammu and Kashmir), **44**, 35.53N 76.32E
Kabul (Afghanistan), **36**, 34.30N 69.10E; **37**
Kabwe (Zambia) **43**
Kaédi (Mauritania), **38**, 16.09N 13.30W; **39**
Kaesong (North Korea), **50**, 37.59N 126.30E; **51**
Kafue (*r.*) (Zambia), **42**, 15.43S 28.55E
Kagoshima (Japan), **50**, 31.37N 130.32E; **51**
Kahoolawe (*i.*) (Hawaii, United States), **14**, 20.30N 156.40W; **15**
Kahului (Hawaii, United States) **15**
Kai Islands (Indonesia), **48**, 5.45S 132.55E; **49**, **52**
Kaikoura (New Zealand), **54**, 42.25S 173.43E
Kakinada (India) **45**
Kalahari Desert, **42**, 23.55S 23.00E; **5**, **7**, 42
Kalámai (Greece), **28**, 37.02N 22.05E; **29**
Kalemie (Democratic Republic of the Congo) **41**
Kalgoorlie (Western Australia) **53**
Kalla (*l.*) (Finland), **20**, 62.40N 27.45E
Kalmar (Sweden), **20**, 56.40N 16.00E; **21**
Kamchatka Peninsula (Russia), **34**, 56.00N 160.00E; **5**, **7**, 34
Kamloops (British Columbia, Canada) **13**
Kampala (Uganda), **40**, 0.19N 32.35E; **41**
Kanaga (Democratic Republic of the Congo), **40**, 5.53S 22.26E; **41**
Kanazawa (Japan), **50**, 36.35N 136.40E
Kanchenjunga (*mt.*)(India/Nepal), **44**, 27.44N 88.11E
Kandahar (Afghanistan), **36**, 31.36N 65.47E; **37**
Kandy (Sri Lanka), **44**, 7.18N 80.43E; **45**
Kangaroo Island (Australia), **52**, 35.50S 137.06E
Kankan (Guinea) **41**
Kano (Nigeria), **40**, 12.00N 8.31E; **41**
Kanpur (India), **44**, 26.27N 80.14E; **45**
Kansas (*s.*) (United States) **15**
Kansas City (Kansas/Missouri, United States), **14**, 39.05N 94.35W
Kanto Plain (Japan), **50**, 36.00N 140.00E
Kaohsiung (Taiwan), **46**, 22.36N 120.17E; **47**
Karachi (Pakistan), **44**, 24.51N 67.02E; **45**
Karaganda (Kazakhstan) **35**
Karagiye Depression, **34**, 44.00N 52.30E
Karakoram Range (Jammu and Kashmir), **44**, 35.30N 76.30E
Kara Kum (*des.*) (Turkmenistan), **34**, 38.45N 58.00E; 34
Kara Sea **5**, **7**, **34**
Kariba (Zimbabwe) **43**
Kariba, Lake (Zambia/Zimbabwe), **42**, 16.50S 28.00E
Karlsruhe (Germany) **31**
Karlstad (Sweden) **21**

Karpathos (*i.*) (Greece), **28**, 35.35N 27.08E; **29**
Karun (*r.*) (Iran), **36**, 30.25N 48.12E
Kasai (*r.*) (Democratic Republic of the Congo), **40**, 3.10S 16.13E
Kasama (Zambia), **42**, 10.10S 31.11E; **43**
Kashi (Xinjiang, China) **47**
Kassel (Germany) **31**
Kastoría (Greece) **29**
Katherine (Northern Territory, Australia) **53**
Kathmandu (Nepal), **44**, 27.42N 85.19E; **45**
Katowice (Poland) **33**
Kattegat (*str.*), **20**, 57.25N 11.30E
Kauai (*i.*) (Hawaii, United States), **14**, 22.05N 159.30W; **15**
Kaula (*i.*) (Hawaii, United States), **14**, 21.40N 160.33W; **15**
Kavála (Greece) **29**
Kawasaki (Japan), **50**, 35.30N 139.45E; **51**
Kayseri (Turkey) **37**
Kazakh language 35
Kazakhstan (*c.*), **34**, 48.00N 70.00E; **5**, 34, *35*, **36**, **46**
Kazan (Russia) **35**
Kebnekaise (*mt.*) (Sweden), **20**, 67.53N 18.33E
Keeling Islands *see* Cocos Islands
Keetmanshoop (Namibia), **42**, 26.34S 18.07E; **43**
Kékes (*mt.*) (Hungary), **32**, 47.52N 20.01E
Kelang (Malaysia) **49**
Kemi (Finland), **20**, 65.49N 24.32E; **21**
Kemi (*r.*) (Finland), **20**, 65.47N 24.30E
Kemijärvi, **20**, 66.42N 27.30E; **21**
Kendari (Indonesia), **48**, 3.57S 122.36E; **49**
Kentucky (*s.*) (United States) **15**
Kenya (*c.*), **40**, 0.00 38.00E; **5**, **38**, 40, *41*
Kenya, Mount (Kenya), **40**, 0.10S 37.19E
Kerguelen Islands (France) **5**
Kerma (Sudan) **39**
Kermadec Islands (New Zealand), **55**, 30.00S 178.15W
Kerman (Iran), **36**, 30.18N 57.05E; **37**
Khabarovsk (Russia), **34**, 48.32N 135.08E; **35**
Khalka Mongolian language 35
Khalkis (Greece), **28**, 38.27N 23.36E; **29**
Khania (Greece), **28**, 35.30N 24.02E; **29**
Khanka (*l.*) (China/Russia), **46**, 45.00N 132.00E
Kharkov (Ukraine) **35**
Khartoum (Sudan), **38**, 15.33N 32.35E; **39**
Khasi Hills (India), **44**, 25.30N 91.00E
Khios (Greece), **28**, 38.23N 26.04E; **29**
Khmer language 49
Khoi-san 43
Kholmsk (Russia) **35**
Kiel (Germany), **30**, 54.20N 10.08E; **31**
Kielce (Poland) **33**
Kiev (Ukraine), **34**, 50.28N 30.29E; **35**
Kigali (Rwanda), **40**, 1.59S 30.05E; **41**
Kii Channel (Japan), **50**, 34.00N 135.00E
Kii Peninsula (Japan), **50**, 34.00N 135.30E
Kilimanjaro (*mt.*) (Tanzania), **40**, 3.02S 37.20E; **5**, **7**, 40
Kimberley (South Africa), **42**, 28.44S 24.44E; **43**
Kimberley Plateau (Australia), **52**, 17.20S 127.20E
Kimbundu language 43
Kimch'aek (North Korea), **50**, 40.41N 129.12E; **51**
Kinabalu, Mount (Malaysia), **48**, 6.10N 116.40E
King Island (Australia), **52**, 39.50S 144.00E
Kingston (Jamaica), **16**, 17.58N 76.48W
Kingston upon Hull (England, United Kingdom), **22**, 23.45N 0.20W
Kingstown (St. Vincent and the Grenadines), **17**, 13.12N 61.14W
Kinshasa (Democratic Republic of the Congo), **40**, 4.18S 15.18E; **41**
Kirghiz language 35
Kirghiz Steppe (*f.*) (Kazakhstan), **34**, 50.00N 57.10E
Kiribati (*c.*), **55**, 1.21N 173.01E; **5**, 55
Kirkpatrick, Mount (Antarctica), **56**, 84.20S 166.19E
Kirkuk (Iraq), **36**, 35.28N 44.26E; **37**
Kirkwall (Scotland, United Kingdom), **22**, 58.59N 2.58W; **23**
Kiruna (Sweden), **20**, 67.51N 20.16E; **21**
Kirundi language 41
Kisangani (Democratic Republic of the Congo), **40**, 0.33N 25.14E; **41**
Kishinev (Moldova), **34**, 47.00N 28.50E; **35**
Kismaayo (Somalia), **38**, 0.25S 42.31E; **39**
Kiso Mountains (Japan), **50**, 35.20N 137.30E
Kitakami (*r.*) (Japan), **50**, 38.25N 141.18E
Kitakyushu (Japan), **50**, 35.50N 130.50E; **51**
Kitchener (Ontario, Canada) **13**
Kithira (*i.*) (Greece), **28**, 36.15N 23.00E; **29**
Kitwe (Zambia) **43**
Kizil Irmak (*r.*) (Turkey), **36**, 41.45N 35.57E
Kjolen Mountains, **20**, 67.30N 17.30E
Klagenfurt (Austria) **31**
Klar (*r.*) (Sweden), **20**, 59.23N 13.32E
Klyuchevskaya, (*mt.*) (Russia), **34**, 55.00N 159.30E
Kobe (Japan), **50**, 34.42N 135.15E; **51**
Koblenz (Germany) **31**
Kochi (Japan), **50**, 33.33N 133.52E; **51**
Kodiak Island (Alaska, United States), **14**, 57.00N 153.50W
Kokenau (Indonesia), **48**, 4.42S 136.25E
Kola Peninsula (Russia), **34**, 67.00N 38.00E
Kolhapur (India) **45**
Kolkata (Calcutta) (India), **44**, 22.35N 88.21E; **45**
Kolyma Range (*mts.*) (Russia), **34**, 68.50N 161.00E
Komatsu (Japan) **51**
Komsomolsk-na-Amure (Russia) **35**
Kópavogur (Iceland) **21**
Korčula (*i.*) (Croatia), **32**, 42.56N 16.53E
Korea 50–51
North *see* North Korea
South *see* South Korea
Korean language 51
Korea Strait, **50**, 35.00N 129.20E
Koror (Palau) **55**, 7.21N 134.31E
Koryak Range (*mts.*) (Russia), **34**, 62.20N 171.00E
Kos (*i.*) (Greece), **28**, 36.48N 27.10E; **29**
Kosciusko (Australia), Mount, **52**, 36.28S 148.17E; **5**, **7**
Košice (Slovakia), **32**, 48.44N 21.15E; **33**
Koszalin (Poland) **33**
Kota Kinabalu (Malaysia) **49**
Kotka (Finland) **21**
Krakatau (*i.*) (Indonesia), **48**, 6.11S 105.26E
Kraków (Poland), **32**, 50.03N 19.55E; **33**
Kras (*mts.*), **32**, 45.20N 14.10E
Krasnodar (Russia) **35**
Krasnovodsk (Turkmenistan) **35**
Krasnoyarsk (Russia), **34**, 56.05N 92.46E; **35**
Krill 57
Krishna (*r.*) (India), **44**, 16.00N 81.00E
Kristiansand (Norway), **20**, 58.10N 8.00E; **21**
Krk (*i.*) (Croatia), **32**, 45.04N 14.36E
Kuala Lumpur (Malaysia), **48**, 3.08N 101.42E; **49**
Kuching (Malaysia), **48**, 1.32N 110.20E; **49**
Kuito (Angola) **43**
Kuju (*mt.*) (Japan), **50**, 33.07N 131.14E
Kula Kangri (*mt.*) (Bhutan), **44**, 28.15N 90.34E
Kumamoto (Japan), **50**, 32.50N 130.42E; **51**
Kunashir (*i.*), **50**, 44.10N 146.00E
Kunlun Shan (*mts.*) (China), **46**, 36.40N 88.00E; **5**, **7**
Kunming (Yunnan, China), **46**, 25.04N 102.41E; **47**
Kunsan (South Korea), **50**, 35.58N 126.41E; **51**
Kuopio (Finland), **20**, 62.51N 27.30E; **21**
Kupang (Indonesia), **48**, 10.13S 123.38E; **49**
Kurds 37
Kuria Muria Islands (Oman), **36**, 17.30N 56.00E
Kuril Islands (Russia), **34**, 46.00N 150.30E; **5**, **7**, **35**, **50**, 51
Kuroshio Current **7**
Kushiro (Japan), **50**, 42.58N 144.24E; **51**
Kuskokwim Mountains (Alaska, United States), **14**, 62.00N 156.00W
Kutch, Rann of, (*f.*), **44**, 23.50N 69.50E
Kuujjuaq (Quebec, Canada) **13**
Kuwait (*c.*), **36**, 29.20N 47.40E; **5**, 36, *37*
Kuwait (*city*) (Kuwait), **36**, 29.20N 48.00E; **37**
Kwangju (South Korea), **50**, 35.01N 126.44E; **51**
Kyoga, Lake (Uganda), **40**, 1.30N 33.00E
Kyoto (Japan), **50**, 35.04N 135.50E; **51**
Kyrgyzstan (*c.*), **34**, 41.30N 75.00E; **5**, 34, *35*, **36**, **46**
Kyushu (*i.*) (Japan), **50**, 33.30N 131.00E; **51**
Kyushu Mountains (Japan), **50**, 32.20N 131.20E
Kyzyl Kum (*des.*) (Kazakhstan/Uzbekistan), **34**, 42.00N 64.30E; 34

Labrador (*f.*) (Canada), **12**, 57.00N 62.00W
Labrador Current 6, **7**
Labrador Sea **4**, **6**
La Coruña (Spain), **26**, 43.22N 8.24W; **27**
La Digue (*i.*) (Seychelles), **40**, 4.20S 55.51E
Ladin language 29
Ladoga (*l.*) (Russia), **34**, 61.00N 32.00E; **20**
Lae (Papua New Guinea) **53**
Lagos (Nigeria), **40**, 6.27N 3.28E; **41**
Lahn (*r.*) (Germany), **30**, 50.18N 7.36E
Lahore (Pakistan), **44**, 31.34N 74.22E; **45**
Lahti (Finland) **21**
Lakshadweep (*isls.*) (India), **44**, 11.00N 72.00E; **45**, 45
Lambaréné (Gabon) **41**
Lanai (*i.*) (Hawaii, United States), **14**, 20.50N 156.55W; **15**
Land reclamation 30
Land's End, (*f.*) (England, United Kingdom), **22**, 50.03N 5.45W
Langjökull (*mt.*) (Iceland), **20**, 63.43N 20.03W
Langkawi Islands (Malaysia), **48**, 6.20N 99.30E; **49**
Langreo (Spain) **27**
Langres Plateau (France), **24**, 47.41N 5.00E
Languedoc-Roussillon (*d.*) (France) **25**
Lansing (Michigan, United States) **15**
Lanzhou (Gansu, China), **46**, 36.01N 103.45E; **47**
Lao language 49
Laos (*c.*), **48**, 19.00N 104.00E; **5**, **46**, 48, *49*
La Paz (Bolivia), **18**, 16.30S 68.10W; **19**
Lapland (*f.*), **20**, 68.10N 24.10E
La Plata (Argentina) **19**
Lappeenranta (Finland) **21**
Lapps 20
Laptev Sea **5**, **7**, **34**
Lárisa (Greece), **28**, 39.36N 22.24E; **29**
Larnaca (Cyprus) **29**
La Rochelle (Poitou-Charentes, France) **25**
Larsen Ice Shelf (Antarctica), **56**, 68.30S 62.30W
La Spezia (Italy), **28**, 44.07N 9.49E; **29**
Las Vegas (Nevada, United States), **14**, 36.11N 115.08W; **15**
Latakia (Syria) **37**
Latin America 17, 18
Latin language 29
Latitude and climate 6
Latvia (*c.*), **34**, 57.00N 25.00E; **5**, **20**, 34, *35*
Latvian language 35
Launceston (Tasmania, Australia) **53**
Laurentian Highlands (Canada), **12**, 52.15N 70.00W
Lausanne (Switzerland), **30**, 46.31N 6.38E; **31**
Lead 10
Lebanon (*c.*), **36**, 34.00N 36.00E; **5**, **28**, 36, *37*, **38**
Lech (*r.*) (Germany) **30**
Leeds (England, United Kingdom), **22**, 53.48N 1.34W; **23**
Leghorn (Italy) *see* Livorno
Le Havre (Upper Normandy, France), **24**, 49.30N 0.06E; **25**
Leipzig (Germany), **30**, 51.19N 12.20E; **31**
Leizhou Peninsula (China), **46**, 20.40N 109.30E
Le Mans (Pays de la Loire, France) **24**, 48.00N 0.12E; **25**
Lena (*r.*) (Russia), **34**, 72.00N 127.10E; **5**, **7**
Lengua language 19
Lens (Nord-Pas-de-Calais, France) **25**
León (Mexico), **16**, 21.10N 101.42W
León (Spain), **26**, 42.35N 5.34W; **27**
Lérida (Spain), **26**, 41.37N 0.38E; **27**
Lerwick (Scotland, United Kingdom), **22**, 60.09N 1.09W; **23**
Lesbos (*i.*) (Greece), **28**, 39.10N 26.16E; **29**
Les Landes (*f.*) (France), **24**, 44.00N 1.00W
Lesotho (*c.*), **42**, 29.30S 28.00E; **5**, 42, *43*
Lesser Antarctica 57
Lesser Antilles (*isls.*), **17**, 16.00N 62.00W; **4**, **6**, **10**
Levkas (*i.*) (Greece), **28**, 38.44N 20.37E; **29**
Lewis (*i.*) (Scotland, United Kingdom), **22**, 58.10N 6.40W; **23**
Leyte (*i.*) (Philippines), **48**, 10.40N 124.50E
Lhasa (Tibet, China), **46**, 29.41N 91.10E; **47**
Lhotsam language 45
Liao (*r.*) (China), **46**, 42.00N 122.00E
Liaoning (*d.*) (China) **47**
Liberia (*c.*), **40**, 6.30N 9.30W; **5**, 40, *41*
Libreville (Gabon), **40**, 0.30N 9.25E; **41**
Libya (*c.*), **38**, 26.30N 17.00E; **5**, **28**, 38, *39*
Libyan Desert, **38**, 26.00N 24.00E; **5**, **7**
Lichen 57
Lichinga (Mozambique) **43**
Liechtenstein (*c.*), **30**, 47.09N 9.32E; **5**, **24**, **28**, 30, **31**, **32**
Liège (Belgium), **30**, 50.38N 5.35E; **31**
Lienz (Austria) **31**
Ligurian Sea **28**
Lille (Nord-Pas-de-Calais, France), **24**, 50.39N 3.05E; **25**
Lillehammer (Norway), **20**, 61.06N 10.27E
Lilongwe (Malawi), **42**, 13.58S 33.49E; **43**
L'Ilôt (*i.*) (Seychelles), **40**, 4.36S 55.54E
Lima (Peru), **18**, 12.06S 77.03W; **19**
Limassol (Cyprus), **28**, 34.40N 33.03E; **29**
Limerick (Ireland), **22**, 52.40N 8.37W; **23**
Límnos (*i.*) (Greece), **28**, 39.55N 25.14E; **29**
Limoges (Limousin, France), **24**, 45.50N 1.15E; **25**
Limousin (*d.*) (France) **25**
Limpopo (*r.*), **42**, 25.14S 33.33E; **5**, **7**
Linares (Spain) **27**
Lincoln (Nebraska, United States) **15**
Lindi (Tanzania) **41**
Lingga (*i.*) (Indonesia), **48**, 0.20S 104.30E; **49**
Linköping (Sweden) **21**
Linz (Austria), **30**, 48.18N 14.18E; **31**
Lipari Islands (Italy), **28**, 38.35N 14.45E; **29**, 29
Lisbon (Portugal), **26**, 38.44N 9.08W; **27**
Lithosphere 4
Lithuania (*c.*), **34**, 55.00N 24.00E; **32**, **5**, **20**, 34, *35*
Lithuanian language 35
Little Andaman (*i.*) (India), **44**, 10.50N 92.38E
Little Karroo (*f.*) (South Africa), **42**, 33.40S 21.40E
Little Rock (Arkansas, United States) **15**
Liverpool (England, United Kingdom), **22**, 53.25N 3.00W; **23**
Livingstone (Zambia), **42**, 17.50S 25.53E; **43**
Livorno (Leghorn) (Italy), **28**, 43.33N 10.18E; **29**
Ljubljana (Slovenia), **32**, 46.04N 14.28E; **33**
Ljusnan (*r.*) (Sweden), **20**, 61.12N 17.08E
Llanos (*f.*), **18**, 7.30N 70.00W
Llullaillaco (*mt.*) (Chile), **18**, 24.38S 68.38W
Lobamba (Swaziland), **42**, **43**
Lobatse (Botswana), **42**, 25.12S 25.39E; **43**
Lobito (Angola), **42**, 12.20S 13.34E; **43**
Łódź (Poland), **32**, 51.49N 19.28E; **33**
Lofoten (*isls.*) (Norway), **20**, 68.15N 13.50E
Logan, Mount (Canada), **12**, 60.34N 140.24W
Loire (*r.*) (France), **24**, 47.16N 2.11W
Lokka Reservoir (Finland), **20**, 67.55N 27.30E
Lolland (*i.*) (Denmark), **20**, 54.46N 11.30E
Lombok (*i.*) (Indonesia), **48**, 8.30S 116.20E; **49**
Lomé (Togo), **40**, 6.10N 1.21E; **41**
London (England, United Kingdom), **22**, 51.32N 0.06W; **23**
London (Ontario, Canada) **13**
Londonderry (Northern Ireland, United Kingdom), **22**, 55.00N 7.20W; **23**
Long Beach (California, United States) **15**
Long Island (Bahamas), **16**, 23.00N 75.00W
Long Island (New York, United States), **14**, 40.50N 73.00W
Longroño (Spain) **27**
Lopez, Cape (Gabon), **40**, 0.36S 8.45E
Lop Nur (*l.*) (Xinjiang, China), **46**, 40.30N 90.30E
Lord Howe Island (Australia), **52**, 31.28S 159.09E
Lorient (Brittany, France) **25**
Lorraine (*d.*) (France) **25**

Los Angeles (California, United States), **14**, 34.00N 118.17W; **15**
Lot (*r.*) (France), **24**, 44.18N 0.20E
Louisiade Archipelago (Papua New Guinea), **52**, 11.10S 153.00E
Louisiana (*s.*) (United States) **15**
Lourdes (Midi-Pyrénées, France) **25**
Low Countries 30–31
Luanda (Angola), **42**, 8.50S 13.20E; **43**
Luang Prabang (Laos), **48**, 19.53N 102.10E; **49**
Luangwa (*r.*) (Zambia), **42**, 15.32S 30.28E
Lubango (Angola) **43**
Lübeck (Germany) **31**
Lublin (Poland), **32**, 51.18N 22.31E; **33**
Lubumbashi (Democratic Republic of the Congo), **40**, 11.41S 27.29E; **41**
Lucania, Mount (Canada), **12**, 61.01N 140.28W
Lucerne (Switzerland) **31**
Lucknow (India) **45**
Lüderitz (Namibia) **43**
Luena (Angola), **42**, 11.46S 19.55E; **43**
Lule (*r.*) (Sweden), **20**, 65.35N 22.03E
Luleå (Sweden), **20**, 65.34N 22.10E; **21**
Luliang Shan (*mts.*) (China) **46**, 38.30N 111.30E
Lunda language 43
Lüneburg Heath (*f.*) (Germany), **30**, 53.06N 10.30E
Luoyang (Henan, China) **47**
Lúrio (*r.*) (Mozambique), **42**, 13.32S 40.31E
Lusaka (Zambia), **42**, 15.26S 28.20E; **43**
Luxembourg (*c.*), **30**, 49.50N 6.15E; **5**, **24**, 30, *31*
Luxembourg (Luxembourg), **30**, 49.37N 6.08E; **31**
Luxor (Egypt) **39**
Luzon (*i.*) (Philippines), **48**, 17.50N 121.00E; **49**
Lvov (Ukraine) **35**
Lyon (Rhône-Alpes, France), **24**, 45.46N 4.50E; **25**

Macao (China), **46**, 22.13N 113.36E; **47**, 47
Macapá (Brazil) **19**
Macchu Picchu (Antarctica), **56**, 62.12S 58.54W
McDonald Islands (Australia) 53
Macdonnell Ranges (*mts.*) (Australia), **52**, 23.45S 133.20E; **5**, **7**
Macedonia (*c.*), **32**, 41.30N 21.30E; **5**, **28**, 32, *33*
Macedonian language 29, 33
Macgillycuddy's Reeks (*mts.*) (Ireland), **22**, 52.00N 9.45W
Machilipatnam (India) **45**
Mackay (Queensland, Australia), **52**, 21.08S 149.11E; **53**
Mackay, Lake (dry) (Australia), **52**, 22.30S 129.00E
Mackenzie (*r.*) (Canada), **12**, 69.20N 134.00W
Mackenzie Bay (Antarctica), **56**, 68.00S 72.00E
Mackenzie Mountains (Canada), **12**, 64.00N 130.00W
McKinley, Mount (Alaska, United States), **14**, 63.00N 151.00W; **4**, **6**, **10**
McMurdo (Antarctica), **56**, 77.50S 166.25E
Madagascar (*c.*), **42**, 20.00S 47.30E; **5**, **7**, 42, *43*
Madang (Papua New Guinea), **52**, 5.14S 145.45E; **53**
Madeira (*i.*) (Portugal), 26, 27
Madeira (*r.*) (Brazil), **18**, 3.20S 59.00W
Madison (Wisconsin, United States) **15**
Madraka, Cape (Oman), **36**, 19.00N 57.50E
Madrid (Spain), **26**, 40.25N 3.43W; **27**
Madura (*i.*) (Indonesia), **48**, 7.00S 113.30E; **49**
Madurai (India) **45**
Maebashi (Japan) **51**
Magadan (Russia) **35**
Magdeburg (Germany), **30**, 52.08N 11.38E; **31**
Magellan, Strait of, **18**, 53.00S 71.00W
Maggiore, Lake (Italy/Switzerland), **28**, 45.57N 8.37E; **30**
Mahajanga (Madagascar), **42**, 15.43S 46.19E; **43**
Mahanadi (*r.*) (India), **44**, 20.17N 86.43E
Mahavavy (*r.*) (Madagascar), **42**, 15.57S 45.54E
Mahé (*i.*) (Seychelles), **40**, 5.00S 55.30E
Mahón (Spain), **26**, 39.55N 4.18E
Main (*r.*) (Germany), **30**, 50.00N 8.18E
Maiduguri (Nigeria) **41**
Mai-Ndombe, Lake (Democratic Republic of the Congo), **40**, 2.00S 18.20E
Maine (*s.*) (United States) **15**
Mainland (Orkney) (*i.*) (Scotland, United Kingdom), **22**, 59.00N 3.10W
Mainland (Shetland) (*i.*) (Scotland, United Kingdom), **22**, 60.15N 1.22W
Mainz (Germany), **30**, 50.00N 8.16E; 31
Maio (*i.*) (Cape Verde), **40**, 15.15N 23.10W
Majorca (*i.*) (Spain), **26**, 39.35N 3.00E; **27**
Majuro (Marshall Islands) **55**, 7.05N 171.08E
Makassar Strait, **48**, 3.00S 118.00E
Makgadikgadi Pan (*f.*) (Botswana), **42**, 20.50S 25.45E
Makran Coast Range (*mts.*) (Pakistan), **44**, 25.40N 65.00E
Makua language 43
Malabo (Equatorial Guinea), **40**, 3.45N 8.48E; **41**
Malacca, Strait of, **48**, 3.00N 100.30E
Málaga (Spain), **26**, 36.43N 4.25W; **27**
Malagasy language 43
Malakal (Sudan), **38**, 9.31N 31.40E; **39**
Malang (Indonesia), **48**, 7.59S 112.45E; **49**
Malanje (Angola), **42**, 9.36S 16.21E; **43**
Mälaren (*l.*) (Sweden), **20**, 59.30N 17.12E
Malatya (Turkey) **37**
Malawi (*c.*), **42**, 13.00S 34.00E; **5**, **40**, 42, *43*
Malawi, Lake, (Malawi/Tanzania), **42**, 12.00S 34.30E; **5**, **7**, 42
Malayalam language 45
Malay language 49
Malay Peninsula, **48**, 4.00N 102.00E
Malaysia (*c.*), **48**, 5.00N 110.00E; **5**, 48, *49*
Maldives (*c.*), **44**, 6.20N 73.00E; **5**, **7**, 44, *45*
Male (Maldives), **44**, 4.00N 73.28E; **45**
Mali (*c.*), **38**, 18.00N 1.00W; **5**, 38, *39*, **40**
Malindi (Kenya) **41**
Malin Head (Northern Ireland, United Kingdom), **22**, 55.22N 7.24W
Malmö (Sweden), **20**, 55.36N 13.00E; **21**
Malpelo Island (Colombia), **18**, 2.00N 81.43W
Malta (*c.*), **28**, 35.55N 14.25E; 28, *29*
Malta (*i.*) (Malta), **28**, 35.55N 14.25E; **5**, **28**, **29**, **38**
Mamelle (*i.*) (Seychelles), **40**, 4.29S 55.31E
Man, Isle of (United Kingdom), **22**, 54.15N 4.30W; 23
Manado (Indonesia), **48**, 1.30N 124.58E; **49**
Managua (Nicaragua), **16**, 12.06N 86.18W
Managua, Lake (Nicaragua), **16**, 12.10N 86.30W
Manama (Bahrain), **36**, 26.12N 50.36E; **37**
Manaus (Brazil), **18**, 3.06S 60.00W; **19**
Manchester (England, United Kingdom), **22**, 53.30N 2.15W; **23**
Manchu language 47
Manchurian Plain (China), **46**, 42.00N 122.00E
Mandalay (Myanmar), **48**, 21.57N 96.04E; **49**
Mandarin Chinese language 47
Mangalore (India), **44**, 12.54N 74.51E; **45**
Mangoky (*r.*) (Madagascar), **42**, 21.29S 43.41E
Manila (Philippines), **48**, 14.36N 120.59E; **49**
Manitoba (*p.*) (Canada) **13**
Manitoba, Lake (Canada), **12**, 51.00N 98.45W
Mannar, Gulf of, **44**, 8.20N 79.00E
Mannheim (Germany), **30**, 49.30N 8.28E; **31**
Manokwari (Indonesia), **48**, 0.53S 134.05E
Mansa (Zambia) **43**
Maoke Mountains (Indonesia), **48**, 4.00S 137.30E
Maoris 54, 55
Maple 6, 8
Mapuche language 19
Maputo (Mozambique), **42**, 25.58S 32.35E; **43**
Maracaibo (Venezuela), **18**, 10.44S 71.37W; **19**
Maracaibo, Lake (Venezuela), **18**, 9.50N 71.30W
Maradi (Niger), **38**, 13.29N 7.10E; **39**
Marambio (Antarctica), **56**, 64.14S 56.38W
Marañón (Peru) (*r.*), **18**, 4.40S 73.20W
Marathi language 45
Mar del Plata (Argentina) **19**
Mariana Islands (United States) **5**, **7**, 15, **55**
Marie Byrd Land, **56**, 79.30S 125.00W; **6**
Maritime Alps (*mts.*) (France), **24**, 44.30N 7.15E
Maritsa (*r.*) (Bulgaria), **32**, 41.40N 26.16E
Markham, Mount (Antarctica), **56**, 82.51S 161.21E
Marmara, Sea of **32**
Marne (*r.*) (France), **24**, 48.49N 2.24E
Maromokotro (*mt.*) (Madagascar), **42**, 14.00S 49.00E
Marrakesh (Morocco), **38**, 31.49N 8.00W; **39**
Marseille (Provence-Alpes-Côtes-d'Azur), **24**, 43.18N 5.24E; **25**
Marshallese language 55
Marshall Islands, **55**, 7.05N 171.08E; **5**, **7**, 55
Martinique (*i.*) (France), **17**, 14.40N 61.00W; 17, 25
Maryland (*s.*) (United States) **15**
Masan (South Korea), **50**, 35.10N 128.35E; **51**
Maseru (Lesotho), **42**, 29.18S 27.28E; **43**
Mashhad (Iran), **36**, 36.16N 59.34E; **37**
Masirah (*i.*) (Oman), **36**, 20.30N 58.50E; **37**
Mask, Lough (Ireland), **22**, 53.38N 9.22W
Masoala, Cape (Madagascar), **42**, 15.59S 50.13E
Massachusetts (*s.*) (United States) **15**
Massif Central (*mts.*) (France), **24**, 45.00N 3.10E
Matadi (Democratic Republic of the Congo) **41**
Matapán, Cape (Greece), **28**, 36.23N 22.29E
Mato Grosso, Plateau of (Brazil), **18**, 16.00S 54.00W
Matopo Hills (Zimbabwe), **42**, 20.45S 28.30E
Matsue (Japan), **50**, 35.29N 133.04E; **51**
Matsuyama (Japan) **51**
Matterhorn (*mt.*) (Switzerland), **30**, 45.59N 7.43E
Maui (*i.*) (Hawaii, United States), **14**, 20.45N 156.15W; **15**
Mauna Kea (*mt.*) (Hawaii, United States), **14**, 19.50N 155.25W
Mauritania (*c.*), **38**, 19.00N 10.00W; **5**, 38, *39*, **40**
Mauritius (*c.*), **42**, 20.08S 57.30E; **5**, **7**, 42, *43*
Mawson (Antarctica) **56**, 67.36S 62.53E
Mayan empire 16
Mayon, Mount (Philippines), **48**, 13.14N 123.45E
Mayotte (*i.*) (France), **42**, 12.50S 45.10E; 25, **43**
Mazar-e Sharif (Afghanistan) **37**
Mbabane (Swaziland), **42**, 26.19S 31.08E; **43**
Mbala (Zambia) **43**
Mbandaka (Democratic Republic of the Congo) **41**
Mbeya (Tanzania) **41**
Mbuji-Mayi (Democratic Republic of the Congo) **41**
Mecca (Saudi Arabia), **36**, 21.26N 39.49E; **37**
Mecklenburg Bay, **30**, 54.20N 11.50E
Medan (Indonesia), **48**, 3.35N 98.39E; **49**
Medellín (Colombia), **18**, 6.15N 75.36W; **19**
Medicine Hat (Alberta, Canada) **13**
Medina (Saudi Arabia), **36**, 24.30N 39.35E; **37**
Mediterranean Sea **5**, **7**, **24**, **26**, **28**, **36**, **38**
Mekong (*r.*), **48**, 10.00N 106.20E; **5**, **7**, **46**
Melanesia 55
Melbourne (Victoria, Australia), **52**, 37.45S 144.58E; **53**
Melilla (Spain), **26**, 35.17N 2.51W; 27
Melville Island (Australia), **52**, 11.30S 131.00E
Melville Peninsula (Canada), **12**, 68.00N 84.00W
Memphis (Tennessee, United States), **14**, 35.08N 90.03W; **15**
Mendip Hills (England, United Kingdom), **22**, 51.15N 2.40W
Mendoza (Argentina) **19**
Mentawai Islands (Indonesia), **48**, 2.50S 99.00E; **49**
Menzies, Mount (Antarctica) **56**, 7.30S 62.00E
Merauke (Indonesia), **48**, 8.30S 140.22E
Mergui Archipelago (Myanmar), **48**, 11.30N 98.30E
Mérida (Mexico), **16**, 20.59N 89.39W
Mérida (Spain) **27**
Merowe (Sudan) **39**
Mersey (*r.*) (England, United Kingdom), **22**, 53.20N 2.30W
Meseta (*f.*) (Spain), **26**, 40.15N 3.30W; 26, 27
Mesolóngion (Greece) **29**
Messina (Italy), **28**, 38.13N 15.34E; **29**, 29
Messina (South Africa) **43**
Metals 10
Metz (Lorraine, France), **24**, 49.07N 6.11E; **25**
Meuse (*r.*) (France/Belgium), **24**, 51.49N 5.01E
Mexico (*c.*), **16**, 22.00N 101.40W; **4**, 16, *17*
Mexico City (Mexico), **16**, 19.25N 99.10W
Mexico, Gulf of, 16, 25.00N 90.00W; **4**, **6**, **10**, 14, **16**
Meymaney (Afghanistan) **37**
Miami (Florida, United States), **14**, 25.45N 80.15W; **15**
Miao language 47
Michigan (*s.*) (United States) **15**
Michigan, Lake (United States), **14**, 44.00N 87.00W
Micronesia, Federated States of (*c.*) **55**
Middle Andaman (*i.*) (India), **44**, 12.35N 93.00E
Middle East *see* Southwest Asia
Middlesbrough (England, United Kingdom), **22**, 54.34N 1.13W; **23**
Midi-Pyrénées (*d.*) (France) **25**
Midway (*i.*) (United States), **55**, 28.13N 177.22W; 15
Migration 14, 24
Mikuni Mountains (Japan), **50**, 37.00N 139.20E
Milan (Italy), **28**, 45.28N 9.16E; **29**
Mildura (Victoria, Australia) **53**
Milos (*i.*) (Greece), **28**, 36.40N 24.26E; **29**
Milwaukee (Wisconsin, United States), **14**, 43.02N 87.55W; **15**
Minami Tori Shima (*i.*) (Japan), **55**, 24.00N 153.45E
Mindanao (*i.*) (Philippines), **48**, 7.30N 125.00E; **49**
Mindoro (*i.*) (Philippines), **48**, 13.00N 121.00E; **49**
Minerals;
reserves **10**, 10
Minho (*r.*) (Portugal/Spain), **26**, 41.52N 8.51W
Minneapolis (Minnesota, United States), **14**, 44.59N 93.13W; **15**
Minnesota (*s.*) (United States) **15**
Minorca (*i.*) (Spain), **26**, 40.00N 4.00E; **27**
Minsk (Belarus), **34**, 53.51N 27.30E; **35**
Mirnyy (Antarctica), **56**, 66.33S 93.00E
Miskolc (Hungary), **32**, 48.07N 20.47E; **33**
Misool (*i.*) (Indonesia), **48**, 1.50S 130.10E; **49**
Misratah (Libya), **38**, 32.24N 15.04E; **39**
Mississippi (*s.*) (United States) **15**
Mississippi (*r.*) (United States), **14**, 29.00N 89.15W; **4**, **6**, **10**
Mississippi Delta (United States), **14**, 29.00N 89.15W
Missouri (*s.*) (United States) **15**
Missouri (*r.*) (United States), **14**, 38.50N 90.08W; **4**, **6**, **10**
Mitchell, Mount (United States), **14**, 35.47N 82.16W
Mitilíni (Greece), **28**, 39.06N 26.34E; **29**
Miyazaki (Japan), **50**, 31.58N 131.50E; **51**
Mljet (*i.*) (Croatia), **32**, 42.45N 17.30E
Modena (Italy) **29**
Mogadishu (Somalia), **38**, 2.02N 45.21E; **39**
Mo-i Rana (Norway) **21**
Mojave Desert (United States), **14**, 35.00N 117.00W
Mokp'o (South Korea), **50**, 34.48N 126.22E; **51**
Moldavian language 35
Moldova (*c.*), **34**, 47.30N 28.30E; **5**, **28**, **32**, **34**, 34, *35*
Moldoveanu (*mt.*) (Romania), **32**, 45.36N 24.44E
Molds 57
Molodeznaja (Antarctica), **56**, 67.40S 45.50E
Molokai (*i.*) (Hawaii, United States), **14**, 21.20N 157.00W; **15**
Moluccas (*isls.*) (Indonesia), **48**, 4.00S 128.00E; **49**
Molucca Sea **48**
Mombasa (Kenya), **40**, 4.04S 39.40E; **41**
Monaco (*c.*), **24**, 43.40N 7.25E; 24, *25*, **28**
Monaco (Monaco), **24**, 43.40N 7.25E; **25**
Monégasque language 25
Mongolia (*c.*), **34**, 46.30N 104.00E; **5**, 34, *35*, **46**
Mongolia (Inner) (*d.*) (China) **47**
Mongol language 47
Mongu (Zambia), **42**, 15.10S 23.09E; **43**

Monrovia (Liberia), **40**, 6.20N 10.46W; **41**
Mons (Belgium) **31**
Monsoon **6–7**, 44, 48, 50
Monsoon Drift **7**
Montana (*s.*) (United States) **15**
Monte Corno (Italy), **28**
Montego Bay (*town*) (Jamaica), **16**, 18.27N 77.56W
Monte Rosa (*mt.*) (Italy/Switzerland), **28**, 29, **30**
Monterrey (Mexico), **16**, 25.40N 100.20W
Montevideo (Uruguay), **18**, 34.55S 56.10W; **19**
Montgomery (Alabama, United States) **15**
Montpelier (Vermont, United States) **15**
Montpellier (Languedoc-Roussillon, France), **24**, 43.36N 3.53E; **25**
Montreal (Quebec, Canada), **12**, 45.31N 73.34W; **13**
Montserrat (*i.*) (United Kingdom), **17**, 16.45N 62.14W; 17
Moore, Lake (dry) (Australia), **52**, 29.30S 117.30E
Moose Jaw (Saskatchewan, Canada) **13**
Mopti (Mali) **39**
Morava (*r.*) (Yugoslavia), **32**, 44.43N 21.02E
Moray Firth (*est.*) (Scotland, United Kingdom), **22**, 57.35N 3.50W
Mordavian language 35
Morioka (Japan), **50**, 39.43N 141.10E; **51**
Morocco (*c.*), **38**, 32.00N 8.00W; **5**, **26**, 38, *39*
Morondava (Madagascar), **42**, 20.17S 44.17E
Moroni (Comoros), **42**, 11.40S 43.19E; **43**
Morvan (*f.*) (France), **24**, 47.00N 4.50E
Moscow (Russia), **34**, 55.45N 37.42E; **35**
Moscow University Ice Shelf (Antarctica), **56**, 66.20S 120.00E
Moselle (*r.*) (France/Germany), **30**, 50.22N 7.36E
Moss 57
Mosselbaai (South Africa) **43**
Mostar (Bosnia and Herzegovina), **32**, 43.20N 17.50E; **33**
Mosul (Iraq), **36**, 36.21N 43.08E; **37**
Motherwell (Scotland, United Kingdom) **23**
Moulmein (Myanmar) **49**
Mountains;
  habitats **6–7**, 6
  mountain building 4, 24
Mount Hagen (Papua New Guinea) **53**
Mount Isa (Queensland, Australia) **53**
Mourne Mountains (Northern Ireland, United Kingdom), **22**, 54.10N 6.02W
Mozambique (*c.*), **42**, 19.00S 35.00E; **5**, **40**, 42, *43*
Mozambique Channel, **42**, 16.00S 42.30E; **5**, **7**
Mpika (Zambia) **43**
Mtwara (Tanzania) **41**
Muchinga Mountains (Zambia), **42**, 12.00S 31.00E
Mui Bai Point (Vietnam), **48**, 8.30N 104.35E
Mulanje, Mount (Malawi), **42**, 15.57S 35.33E
Mulhacén (*mt.*) (Spain), **26**, 37.04N 3.22W; 27
Mulhouse (Alsace, France), **24**, 47.45N 7.21E; **25**
Mull (*i.*) (Scotland, United Kingdom), **22**, 56.28N 5.56W; **23**
Multan (Pakistan), **44**, 30.10N 71.36E; **45**
Mumbai (Bombay) (India), **44**, 18.56N 72.51E; **45**
Munich (Germany), **30**, 48.08N 11.34E; **31**
Münster (Germany) **31**
Mur (*r.*) (Austria), **30**, 47.05N 15.27E
Murcia (Spain), **26**, 37.59N 1.08W; **27**
Mures (*r.*) (Romania), **32**, 46.16N 20.10E
Müritz, Lake (Germany), **30**, 53.25N 12.43E
Murmansk (Russia), **34**, 68.59N 33.08E; **35**
Muroran (Japan), **50**, 42.21N 140.59E; **51**
Murray (*r.*) (Australia), **52**, 35.23S 139.20E
Murrumbidgee (*r.*) (Australia), **52**, 34.38S 143.10E
Musala (*mt.*) (Bulgaria), **32**, 42.11N 23.35E
Muscat (Oman), **36**, 23.36N 58.37E; **37**
Musgrave Ranges (*mts.*) (Australia), **52**, 26.10S 131.50E
Mutare (Zimbabwe), **42**, 18.58S 32.40E; **43**
Muztag (*mt.*) (China), **46**, 36.25N 87.25E
Mwanza (Tanzania) **41**
Mweru, Lake, **40**, 9.00S 28.40E; **42**
Myanmar (Burma) (*c.*), **48**, 22.00N 98.00E; **5**, **44**, **46**, 48, *49*
Myingyan (Myanmar), **48**, 21.25N 95.20E; **49**
Myitkyina (Myanmar) **49**
Mymensingh (Bangladesh) **45**
Mzuzu (Malawi), **42**, 11.50S 33.39E; **43**

Nacala (Mozambique), **42**, 14.31S 40.34E
Naga Hills (India), **44**, 26.10N 94.30E
Nagano (Japan) **51**
Nagaoka (Japan) **51**
Nagasaki (Japan), **50**, 32.45N 129.52E; **51**
Nagoya (Japan), **50**, 35.08N 136.53E; **51**
Nagpur (India), **44**, 21.10N 79.12E; **45**
Nahua language 17
Nairobi (Kenya), **40**, 1.17S 36.50E; **41**
Najran (Saudi Arabia) **37**
Nakhon Ratchasima (Thailand) **49**
Naktong (*r.*) (South Korea), **50**, 35.10N 128.18E
Nam, Lake (Tibet, China), **46**, 30.40N 90.30E
Namib Desert (Namibia), **42**, 22.50S 14.40E; 42
Namibe (Angola) **43**
Namibia (*c.*), **42**, 22.00S 17.00E; **5**, 42, *43*
Namlea (Indonesia), **48**, 3.15S 127.07E
Namp'o (North Korea), **50**, 38.40N 125.30E; **51**
Nampula (Mozambique), **42**, 15.09S 39.14E; **43**
Namsos (Norway) **21**
Namur (Belgium), **30**, 50.28N 4.52E; **31**
Nanchang (Jiangxi, China), **46**, **47**
Nancy (Lorraine, France), **24**, 48.42N 6.12E; **25**
Nanded (India) **45**
Nangnim Mountains (North Korea), **50**, 40.30N 127.00E
Nanjing, **46**, 32.00N 118.40E
Nanning (Guangxi, China), **46**, 22.50N 108.19E; **47**
Nantes (Pays de la Loire, France), **24**, 47.14N 1.35W; **25**
Napier (New Zealand), **54**, 39.30S 176.54E
Naples (Italy), **28**, 40.50N 14.14E; **29**
Narmada (*r.*) (India), **44**, 21.40N 73.00E
Narvik (Norway), **20**, 68.26N 17.25E; **21**
Nashville (Tennessee, United States) **15**
Näsi (*l.*) (Finland), **20**, 61.58N 23.57E
Nassau (Bahamas), **16**, 25.05N 77.20W
Nasser, Lake (Egypt/Sudan), **38**, 22.40N 32.00E
Native Americans 12, 13, 14, 15, 16, 17, 18, 19
Natuna Besar (*i.*) (Indonesia), **48**, 3.00N 108.50E; **49**
Nauru (*c.*), **55**, 0.31S, 166.56E; **5**, 55
Nauruan language 55
Nawabshah (Pakistan) **45**
Naxos (*i.*) (Greece), **28**, 37.03N 25.30E; **29**
N'djamena (Chad), **38**, 12.10N 14.59E; **39**
Ndola (Zambia), **42**, 13.00S 28.39E; **43**
Neagh, Lough (Northern Ireland, United Kingdom), **22**, 54.36N 6.26W
Neblina Peak (Brazil) (*mt.*), **18**, 0.45N 66.01W
Nebraska (*s.*) (United States) **15**
Neckar (*r.*) (Germany), **30**, 49.31N 8.26E
Negro (*r.*) (Brazil), **18**, 3.00S 59.55W; **4**, **6**, **10**
Negros (*i.*) (Philippines), **48**, 10.00N 123.00E; **49**
Nejd (*des.*) (Saudi Arabia), **36**, 25.00N 43.00E
Nellore (India) **45**
Nelson (New Zealand), **54**, 41.16S 173.15E
Nelson (*r.*) (Canada), **12**, 57.04N 92.30W
Nepal (*c.*), **44**, 28.00N 84.00E; **5**, 44, *45*, **46**
Nepalganj (Nepal) **45**
Nepali language 45
Ness, Loch (Scotland, United Kingdom), **22**, 57.16N 4.30W
Netherlands (*c.*), **30**, 52.00N 5.00E; **5**, **20**, **22**, **24**, 30, *31*
  dependencies 17
Netherlands Antilles (*isls.*), **17**, 12.15N 69.00W; 31
Neuchâtel (Switzerland) **31**
Neuchâtel, Lake (Switzerland), **30**, 46.52N 6.50E
Neusiedler, Lake (Austria/Hungary), **30**, 47.52N 16.45E
Nevada (*s.*) (United States) **15**
Newark (New Jersey, United States) **15**
New Britain (*i.*) (Papua New Guinea), **52**, 6.00S 150.00E
New Brunswick (*p.*) (Canada) **13**
New Caledonia (*i.*) (France) **55**, 21.00S 165.00E; **5**, **7**, 25
Newcastle (New South Wales, Australia), **52**, 32.55S 151.46E; **53**
Newcastle upon Tyne (England, United Kingdom), **22**, 54.58N 1.36W; **23**
New Delhi (India), **44**, 28.37N 77.13E; **45**
Newfoundland (*i.*) (Canada), **12**, 48.30N 56.00W; **4**, **6**, **10**
Newfoundland (*p.*) (Canada) **13**
New Guinea (*i.*) (Indonesia), **52**, 5.00S 140.00E; **5**, **7**, **49**, **52**, **55**
New Hampshire (*s.*) (United States) **15**
New Hebrides (*isls.*) **5**, **7**
New Ireland (*i.*) (Papua New Guinea), **52**, 2.30S 151.30E
New Jersey (*s.*) (United States) **15**
New Mexico (*s.*) (United States) **15**
New Orleans (Louisiana, United States), **14**, 29.58N 90.07W; **15**
New Plymouth (New Zealand), **54**, 39.04S 174.04E
New Siberian Islands (Russia), **34**, 76.00N 144.00E; **5**, **7**, **35**
New South Wales (*d.*) (Australia) **53**
New York (*s.*) (United States) **15**
New York (New York, United States), **14**, 40.43N 74.01W; **15**
New Zealand (*c.*), **54**, 41.30S 175.00E; **5**, **7**, 54, *55*
Nha Trang (Vietnam), **48**, 12.15N 109.10E; **49**
Nhulunbuy (Northern Territory, Australia) **53**
Niagara Falls (New York, United States/Canada), **14**, 43.06N 79.04W; **12**
Niamey (Niger), **38**, 13.32N 2.05E; **39**
Nias (*i.*) (Indonesia), **48**, 1.05N 97.30E; **49**
Nicaragua (*c.*), **16**, 13.00N 85.00W; **4**, 16, *17*
Nicaragua, Lake (Nicaragua), **16**, 11.30N 85.30W
Nice (Provence-Alpes-Côte-d'Azur, France), **24**, 43.42N 7.16E; **25**
Nicobar Islands (India), **44**, 8.00N 94.00E; **5**, **7**, **45**, 45, **48**
Nicosia (Cyprus), **28**, 35.11N 33.23E; **29**
Niger (*c.*), **38**, 17.00N 10.00E; **5**, 38, *39*, **40**
Niger (*r.*), **40**, 4.15N 6.05E; **5**, **7**, **38**
Nigeria (*c.*), **40**, 9.00N 9.00E; **5**, **38**, 40, *41*
Niigata (Japan), **50**, 37.58N 139.02E; **51**
Niihau (*i.*) (Hawaii, United States), **14**, 21.55N 160.10W; **15**
Nijmegen (Netherlands) **31**
Nikolayevsk-na-Amure (Russia) **35**
Nile (*r.*) (Egypt/Sudan), **38**, 31.30N 30.25E; **5**, **7**
Nile, Blue (*r.*) (Sudan/Ethiopia), **38**, 15.45N 32.25E
Nile, White (*r.*) (Sudan), **38**, 15.45N 32.25E; 40
Nimba, Mount, **40**, 7.35N 8.28W
Ningbo (Zhejiang, China) **47**
Ningxia (*d.*) (China) **47**
Nioro du Sahel (Mali) **39**
Niš (Yugoslavia), **32**, 43.20N 21.54E; **33**
Niue (*isls.*) (New Zealand), **55**, 19.02S 169.54W; 55
Nizhniy Novgorod (Russia), **34**, 56.20N 44.00E; **35**
Nobeoka (Japan) **51**
Nomadism 38
Nome (Alaska, United States) **15**
Nordic Council 21
Nordic countries 20–**21**
Nord-Pas-de-Calais (*d.*) (France) **25**
Nordvik (Russia) **35**
Norfolk (Virginia, United States), **14**, 36.54N 76.18W; **15**
Norfolk Island (Australia), **55**, 28.58S 168.03E; 53
Norlisk (Russia) **35**
Normandy;
  Lower (*d.*) (France) **25**
  Upper (*d.*) (France) **25**
Norrköping (Sweden), **20**, 58.36N 16.11E; **21**
Norrland (*f.*) (Sweden), **20**, 63.00N 17.00E
North America **4**, **6**, **7**, **10**, 12–13
Northampton (England, United Kingdom) **23**
North Andaman (*i.*) (India), **44**, 13.14N 94.00E
North Atlantic Current 6, 22
North Atlantic Drift **7**
North Atlantic Ocean **7**
North Atlantic Treaty Organization (NATO) 15, 21, 23, 25
North Cape (Iceland), **20**, 66.30N 23.00W
North Cape (New Zealand), **54**, 34.28S 173.00E
North Cape (Norway), **20**, 71.11N 25.48E
North Carolina (*s.*) (United States) **15**
North China Plain (*f.*) (China) **46**, 37.30N 116.00E
North Dakota (*s.*) (United States) **15**
North Equatorial Current **7**
Northern Africa 38–**39**
Northern European Plain (*f.*) (Russia), **34**, 60.00N 40.00E; **5**, **7**, 24, 30, 32, **39**
Northern Ireland (United Kingdom) **23**
Northern Mariana Islands, **55**, 17.00N 145.00E
Northern Territory (*d.*) (Australia) **53**
North Frisian Islands (Germany) **30**, 54.54N 8.20E; **31**
North Island (*i.*) (Seychelles), **40**, 4.23S 55.15E
North Island (New Zealand), **54**, 39.00S 175.00E
North Korea (*c.*), **50**, 38.30N 127.00E; **5**, **34**, **46**, 50, *51*
North Pacific Drift **7**
North Pacific Ocean **7**
North Pole 12
North Sea **5**, **20**, **22**, 22, **30**
North West Highlands (Scotland, United Kingdom), **22**, 57.30N 5.15W
Northwest Territories (*d.*) (Canada) **13**
North York Moors (England, United Kingdom), **22**, 54.21N 0.50W
Norvegia, Cape (Antarctica), **56**, 71.25S 12.18W
Norway (*c.*), **20**, 63.00N 10.00E; **5**, 20, *21*, **22**
Norwegian language 21
Norwegian Sea **20**
Norwich (England, United Kingdom), **22**, 52.38N 1.17E; **23**
Nosy Bé (*i.*) (Madagascar), **42**, 13.20S 48.15E
Nosy Boraha (*i.*) (Madagascar), **42**, 16.50S 49.55E
Noto Peninsula (Japan), **50**, 37.30N 137.00E
Nottingham (England, United Kingdom), **22**, 52.58N 1.10W
Nouadhibou (Mauritania), **38**, 20.54N 17.01W; **39**
Nouakchott (Mauritania), **38**, 18.09N 15.58W; **39**
Nova Scotia (*p.*) (Canada), **12**, 45.00N 63.30W; **13**
Novaya Zemlya (*i.*) (Russia), **34**, 74.00N 56.00E; **5**, **7**, **35**
Novi Sad (Yugoslavia), **32**, 45.16N 19.52E; **33**
Novokuznetsk (Russia) **35**
Novolazarevskaya (Antarctica), **56**, 70.46S 11.50E
Novosibirsk (Russia), **34**, 55.04N 82.55E; **35**
Nowshak (*mt.*) (Afghanistan), **36**, 36.26N 71.50E
Nubian Desert (Sudan), **38**, 21.00N 34.00E
Nuclear power 8
Nuclear waste 8
Nuevo Laredo (Mexico), **16**, 27.30N 99.30W
Nuku'alofa (Tonga), **55**, 21.09S 175.14W
Nullarbor Plain (Australia), **52**, 31.30S 125.00E
Nunavut (*d.*) (Canada) **13**, 13
Nunivak Island (Alaska, United States), **14**, 60.00N 166.30W
Nuremberg (Germany), **30**, 49.27N 11.04E; **31**
Nuuk (Greenland) *see* Godthåb
Nyainqentanglha Shan (*mts.*) (Tibet, China), **46**, 30.00N 90.00E
Nyala (Sudan) **39**

Oahu (*i.*) (Hawaii, United States), **14**, 21.30N 158.00W; **15**
Oak 6, 8
Oamaru (New Zealand), **54**, 45.05S 170.59E
Ob (*r.*) (Russia), **34**, 66.50N 69.00E; **5**, **7**
Obi (*i.*) (Indonesia), **48**, 1.45S 127.30E; **49**
Obihiro (Japan), **50**, 42.55N 143.00E; **51**
Oceania **55**, 55
Ocean ridges 4
Ocean trenches 48
Ódádahraun (Iceland), **20**, 65.00N 17.30W
Odense (Denmark), **20**, 55.24N 10.23E; **21**

Odenwald (f.) (Germany), 30, 49.35N 9.05E
Oder (r.), 32, 53.30N 14.36E
Odessa (Ukraine), 34, 46.30N 30.46E; 35
Offenbach (Germany) 31
Ogaden (f.) (Ethiopia), 38, 7.50N 45.40E
Ogulin (Croatia) 33
Ohio (s.) (United States) 15
Ohio (r.) (United States), 14, 36.59N 89.08W
Ohrid (Macedonia) 33
Ohrid, Lake (Albania/Macedonia), 32, 41.06N 20.48E
Oil 10, 20, 36, 38
  reserves 10
Oise (r.) (France), 24, 49.00N 2.04E
Oita (Japan), 50, 33.15N 131.40E; 51
Okavango Delta (Botswana), 42, 19.30S 23.00E
Okayama (Japan), 50, 34.40N 133.54E; 51
Okeechobee, Lake (Florida, United States), 14, 27.00N 80.45W
Okha (Russia) 35
Okhotsk (Russia) 35
Oki Islands (Japan), 50, 36.10N 133.10E; 51
Okinawa (i.) (Japan), 48, 26.40N 128.00E; 51
Oklahoma (s.) (United States) 15
Oklahoma City (Oklahoma, United States) 15
Okushiri (i.) (Japan), 50, 42.10N 139.31E; 51
Öland (i.) (Sweden), 20, 56.45N 16.38E; 21
Olbia (Italy) 29
Oldenburg (Germany) 31
Oléron, Ile d', (France), 24, 45.56N 1.15W
Olongapo (Philippines) 49
Olsztyn (Poland), 32, 53.48N 20.29E; 33
Olt (r.) (Romania), 32, 44.13N 24.28E
Olympia (Washington, United States) 15
Olympus (mt.) (Cyprus), 28, 34.55N 32.52E
Olympus (mt.) (Greece), 28, 40.04N 22.20E
Omaha (Nebraska, United States) 15
Oman (c.), 36, 22.30N 57.30E; 5, 36, 37
Omdurman (Sudan), 38, 15.37N 32.59E; 39
Omsk (Russia), 34, 55.00N 73.22E; 35
Onega, Lake (Russia), 34, 62.00N 35.30E
Ontario (p.) (Canada) 13
Ontario, Lake (United States/Canada), 12, 43.45N 78.00W; 14
Oporto (Portugal), 26, 41.09N 8.37W; 27
Oradea (Romania), 32, 47.03N 21.55E; 33
Oran (Algeria), 38, 35.45N 0.38W; 39
Orange (r.) (South Africa), 42, 28.38S 16.38E
Orcadas (Antarctica), 56, 60.45S 44.43W
Ordos (des.) (China), 46, 40.00N 109.00E
Örebro (Sweden), 20, 59.17N 15.13E; 21
Oregon (s.) (United States) 15
Organization of African Unity (OAU) 39, 41, 43
Organization of American States (OAS) 15
Organization for Economic Cooperation and Development (OECD) 15, 21, 23, 25, 51, 53
Organization of Petroleum Exporting Countries (OPEC) 39
Ori (l.) (Finland), 20, 62.21N 29.34E
Orinoco (r.) (Venezuela), 18, 9.00N 61.30W; 4, 6, 10
Orkney Islands (Scotland, United Kingdom), 22, 59.00N 3.00W; 23
Orléans (Centre, France), 24, 47.54N 1.54E; 25
Ortles (mt.) (Italy), 28, 46.31N 10.33E
Osaka (Japan), 50, 34.40N 135.30E; 51
Osijek (Croatia), 32, 45.33N 18.41E; 33
Oslo (Norway), 20, 59.55N 10.45E; 21
Osnabrück (Germany) 31
Ostend (Belgium), 30, 51.13N 2.55E; 31
Östersund (Sweden), 20, 63.10N 14.40E; 21
Ostrava (Czech Republic), 32, 49.50N 18.15E; 33
Osumi (i.) (Japan), 50, 30.30N 130.30E
Otaru (Japan), 50, 43.14N 140.59E; 51
Otranto, Strait of, 28, 40.10N 19.00E
Ottawa (Ontario, Canada), 12, 45.25N 75.42W; 13
Ouagadougou (Burkina Faso), 40, 12.20N 1.40W; 41

Oudtshoorn (South Africa) 43
Oulu (Finland), 20, 65.01N 25.28E; 21
Oulu, Lake (Finland), 20, 64.20N 27.15E
Ouse (r.) (England, United Kingdom), 22, 53.41N 0.42W
Ovamboland (f.) (Namibia), 42, 17.45S 16.00E
Oviedo (Spain), 26, 43.21N 5.50W; 27
Owen Stanley Range (mts.) (Papua New Guinea), 52, 9.30S 148.00E
Oyashio Current 7
Ozark Plateau (United States), 14, 37.00N 93.00W
Ozone layer hole 56

Pacific Coast Range see Coast Range
Pacific Ocean 4, 6, 10, 55
Pacific ring of fire 34, 50
Padang (Indonesia), 48, 0.55S 100.21E; 49
Padua (Italy) 29
Paektu, Mount (North Korea), 50, 42.00N 128.17E
Pag (i.) (Croatia), 32, 44.28N 15.00E
Päijänne (l.) (Finland), 20, 61.22N 25.37E
Pakistan (c.), 44, 30.00N 70.00E; 5, 34, 36, 44, 45
Pakse (Laos), 48, 15.05N 105.50E; 49
Palau (c.), 55, 7.00N 134.25E; 5, 48, 55
Palauan language 55
Palawan (i.) (Philippines), 48, 9.30N 118.30E; 49
Palembang (Indonesia), 48, 2.59S 104.50E; 49
Palermo (Italy), 28, 38.09N 13.22E; 29
Palestinians 37
Palikir (Federated States of Micronesia) 55, 6.55N 158.10E
Palk Strait, 44, 10.00N 79.40E
Palliser, Cape (New Zealand), 54, 41.35S 175.15E
Palma (Spain), 26, 39.36N 2.39E; 27
Palmas, Cape, 40, 4.30N 7.55W
Palmer (Antarctica), 56, 64.46S 64.03W
Palmer Land (Antarctica), 56, 73.00S 67.00W
Palmerston North (New Zealand), 54, 40.21S 175.37E
Palmyra Atoll (United States), 55, 5.52N 162.05W; 15
Palu (Indonesia), 48, 0.54S 119.52E; 49
Pamirs (mts.), 34, 37.50N 73.30E; 34
Pampas (f.) (Argentina), 18, 35.00S 64.00W
Pamplona (Spain), 26, 42.49N 1.39W; 27
Panama (c.), 16, 9.00N 80.00W; 4, 16, 17
Panama Canal, 16, 9.21N 79.54W
Panama City (Panama), 16, 8.57N 79.30W
Panay (i.) (Philippines), 48, 11.10N 122.30E; 49
Pangea 4
Pantelleria (i.) (Italy), 28, 36.48N 12.00E; 29, 29
Panzhihua (Sichuan, China) 47
Paphos (Cyprus) 29
Papua New Guinea (c.), 52, 6.00S 144.00E; 5, 48, 52, 53, 55, 55
  climate 52
Paraguay (c.), 18, 23.00S 57.00W; 4, 18, 19
Paraguay (r.), 18, 27.30S 58.50W; 4, 6, 10
Paramaribo (Suriname), 18, 5.52N 55.14W; 19
Paraná (r.), 18, 34.00S 58.30W; 4, 6, 10
Parece Vela (i.) (Japan), 55, 20.25N 136.00E
Parepare (Indonesia), 48, 4.03S 119.40E
Paris (Ile-de-France, France), 24, 48.52N 2.20E; 24, 25
Parma (Italy), 28, 44.48N 1019E; 29
Pashtu language 37
Passero, Cape (Italy), 28, 36.40N 15.09E
Patagonia (f.) (Argentina), 18, 42.20S 67.00W; 4, 6, 10
Patna (India), 44, 25.37N 85.12E; 45
Pátrai (Greece), 28, 38.15N 21.45E; 29
Pau (Aquitaine, France) 25
Pavlodar (Kazakhstan) 35
Pays de la Loire (d.) (France) 25
Peace (r.) (Canada), 12, 59.00N 111.25W; 4, 6, 10
Peć (Yugoslavia) 33
Pécs (Hungary), 32, 42.40N 20.17E; 33
Pedro Vicente Maldonado (Antarctica), 56, 62.30S 59.41W
Pegu (Myanmar), 48, 17.18N 96.31E; 49
Pegu Yoma (mts.) (Myanmar), 48, 18.40N 96.00E

Pekanbaru (Indonesia) 49
Peking (China) see Beijing
Peloponnese (f.) (Greece), 28, 38.00N 22.00E
Pemba (Mozambique) 43
Pemba (i.) (Tanzania), 40, 5.10S 39.45E; 41
Penguin, Emperor 57
Pennines (mts.) (England, United Kingdom), 22, 54.40N 2.20W
Pennsylvania (s.) (United States) 15
Perigueux (Aquitaine, France) 25
Perm (Russia) 35
Perpignan (Languedoc-Roussillon, France), 24, 42.42N 2.54E; 25
Persian Gulf, 36, 27.00N 50.00E; 5, 7
Perth (Scotland, United Kingdom), 22, 56.24N 3.28W; 23
Perth (Western Australia), 52, 31.58S 115.49E; 53
Peru (c.), 18, 12.00S 75.00W; 4, 18, 19
Peru Current 7
Perugia (Italy), 28, 43.07N 12.23E; 29
Pescara (Italy), 28, 42.27N 14.13E; 29
Peshawar (Pakistan) 45
Peter I (i.) (Antarctica), 56, 68.47S 90.35W
Petrel, Antarctic 57
Petropavlovsk Kamchatskiy (Russia), 34, 53.03N 158.43E; 35
Pevek (Russia) 35
Philadelphia (Pennsylvania, United States), 14, 40.00N 75.10W; 15
Philippines (c.), 48, 13.00N 123.00E; 5, 7, 46, 48, 49
Philippine Sea 48
Phnom Penh (Cambodia), 48, 11.35N 104.55E; 49
Phoenix (Arizona, United States), 14, 33.27N 112.05W; 15
Phosphate 10
Phuket (i.) (Thailand), 48, 8.10N 98.20E; 49
Piacenza (Italy) 29
Picardy (d.) (France) 25
Pico de Teide (mt.) (Tenerife) 27
Pidurutalagala (mt.) (Sri Lanka), 44, 6.56N 80.45E
Pielinen (l.) (Finland), 20, 63.20N 29.50E
Pierre (South Dakota, United States) 15
Pietermaritzburg (South Africa) 43
Pietersburg (South Africa) 43
Pinang (i.) (Malaysia), 48, 5.30N 110.10E
Pindus Mountains (Greece), 28, 39.40N 21.00E; 29
Pingxiang (Jiangxi, China) 47
Pinios (r.) (Greece), 28, 39.51N 22.37E
Piraeus (Greece), 28, 37.56N 23.38E; 29
Pirin (mts.) (Bulgaria), 32, 41.35N 23.24E
Piru (Indonesia), 48, 3.01S 128.10E
Pisa (Italy), 28, 43.43N 10.24E; 29
Pitcairn Island (United Kingdom), 55, 25.05S 130.05W; 23
Piteşti (Romania) 33
Piton des Neiges (mt.) (Réunion), 42, 21.05S 55.28E
Pitt Island (New Zealand), 54, 44.10S 176.30W
Pittsburgh (Pennsylvania, United States), 14, 40.26N 80.00W; 15
Plenty, Bay of (New Zealand), 54, 37.40S 176.50E
Pleven (Bulgaria), 32, 43.25N 24.39E; 33
Ploieşti (Romania) 33
Plovdiv (Bulgaria), 32, 42.09N 24.45E; 33
Plymouth (England, United Kingdom), 22, 50.23N 4.09W; 23
Plzeň (Czech Republic), 32, 49.45N 13.22E; 33
Po (r.) (Italy), 28, 44.51N 12.30E; 28, 29
Pobeda (mt.) (Russia), 34, 65.10N 146.00E
Pobedy Peak (Kyrgyzstan), 34, 42.25N 80.15E
Podgorica (Yugoslavia) 33
P'ohang (South Korea), 50, 36.00N 129.26E; 51
Pointe-Noire (Republic of the Congo) 41
Poitiers (Poitou-Charentes, France), 24, 46.35N 0.20E; 25
Poitou-Charentes (d.) (France) 25
Poland (c.), 32, 52.30N 19.00E; 5, 20, 30, 32, 33, 34
Polar easterlies 6
Polish language 15, 23, 25, 33, 35
Pollution 8–9, 8, 10
  acid rain 8
  sea 6
Polynesia 54, 55
Pontianak (Indonesia), 48, 0.05S 109.16E; 49
Ponza (i.) (Italy), 28, 40.53N 12.58E; 29, 29
Popocatépetl (mt.) (Mexico), 16, 19.02N 98.38W

Population, world 8–9, 8
Pori (Finland), 20, 61.28N 21.45E; 21
Portalegre (Portugal) 27
Port Augusta (South Australia) 53
Port-au-Prince (Haiti), 17, 18.33N 72.20W
Port Blair (Andaman Islands, India), 44, 11.40N 92.30E; 45
Port Elizabeth (South Africa), 42, 33.57S 25.34E; 43
Port Harcourt (Nigeria) 41
Port Hedland (Western Australia), 52, 20.24S 118.36E; 53
Portimão (Portugal) 27
Portland (Oregon, United States), 14, 45.33N 122.50W
Port Lincoln (South Australia) 53
Port Louis (Mauritius), 42, 20.08S 57.30E
Port Macquarie (New South Wales, Australia) 53
Port Moresby (Papua New Guinea), 52, 9.30S 147.07E; 53
Port Nolloth (South Africa) 43
Pôrto Alegre (Brazil), 18, 30.03S 51.10W; 19
Port-of-Spain (Trinidad), 17, 10.38N 61.31W
Porto Novo (Benin), 40, 6.30N 2.47E; 41
Porto Velho (Brazil) 19
Port Pirie (South Australia) 53
Port Said (Egypt), 38, 31.17N 32.18E; 39
Portsmouth (England, United Kingdom) 23
Port Sudan (Sudan), 38, 19.39N 37.01E; 39
Portugal (c.), 26, 39.30N 8.05W; 5, 26, 27, 38
  climate 27
Portuguese language 18, 19, 25, 27, 41, 43, 47
Port-Vila (Vanuatu), 55, 17.45S 168.18E
Poso (Indonesia), 48, 1.23S 120.45E
Potsdam (Germany) 31
Poyang, Lake (China), 46, 29.05N 116.20E
Poznań (Poland), 32, 52.25N 16.53E; 33
Prague (Czech Republic), 32, 50.05N 14.25E; 33
Praia (Cape Verde), 40, 15.04N 23.29W
Praslin (i.) (Seychelles), 40, 4.18S 55.45E
Prato (Italy) 29
Precipitation 6
Prespa, Lake (Albania/Macedonia), 32, 40.53N 21.02E
Pretoria (South Africa), 42, 25.43S 28.11E; 43
Préveza (Greece) 29
Prince Albert (Saskatchewan, Canada) 13
Prince Edward Island (p.) (Canada), 12, 46.15N 63.00W; 13
Prince George (British Columbia, Canada) 13
Prince of Wales Island (Canada), 12, 73.00N 99.00W
Prince Rupert (British Columbia, Canada) 13
Priština (Yugoslavia) 33
Provençal language 25
Provence-Alpes-Côte-d'Azur (d.) (France) 25
Providence (Rhode Island, United States) 15
Ptuj (Slovenia) 33
Puerto Montt (Chile), 18, 41.28S 73.00W; 19
Puerto Princesa (Philippines) 49
Puerto Rico (United States), 17, 18.20N 66.30W; 4, 15, 16, 17
Pula (Croatia) 33
Pune (India), 44, 18.34N 73.58E; 45
Punjabii 33
Punta Arenas (Chile), 18, 53.10S 70.56W; 19
Punta la Marmora (mt.) (Italy), 28, 40.00N 9.07E
Pusan (South Korea), 50, 35.06N 129.03E; 51
Putumayo (r.), 18, 3.05S 68.10W
Puula (l.) (Finland), 20, 61.50N 26.42E
Puy de Dôme (mt.) (France), 24, 45.47N 2.58E
Puy de Sancy (mt.) (France), 24, 18.34N 73.58E
P'yongyang (North Korea), 50, 39.00N 125.47E; 51
Pyrenees (mts.) (France/Spain), 26, 42.40N 0.30W; 5, 7, 24, 26, 27

Qaanaaq (Greenland) see Thule
Qaidam Basin (Qinghai, China), 46, 37.46N 96.00E
Qal'at at Bishah (Saudi Arabia) 37
Qatar (c.), 36, 25.20N 51.10E; 5, 36, 37

Qattara Depression (Egypt), **38**, 29.40N 27.30E
Qian Shan (*mts.*) (China), **46**, 42.00N 125.00E
Qilian Shan (*mts.*) (China), **46**, 38.30N 100.00E
Qingdoa (Shandong, China) **47**
Qinghai (*d.*) (China) **47**
Qinghai, Lake (Qinghai, China), **46**, 36.40N 100.00E
Qin Ling (*mts.*) (China), **46**, 33.40N 109.00E
Qiqihar (Heilongjiang, China) **47**
Qom (Iran) **37**
Quebec (*p.*) (Canada) **13**, 13
Quebec (*city*) (Canada), **12**, 46.50N 71.20W; **13**
Quechua language 19
Queen Charlotte Islands (Canada), **12**, 53.00N 132.00W
Queen Elizabeth Islands (Canada), **12**, 78.30N 99.00W
Queen Maud Land (Antarctica), **56**, 72.30S 12.00E; **7**
Queensland (*d.*) (Australia) **53**
Quelimane (Mozambique) **43**
Quetta (Pakistan), **44**, 30.15N 67.00E; **45**
Quezon City (Philippines) **49**
Quimper (Brittany, France) **25**
Quito (Ecuador), **18**, 0.14S 78.30W; **19**

Raba (Indonesia), **48**, 8.27S 118.45E; **49**
Rabat (Morocco), **38**, 34.02N 6.51W; (Somalia) **39**
Rabaul (Papua New Guinea), **52**, 4.13S 152.11E; **53**
Race, Cape (Canada), **12**, 46.40N 53.10W
Raeside, Lake (dry) (Australia), **52**, 29.20S 122.00E
Rainfall 6
Rain forest 6, **8–9**, 8, 40
Rainier, Mount (Washington, United States), **14**, 46.52N 121.46W
Rajang (*r.*) (Malaysia), **48**, 2.10N 112.45E
Raleigh (North Carolina, United States) **15**
Ranchi (India) **45**
Rangoon *see* Yangon
Rankin Inlet (*town*) (Nunavut, Canada) **13**
Rann of Kutch (India), **44**
Ras Dashan (*mt.*) (Ethiopia), **38**, 13.20N 38.10E
Rasht (Iran), **36**, 37.18N 49.38E; **37**
Rau Islands (Indonesia) **49**
Raurkela (India) **45**
Ravenna (Italy), **28**, 44.25N 12.12E; **29**
Rawalpindi (Pakistan), **44**, 33.35N 73.08E; **45**
Reading (England, United Kingdom), **22**, 51.28N 0.59W; **23**
Recif (*i.*) (Seychelles), **40**, 4.36S 55.42E
Recife (Brazil), **18**, 8.06S 34.53W; **19**
Red (*r.*) (United States), **14**, 31.10N 92.00W
Red (*r.*) (Vietnam/China), **48**, 20.15N 106.32E; **46**
Red Deer (Alberta, Canada) **13**
Red Sea, **5**, **7**, **38**
Ree, Lough (Ireland), **22**, 53.31N 7.58W
Refrigeration 10, 56
Regensburg (Germany), **30**, 49.01N 12.07E; **31**
Reggio di Calabria (Italy), **28**, 38.07N 15.38E; **29**
Regina (Saskatchewan, Canada), **12**, 50.25N 104.39W; **13**
Rehoboth (Namibia) **43**
Ré, Ile de (*i.*) (France), **24**, 46.10N 1.26W
Reims (Champagne-Ardenne, France), **24**, 49.15N 4.02E; **25**
Reindeer Lake (Canada), **12**, 57.15N 102.40W
Rennes (Brittany, France), **24**, 48.06N 1.40W; **25**
Republic of the Congo *see* Congo, Republic of the
Resolute (Nunavut, Canada), **12**, 74.40N 95.00W; **13**
Resources **10**, 10
  nonrenewable 10
  recycling 10
Réunion (*i.*) (France), **42**, 21.00S 55.30E **5**, **7**, 25
Revillagigedo Islands (Mexico), **16**, 19.00N 111.00W
Reykjavik (Iceland), **20**, 64.09N 21.58W; **21**
Rhine (*r.*), **30**, 51.53N 6.03E; **24**
Rhode Island (*s.*) (United States) **15**
Rhodes (Greece), **28**, 36.24N 28.15E; **29**
Rhodes (*i.*) (Greece), **28**, 36.12N 28.00E; **29**
Rhodope Mountains (Bulgaria), **32**, 41.35N 24.35E
Rhône (*r.*) (France/Switzerland), **24**, 43.20N 4.50E
Rhône-Alpes (*d.*) (France) **25**
Rhum (*i.*) (Scotland, United Kingdom), **22**, 57.00N 6.20W
Richmond (Virginia, United States) **15**
Rift Valley, **40**, 0.00 29.00E; **5**, **7**, 38, 40, **42**, 42
Riga (Latvia), **34**, 56.53N 24.08E; **35**
Rijeka (Croatia), **32**, 45.20N 14.25E; **33**
Rimini (Italy) **29**
Rimouski (Quebec, Canada) **13**
Rinkøbing (Denmark) **21**
Rio Branco (*city*) (Brazil) **19**
Rio de Janeiro (Brazil), **18**, 22.50S 43.17W; **19**, 19
Rio de la Plata (*r.*) (Argentina), **18**, 35.15S 56.45W
Rio Gallegos (*town*) (Argentina) **19**
Rio Grande (*r.*) (United States/ Mexico), **14**, 25.55N 97.08W; **4**, **6**, **10**, **16**
Rio Grande de Santiago (*r.*) (Mexico), **16**, 21.43N 105.14W
Riyadh (Saudi Arabia), **36**, 24.39N 46.44E; **37**
Robson, Mount (Canada), **12**, 53.10N 119.10W
Rockhampton (Queensland, Australia) **53**
Rocky Mountains, **14**, 50.00N 115.00W; **4**, **6**, **10**
Romania (*c.*), **32**, 46.30N 24.00E; **5**, **28**, 32, *33*, **34**, **36**
Romanian language 33
Rome (Italy), **28**, 41.54N 12.29E; **29**
Ronne Ice Shelf (Antarctica) **56**, 78.00S 60.00W
Roosevelt (*i.*) (Antarctica), **56**, 79.30S 162.00W
Roraima (*mt.*) (Brazil/Venezuela/ Guyana), **18**, 5.14N 60.44W
Rosa, Monte, (*mt.*), **28**, 45.57N 7.53E
Rosario (Argentina), **18**, 33.00S 60.40W; **19**
Roseau (Dominica), **17**, 15.18N 61.23W
Ross Ice Shelf (Antarctica), **56**, 81.30S 175.00W
Ross Island (Antarctica), **56**, 77.40S 168.00E
Rostock (Germany) **31**
Rostov (Russia), **34**, 57.11N 39.23E; **35**
Rothera (Antarctica), **56**, 67.34S 60.74W
Roti (*i.*) (Indonesia), **52**, 10.50S 123.00E
Rotorua, Lake (New Zealand), **54**, 38.00S 176.00E
Rotterdam (Netherlands), **30**, 51.55N 4.29E; **31**
Rouen (Upper Normandy, France), **24**, 49.26N 1.05E; **25**
Ruahine Range (*mts.*) (New Zealand), **54**, 40.00S 176.00E
Ruapehu (*mt.*) (New Zealand), **54**, 39.20S 175.30E
Rub al-Khali (*des.*), **36**, 19.30N 50.00E
Rufiji (*r.*) (Tanzania), **40**, 8.02S 39.17E
Rügen (*i.*) (Germany), **30**, 54.25N 13.24E
Ruhr (*r.*) (Germany), **30**, 51.27N 6.44E
Ruse (Bulgaria), **32**, 43.50N 25.59E; **33**
Russia (*c.*), **34**, 57.30N 87.00E; **5**, **12**, **14**, **20**, **32**, 34, *35*, **36**, **46**, **50**
Russian language 35
Ružomberok (Slovakia) **33**
Rwanda (*c.*), **40**, 2.00S 3.00E; **5**, 40, *41*
Rwandan language 41
Ryukyu Islands (Japan), **48**, 26.30N 128.00E; **46**, **48**, 51

Saale (*r.*) (Germany), **30**, 51.57N 11.55E
Saarbrücken (Germany) **31**
Sabha (Libya), **38**, 27.02N 14.26E; **39**
Sable, Cape (Canada), **12**, 43.25N 65.35W
Sable, Cape (Florida, United States), **14**, 25.00N 81.20W
Sachs Harbour (Northwest Territories, Canada) **13**
Sacramento (California, United States), **14**, 38.33N 121.30W; **15**
Sa'dah (Yemen) **37**
Sado (*i.*) (Japan), **50**, 38.00N 138.20E; **51**
Saga (Japan) **51**
Sahara (*des.*), **38**, 20.50N 5.50E; **5**, **7**, 8, 38
Saharan Atlas (*mts.*) (Algeria), **38**, 34.20N 2.00E; **5**, **7**, 38
Sahel (*f.*), **38**, 14.00N 7.50E; **5**, **7**, 8, 38, **40**
Saimaa (*l.*) (Finland), **20**, 61.28N 28.07E
St. Anne (*i.*) (Seychelles), **40**, 4.36S 55.30E
St. Catherines-Niagara (Ontario, Canada) **13**
Saint Denis (Réunion, France), **42**, 20.52S 55.27E
St. Elias, Mount (United States/ Canada), **14**, 60.18N 140.55W; **12**
Saintes (Poitou-Charentes, France) **25**
St.-Étienne (Rhône-Alpes, France), **24**, 45.26N 4.26E; **25**
St. Gall (Switzerland) **31**
St. George's (Grenada), **17**, 12.04N 61.44W
St. George's Channel, **22**, 52.00N 6.00W
St. Helena (*i.*) (United Kingdom) **23**
St. John (New Brunswisk, Canada) **13**
St. John's (Antigua and Barbuda), **17**, 17.07N 61.51W
St. John's (Newfoundland, Canada), **12**, 47.34N 52.43W; 12, **13**
St. Kitts-Nevis (*c.*), **17**, 17.20N 62.45W; **4**, 16, *17*
St. Lawrence (*r.*) (Canada), **12**, 44.15N 76.10W; **4**, **6**, **10**
St. Lawrence, Gulf of (Canada), **12**, 48.00N 62.00W
St. Lawrence Island (United States), **14**, 63.00N 170.00W
St. Louis (Missouri, United States), **14**, 38.38N 90.11W; **15**
St. Louis (Senegal) **41**
St. Lucia (*c.*), **17**, 14.05N 61.00W; **4**, 16, *17*
St.-Malo (Brittany, France) **25**
St.-Nazaire (Pays de la Loire, France) **25**
St. Peter and St. Paul Rocks (Brazil), **18**, 1.00N 29.23W
St. Petersburg (Russia), **34** 59.55N 30.25E; **35**
St. Pierre and Miquelon (*isls.*) (France), **12**, 46.55N 56.10W; **13**
St. Pölten (Austria) **31**
St. Vincent and the Grenadines (*c.*), **17**, 13.10N 61.15W; **4**, 16, *17*
Sajama (*mt.*) (Bolivia), **18**, 18.06S 69.00W
Sakai (Japan), **50**, 34.37N 135.28E
Sakhalin (*i.*) (Russia), **34**, 50.00N 143.00E; **5**, **7**, 51
Sal (*i.*) (Cape Verde), **40**, 16.50N 22.50W
Salado (*r.*) (Argentina), **18**, 27.50S 62.50W
Salalah (Oman), **36**, 17.00N 54.04E; **37**
Salamanca (Spain), **26**, 40.58N 5.40W; **27**
Salem (Oregon, United States) **15**
Salerno (Italy), **28**, 40.41N 14.45E; **29**
Salinas Grande (Argentina), **18**, 23.30S 68.20W
Salonika (Greece), **28**, 40.38N 22.56E; **29**, 29
Salt Lake City (Utah, United States), **14**, 40.46N 111.53W; **15**
Salvador (Brazil), **18**, 12.58S 38.20W; **19**
Salween (*r.*) (China/Myanmar), **48**, 16.30N 97.33E; **5**, **7**, **48**
Salzach (*r.*) (Austria), **30**, 48.12N 12.56E
Salzburg (Austria), **30**, 47.48N 13.02E; **31**
Samar (*i.*) (Philippines), **48**, 11.45N 125.15E; **49**
Samara (Russia) **35**
Samarinda (Indonesia), **48**, 0.30S 117.09E; **49**
Samarkand (Uzbekistan) **35**
Samoa (*c.*), **55**, 13.50S 171.44W; **5**, **7**, 55
Samoan language 55
Samos (*i.*) (Greece), **28**, 37.44N 26.45E; **29**
Samsun (Turkey), **36**, 41.17N 36.22E; **37**
Sanae (Antarctica), **56**, 70.18S 2.24W
San'a (Yemen), **36**, 15.23N 44.14E; **37**
San Antonio (Texas, United States), **14**, 29.28N 98.31W; **15**
San Carlos de la Rapita (Spain) **27**
Sancy, Puy de (*mt.*) (France) **24**, 45.32N 2.49E
Sandakan (Malaysia) **49**
Sanday (*i.*) (Scotland, United Kingdom), **22**, 59.15N 2.33W
San Diego (California, United States), **14**, 32.43N 117.09W; **15**
Sandnes (Norway) **21**
Sandy Desert (Pakistan), **44**, 28.00N 64.00E
San Félix Island (Chile), **18**, 26.23S 80.05W
San Francisco (California, United States), **14**, 37.48N 122.24W; **15**
San Jose (California, United States) **15**
San José (Costa Rica), **16**, 9.59N 84.04W
San Juan (Puerto Rico), **17**, 18.29N 66.08W
San Juan Mountains (United States), **14**, 37.35N 107.10W
San Lucas, Cape (Mexico), **16**, 22.50N 110.00W
San Marino (*c.*), **28**, 43.55N 12.27E; 28, *29*, **32**
San Marino (San Marino), **28**, 43.55N 12.27E; **29**
San Martín (Antarctica), **56**, 68.07S 67.08W
San Miguel de Tucumán (Argentina), **18**, 26.47S 65.15W; **19**
San Pedro Sula (Honduras), **16**, 15.26N 88.01W
San Salvador (El Salvador), **16**, 13.40N 89.10W
San Sebastián (Spain), **26**, 43.19N 1.59W; **27**
Santa Cruz (Bolivia), **18**, 17.45S 63.14W; **19**
Santa Fe (New Mexico, United States) **15**
Santa Isabel (*i.*) (Solomon Islands), **52**, 8.00S 159.00E
Santa Luzia (*i.*) (Cape Verde), **40**, 16.50N 24.55W
Santander (Spain), **26**, 43.28N 3.48W; **27**
Santarém (Brazil) **19**
Santarém (Portugal) **27**
Santiago (Chile), **18**, 33.30S 70.40W; **19**
Santiago de Cuba (Cuba), **17**, 20.00N 75.49W
Santiago de Compostela (Spain) **27**
Santo Antão (*i.*) (Cape Verde), **40**, 17.10N 25.10W
Santo Domingo (Dominican Republic), **17**, 18.30N 69.57W
São Francisco (*r.*) (Brazil), **18**, 10.20S 36.20W
Saône (*r.*) (France), **24**, 45.44N 4.50E
São Nicolau (*i.*) (Cape Verde), **40**, 16.45N 24.20W
São Paulo (Brazil), **18**, 23.33S 46.39W; **19**
São Roque, Cape of (Brazil), **18**, 4.00S 35.00W
São Tiago (*i.*) (Cape Verde), **40**, 15.10N 23.35W
São Tomé (*town*) (São Tomé and Príncipe), **40**, 0.19N 6.43E **41**
São Tomé and Príncipe (*c.*), **40**, 1.00N 7.00E; **5**, 40, *41*
São Vicente (*i.*) (Cape Verde) **40**, 17.00N 25.00W
São Vicente, Cape (Portugal), **26**, 37.01N 8.59W
Sapporo (Japan), **50**, 43.05N 141.21E; **51**
Sarajevo (Bosnia and Herzegovina), **32**, 43.52N 18.26E; **33**
Saratov (Russia) **35**
Sardinia (*i.*) (Italy), **28**, 40.00N 9.00E; **29**, 29
Sardinian language 29
Sargodha (Pakistan) **45**
Sarh (Chad) **39**
Sasebo (Japan), **50**, 33.10N 129.42E
Saskatchewan (*p.*) (Canada) **13**
Saskatchewan (*r.*) (Canada), **12**, 53.12N 99.16W
Saskatchewan, South (*r.*) (Canada), **12**, 53.12N 105.07W
Saskatoon (Saskatchewan, Canada), **12**, 52.07N 106.38W; **13**
Sassari (Italy), **28**, 40.43N 8.33E; **29**
Sata, Cape (Japan), **50**, 31.00N 130.39E
Satpura Range (*mts.*) (India), **44**, 21.50N 76.00E
Satu Mare (Romania) **33**
Saudia Arabia (*c.*), **36**, 26.00N 44.00E; **5**, 36, *37*, **38**
Sault Sainte Marie (Ontario, Canada), **12**, 46.31N 84.20W; **13**
Saumlakki (Indonesia), **48**, 7.59S 131.22E
Saurimo (Angola) **43**
Sava (*r.*) (Croatia/Bosnia and Herzegovina), **32**, 44.50N 20.26E
Savanna 6, 42
Save (*r.*) (Zimbabwe/Mozambique), **42**, 20.59S 35.02E
Sayan, Eastern (*mts.*) (Russia), **34**, 53.30N 98.00E
Sayan, Western (*mts.*) (Russia), **34**, 53.00N 92.00E
Saywun (Yemen) **37**
Scafell Pike (*mt.*) (England, United Kingdom), **22**, 54.27N 3.12W
Scandinavia *see* Nordic countries
Schelde (*r.*) (Belgium), **30**, 51.13N 4.25E
Schwaner Range (*mts.*) (Indonesia), **48**, 0.45S 113.20E
Schwerin (Germany) **31**
Scilly, Isles of (United Kingdom), **22**, 49.55N 6.20W
Scotland (United Kingdom) 22, **23**
Scott Base (Antarctica), **56**, 77.50S 166.25E
Sea, influence on climate 6

Seattle (Washington, United States), **14**, 47.36N 122.20W; **15**
Ségou (Mali), **38**, 13.28N 6.18W; **39**
Segovia (Spain) **27**
Segre (*r.*) (Spain), **26**, 41.40N 0.40E
Seine (*r.*) (France), **24**, 49.28N 0.25E
Seistan (*f.*) (Iran), **36**, 31.00N 61.00E
Selkirk Mountains (Canada), **12**, 51.00N 118.00W
Selvas (*f.*) (Brazil), **18**, 9.00S 68.00W
Selwyn Mountains (Canada), **12**, 62.00N 130.00W
Selwyn Range (*mts.*) (Australia), **52**, 21.35S 140.35E
Semipalatinsk (Kazakhstan) **35**
Sendai (Japan), **50**, 38.20N 140.50E; **51**
Senegal (*c.*), **40**, 14.15N 14.15W; **5**, **38**, 40, *41*
Senegal (*r.*), **40**, 16.00N 16.28W; **38**
Senja (*i.*) (Norway), **20**, 69.15N 17.20E
Seoul (South Korea), **50**, 37.30N 127.00E; **51**
Sepik (*r.*) (Papua New Guinea), **52**, 3.54S 144.30E
Sept-Iles (Quebec, Canada), **12**, 50.12N 66.23W; **13**
Serbian language 33
Serowe (Botswana), **42**, 22.25S 26.44E
Serra da Estrela (*mts.*) (Portugal), **26**, 40.20N 7.40W
Serra da Mantiqueira (*mts.*) (Brazil), **18**, 22.25S 45.00W
Serra do Mar (*mts.*) (Brazil), **18**, 24.00S 44.40W
Serranía de Cuenca (*mts.*) (Spain), **26**, 40.25N 2.00W
Sesotho language 43
Setúbal (Portugal) **27**
Setwana language 43
Severn (*r.*) (England, United Kingdom), **22**, 51.50N 2.21W
Severnaya Zemlya (*i.*) (Russia), **34**, 80.00N 96.00E; **5**, **7**, **35**
Seville (Spain), **26**, 37.24N 5.59W; **27**
Seward (Alaska, United States), **15**
Seward Peninsula (Alaska, United States), **14**, 65.00N 164.10W; **15**
Seychelles (*c.*), **40**, 4.35S 55.40E; **5**, **7**, 40, *41*
Sfax (Tunisia), **38**, 34.54N 10.43E; **39**
Shaanxi (*d.*) (China) **47**
Shache (Xinjiang, China) **47**
Shackleton Ice Shelf (Antarctica), **56**, 66.00S 100.00E
Shah Fuladi (*mt.*) (Afghanistan), **36**, 34.38N 67.32E
Shandong (*d.*) (China) **47**
Shandong Peninsula (China), **46**, 37.00N 121.30E
Shanghai (China), **46**, 31.13N 121.25E; **47**
Shannon (*r.*) (Ireland), **22**, 52.39N 8.43W
Shan Plateau (Myanmar), **48**, 18.40N 98.00E
Shantou (Guangdong, China) **47**
Shanxi (*d.*) (China) **47**
Shebelle (*r.*) (Ethiopia/Somalia), **38**, 0.30N 43.10E
Sheffield (England, United Kingdom), **22**, 53.23N 1.28W; **23**
Shenyang (Liaoning, China), **46**, 41.50N 123.26E; **47**
Shetland Islands (Scotland, United Kingdom), **22**, 60.20N 1.15W; **23**
Shibotsu (*i.*), **50**, 43.30N 146.09E
Shihezi (Xinjiang, China) **47**
Shijiazhuang (Hebei, China) **47**
Shikoku (*i.*) (Japan), **50**, 33.30N 133.00E; **51**
Shikoku Mountains (Japan), **50**, 33.33N 133.52E
Shikotan (*i.*) (Russia), **50**, 43.47N 146.45E
Shinano (*r.*) (Japan), **50**, 37.58N 139.02E
Shiono (Japan), Cape, **50**, 33.28N 135.47E
Shiraz (Iran), **36**, 29.36N 52.33E; **37**
Shire (*r.*) (Malawi/Mozambique), **42**, 17.46S 35.20E
Shkodër (Albania), **32**, 42.03N 19.30E; **33**
Shkodër, Lake (Yugoslavia/Albania), **32**, 42.03N 19.30E
Siberia 8
see also Central Siberian Plain; West Siberian Plain
Siberut (*i.*) (Indonesia), **48**, 1.30S 99.00E; **49**
Sibiu (Romania) **33**
Sibu (Malaysia) **49**
Sichuan (*d.*) (China) **47**
Sichuan Basin (China), **46**, 30.00N 105.00E
Sicily (*i.*) (Italy), **28**, 37.30N 14.00E; **29**, 29
Sidley, Mount (Antarctica), **56**, 77.12S 129.00W
Sierra de Gata (*mts.*) (Spain), **26**, 40.20N 6.30W
Sierra de Gredos (*mts.*) (Spain), **26**, 40.18N 5.20W
Sierra de Guadarrama (*mts.*) (Spain), **26**, 41.00N 3.50W
Sierra de la Demanda (*mts.*) (Spain), **26**, 42.10N 3.00W
Sierra de San Just (*mts.*) (Spain), **26**, 41.00N 1.00W
Sierra de Segura (*mts.*) (Spain), **26**, 38.00N 2.50W
Sierra Leone (*c.*), **40**, 8.30N 12.00W; **5**, 40, *41*
Sierra Madre (*mts.*) (Mexico), **16**, 15.00N 92.00W
Sierra Madre del Sur (*mts.*) (Mexico), **16**, 16
Sierra Madre Occidental (*mts.*) (Mexico), **16**, 25.00N, 107.00W; **4**, **6**, **10**
Sierra Madre Oriental (*mts.*) (Mexico), **16**, 23.00N 99.00W
Sierra Morena (*mts.*) (Spain), **26**, 38.10N 5.00W
Sierra Nevada (*mts.*) (Spain), **26**, 37.04N 3.20W; 27
Sierra Nevada (*mts.*) (United States), **14**, 37.45N 119.30W
Signy (Antarctica), **56**, 60.43S 45.36W; **57**
Sikhote-Alin (*mts.*) (Russia), **34**, 45.00N 136.00E
Silesian Plain, **32**, 50.30N 19.30E
Silhouette (*i.*) (Seychelles), **40**, 4.29S 55.12E
Siling, Lake (Tibet, China), **46**, 31.40N 88.30E
Siljan (*l.*) (Sweden), **20**, 60.50N 14.45E
Simbirsk (Russia) **35**
Simeulue (*i.*) (Indonesia), **48**, 2.30N 96.00E; **49**
Simpson Desert (Australia), **52**, 25.00S 136.50E
Sinai (*pen.*) (Egypt), **38**, 29.00N 34.00E
Si Ndebele language 43
Singapore (*c.*), **48**, 1.20N 103.45E; **5**, 48, *49*
Singapore (*city*) (Singapore), **48**, 1.20N 103.45E; **49**
Singkep (*i.*) (Indonesia), **48**, 0.30S 104.20E; **49**
Sinhalese language 45
Sinuiju (North Korea), **50**, 40.04N 124.25E; **51**
Sion (Switzerland) **31**
Siple Island (Antarctica), **56**, 73.25S 122.50W
Siret (*r.*) (Romania), **32**, 45.28N 27.56E
siSwati language 43
Sisters, The (*isls.*) (Seychelles), **40**, 4.16S 55.52E
Sittwe (Myanmar) **49**
Siwalik Range (*mts.*) (India/Nepal), **44**, 31.15N 77.45E
Sjaelland (*i.*) (Denmark), **20**, 55.30N 11.45E
Skagerrak (*str.*), **20**, 58.00N 9.30E
Skellefteå (Sweden), **20**, 64.46N 20.57E; **21**
Skien (Norway) **21**
Skopje (Macedonia), **32**, 41.58N 21.29E; **33**
Skovorodino (Russia) **35**
Skye (*i.*) (Scotland, United Kingdom), **22**, 57.20N 6.15W; **22**, **23**
Sligo (Ireland), **22**, 54.17N 8.28W; **23**
Slovakia (*c.*), **32**, 48.50N 20.00E; **5**, **28**, 32, *33*, 34
Slovakian Ore Mountains (Slovakia), **32**, 48.30N 20.00E
Slovak language 33
Slovenia (*c.*), **32**, 45.50N 14.30E; **5**, **28**, **30**, 32, *33*
Slovenian language 29, 33
Smog 8
Smólikas (*mt.*) (Greece), **28**, 40.06N 20.55E
Snake (*r.*) (United States), **14**, 46.12N 119.02W
Sněžka, Mount (Poland/Czech Republic), **32**, 50.45N 15.37E
Snowdon (*mt.*) (Wales, United Kingdom), **22**, 53.05N 4.05W
Sobaek Mountains (South Korea), **50**, 35.50N 127.45E
Sochi (Russia), **34**, 43.35N 39.46E; **35**
Socotra (*i.*) (Yemen), **36**, 12.30N 54.00E; **5**, **37**
Sofia (Bulgaria), **32**, 42.41N 23.19E; **33**
Sofia (*r.*) (Madagascar), **42**, 15.27S 47.23E
Sogne Fjord (Norway), **20**, 61.06N 5.10E
Soil;
erosion 4, 8
Solar power 10
Sologne (*f.*)(France), **24**, 47.20N 2.00E
Solomon Islands, **55**, 9.28S 159.52E; **5**, **7**, **52**, 55
Somalia (*c.*), **38**, 4.00N 47.00E; **5**, **36**, 38, *39*
Somali language 39
Somerset Island (Canada), **12**, 73.00N 93.30W
Somes (*r.*) (Romania), **32**, 48.04N 22.30E
Songhua (*r.*) (China), **46**, 47.46N 132.30E
Songkhla (Thailand), **48**, 7.12N 100.35E; **49**
Soria (Spain) **27**
Sorong (Indonesia), **48**, 0.50S 131.17E; **49**
Sosnoweic (Poland) **33**
South Africa (*c.*), **42**, 30.00S 22.00E; **5**, 42, *43*
South America **4**, **6**, **7**, **10**, 16, 18
Southampton (England, United Kingdom), **22**, 50.54N 1.23W; **23**
Southampton Island (Canada), **12**, 64.30N 84.00W
South Andaman (*i.*) (India), **44**, 11.41N 92.40E
South Asia Association for Regional Cooperation Committee (SAARC) 45
South Atlantic Ocean **7**
South Australia (*d.*) (South Australia) **53**
South Carolina (*s.*) (United States) **15**
South China Sea **5**, **7**, **46**, **48**
South Dakota (*s.*) (United States) **15**
Southeast Asia **48**, **49**
South Equatorial Current **7**
Southern Africa 42, **43**
Southern Africa Development Community (SADC) 43
Southern Alps (New Zealand), **54**, 43.20S 170.45E; 54
Southern Uplands (Scotland, United Kingdom), **22**, 55.30N 3.30W
South Georgia (*i.*) (United Kingdom), **18**, 54.00S 37.00W; **5**, **7**, 19
South Island (New Zealand), **54**, 43.00S 171.00E
South Korea (*c.*), **50**, 37.00N 128.00E; **5**, **46**, 50, *51*
South Orkney Islands (Antarctica), **56**, 60.35S 45.30W
South Pacific Ocean **7**
South Pole (Antarctica), **56**, 90.00S 0.00; 56, 57
South Sandwich Islands (United Kingdom) 19, 23
South Shetland Islands (Antarctica), **56**, 62.00S 58.00W
Southwest Asia **36–37**
Southwest Cape (New Zealand), **54**, 47.15S 167.30E
Sovereignty 4
Soviet Union *see* Union of Soviet Socialist Republics
Soya, Cape (Japan), **50**, 45.33N 141.58E
Spain (*c.*), **26**, 40.00N 4.00W; **5**, **24**, 26, *27*, **38**
climate 27
Spanish language 15, 16, 17, 18, 19, 25, 27, 41
Spanish Sahara *see* Western Sahara
Sparta (Greece) **29**
Spartivento, Cape (Italy), **28**, 37.55N 16.04E
Spartivento, Cape (Sardinia, Italy), **28**, 38.53N 8.52E
Spenser Mountains (New Zealand), **54**, 42.12S 172.36E
Spessart (*mts.*) (Germany), **30**, 50.07N 9.35E
Split (Croatia), **32**, 43.31N 16.28E; **33**
Sporades, Northern (*isls.*) (Greece), **28**, 39.20N 23.30E; **29**
Spree (*r.*) (Germany), **30**, 51.30N 14.10E
Springfield (Illinois, United States) **15**
Sranang Tongo language 19
Sri Lanka (*c.*), **44**, 7.30N 80.50E; **5**, **7**, 44, *45*
Srinagar (Jammu and Kashmir), **44**, 34.08N 74.50E; **45**
Stanley (Falkland Islands) **18**, 51.45S 57.56W; **19**
Stanley, Mount (Uganda/Democratic Republic of the Congo), **40**, 0.20N 30.50E
Stanovoy Range (*mts.*) (Russia), **34**, 56.00N 125.40E
Stara Zagora (Bulgaria), **32**, 42.26N 25.37E; **33**
Stavanger (Norway), **20**, 58.58N 5.45E; **21**
Steppe
tropical **6–7**
Stewart Island (New Zealand), **54**, 47.02S 167.51E
Stockholm (Sweden), **20**, 59.20N 18.03E; **21**
Stoke on Trent (England, United Kingdom) **23**
Stormberg (*mts.*) (South Africa), **42**, 30.45S 25.00E
Storsjön (*l.*) (Sweden), **20**, 63.10N 14.20E
Strasbourg (Alsace, France), **24**, 48.35N 7.45E; **25**
Straumnes (Iceland), **20**, 66.30N 23.05W
Struma (*r.*) (Greece), **28**, 40.45N 23.51E
Stuttgart (Germany), **30**, 48.46N 9.11E; **31**
Subarctic climate **6–7**
Subotica (Yugoslavia), **32**, 46.04N 19.41E; **33**
Subtropical climate **6–7**
Sucre (Bolivia), **18**, 19.05S 65.15W; **19**
Sudan (*c.*), **38**, 14.00N 28.00E; **5**, **36**, 38, *39*, **40**
Sudbury (Ontario, Canada) **13**
Sudd (*f.*) (Sudan), **38**, 7.50N 30.00E
Sudetic Mountains (Poland/Czech Republic), **32**, 50.30N 16.30E
Suez (Egypt) **38**, 29.59N 32.33E; **39**
Suir (*r.*) (Ireland), **22**, 52.17N 7.00W
Sukkur (Pakistan), **44**, 27.42N 68.54E; **45**
Sulaiman Range (*mts.*) (Pakistan), **44**, 30.50N 70.20E
Sula Islands (Indonesia), **48**, 1.50S 125.10E; **48**, **49**
Sulawesi (*i.*) (Indonesia), **48**, 2.00S 120.30E; **5**, **7**, **49**, **52**
Sulu Archipelago (Philippines), **48**, 5.30N 121.00E
Sulu Sea **48**
Sumatra (*i.*) (Indonesia), **48**, 2.00S 102.00E; **5**, **7**, **49**
Sumba (*i.*) (Indonesia), **48**, 9.30S 119.55E; **49**
Sumbawa (*i.*) (Indonesia), **48**, 8.45S 117.50E; **49**
Sundsvall (Sweden), **20**, 62.23N 17.18E; **21**
Supercontinents 4, 18
Superior, Lake (United States/ Canada), **12**, 48.00N 88.00W; **14**
Sur (Oman), **36**, 22.23N 59.32E; **37**
Surabaya (Indonesia), **48**, 7.14S 112.45E; **49**
Surat (India), **44**, 21.10N 72.54E; **45**
Surgut (Russia) **35**
Suriname (*c.*), **18**, 4.00N 56.00W; **4**, **17**, 18, *19*
Surtsey (*i.*) (Iceland), **20**, 63.18N 20.30W
Sutlej (*r.*) (China/India/Pakistan), **44**, 29.26N 71.09E
Suva (Fiji), **55**, 18.08S 178.25E
Svalbard (*isls.*) (Norway), **34**, 78.00N 20.00E; **5**, **7**, 20, 21
Svartisen (*mt.*) (Norway), **20**, 66.40N 13.56E
Swabian Jura (*mts.*) (Germany), **30**, 48.30N 9.38E
Swahili language 41
Swakopmund (Namibia) **43**
Swansea (Wales, United Kingdom), **22**, 51.37N 3.57W; **23**
Swaziland (*c.*), **42**, 26.30S 32.00E; **5**, 42, *43*
Sweden (*c.*), **20**, 63.00N 16.00E; **5**, 20, *21*, **30**
Swedish language 21
Switzerland (*c.*), **30**, 46.45N 8.30E; **5**, **24**, **28**, 30, *31*, **32**
Sydney (New South Wales, Australia), **52**, 33.55S 151.10E; **53**
Sydney (Nova Scotia, Canada) **13**
Syowa (Antarctica) **56**, 69.00S 39.35E
Syracuse (Italy), **28**, 37.05N 15.17E; **29**
Syr Darya (*r.*), **34**, 46.00N 61.12E; **5**, **7**
Syria (*c.*), **36**, 35.00N 38.00E; **5**, **28**, 36, *37*, **38**
Syrian Desert, **36**, 32.00N 39.00E
Szczecin (Poland), **32**, 53.25N 14.32E; **33**

Tabriz (Iran), **36**, 38.05N 46.18E; **37**
Tabuk (Saudi Arabia) **37**
Tademait, Plateau of (Algeria), **38**, 28.45N 2.10E
Tadzhik language 35
Taebaek Mountains (North Korea/ South Korea), **50**, 36.40N 129.00E
Taedong (*r.*) (North Korea), **50**, 39.30N 126.00E
Taegu (South Korea), **50**, 35.52N 128.36E; **51**
Taejon (South Korea), **50**, 36.20N 127.26E; **51**
Tagus (*r.*) (Spain/Portugal), **26**, 39.00N 8.57W; 27
Tahat, Mount (Algeria), **38**, 23.20N 5.40E
Taihang Shan (China) (*mts.*), **46**, 36.40N 113.35E
Taipei (Taiwan), **46**, 25.05N 121.32E; **47**
Taiwan (*c.*), **46**, 23.30N 121.00E; **5**, **7**, 46, *47*, **48**
Taiwan Strait, **46**, 25.00N 120.00E; **47**
Taiyuan (Shanxi, China), **46**, 37.50N 112.30E; **47**
Ta'izz (Yemen) **37**
Tajikistan (*c.*), **34**, 39.00N 70.30E; **5**, 34, *35*, **36**
Tajumalco (*mt.*) (Guatemala), **16**, 15.02N 91.55W
Takamatsu (Japan), **50**, 34.28N 134.05E; **51**

Takaoka (Japan), **50**, 36.47N 137.00E; **51**
Takla Makan (*des.*) (Xinjiang, China), **46**, 38.10N 82.00E
Taliban 37
Tallahassee (Florida, United States) **15**
Tallinn (Estonia), **34**, 59.22N 24.48E; **35**
Tamanrasset (Algeria), **38**, 22.50N 5.31E; **39**
Tamil language 45
Tampa (Florida, United States), **14**, 27.58N 82.38W; **15**
Tampere (Finland), **20**, 61.30N 23.45E; **21**
Tampico (Mexico), **16**, 22.18N 97.52W
Tana, Lake (Ethiopia), **38**, 12.00N 37.20E
Tanami Desert (Australia), **52**, 19.50S 130.50E
Tanega (*i.*) (Japan), **50**, 30.32N 131.00E
Tanen Range (*mts.*) (Myanmar/ Thailand), **48**, 20.00N 98.30E
Tanga (Tanzania) **41**
Tanganyika, Lake, **40**, 5.37S 29.30E; **5**, **7**, 40
Tanggula Shan (*mts.*) (Tibet, China), **46**, 32.40N 92.30E
Tangier (Morocco), **38**, 35.48N 5.45W; **39**
Tangra Yumco (*l.*) (Tibet, China), **46**, 31.00N 86.00E
Tangshan (Hebei, China) **47**
Tanimbar Islands (Indonesia), **48**, 7.50S 131.30E; **49**
Tanjungkarang (Indonesia), **48**, 5.28S 105.16E; **49**
Tanzania (*c.*), **40**, 5.00S 35.00E; **5**, 40, *41*, **42**
Tapajós (*r.*) (Brazil), **18**, 2.25S 54.40W
Tapi (*r.*) (India), **44**, 21.30N 75.00E
Tarakan (Indonesia) **49**
Taranto (Italy), **28**, 40.28N 17.14E; **29**
Taranto, Gulf of, **28**, 40.00N 17.20E
Tararua Range (*mts.*) (New Zealand), **54**, 40.50S 175.25E
Tarawa (Kiribati), **55**, 1.30N 173.00E
Tarim (*r.*) (China), **46**, 41.00N 83.30E
Tarim Basin (Xinjiang, China), **46**, 40.00N 83.00E
Tarn (*r.*) (France), **24**, 44.05N 1.06E
Tarragona (Spain), **26**, 41.07N 1.15E; **27**
Tashkent (Uzbekistan), **34**, 41.16N 69.13E; **35**
Tasmania (*i.*) (Australia), **52**, 42.00S 147.00E; **5**, **7**, 52, **53**
Tasman Mountains (New Zealand), **54**, 41.06S 172.30E
Tasman Sea **5**, **7**, **52**, **54**, **55**
Tatar language 35
Tatra Mountains (Slovakia/Poland), **32**, 49.10N 20.00E
Tauern (*mts.*) (Austria), **30**, 47.00N 13.00E
Taunus (*mts.*) (Germany), **30**, 50.10N 8.30E
Taupo, Lake (New Zealand), **54**, 38.48S 175.55E
Tauranga (New Zealand), **54**, 37.42S 176.11E
Taurus Mountains (Turkey), **36**, 37.15N 34.15E
Tavoy (Myanmar), **48**, 14.07N 98.18E; **49**
Tawau (Malaysia) **49**
Tay (Scotland, United Kingdom), Firth of (*est.*), **22**, 56.24N 3.08W
Taymyr Peninsula (Russia), **34**, 74.50N 100.00E
Tbilisi (Georgia), **34**, 41.43N 44.48E; **35**
Te Anau, Lake (New Zealand), **54**, 45.14S 167.46E
Tectonic plates 4
Tegucigalpa (Honduras), **16**, 14.05N 87.14W
Tehran (Iran), **36**, 35.40N 51.26E; **37**
Tehuantepec, Gulf of, **16**, 16.00N 95.00W
Tehuantepec, Isthmus of (Mexico), **16**, 17.00N 95.00W
Tel Aviv (Israel), **36**, 32.05N 34.46E; **37**
Telugu language 45
Temperate climate **6–7**
Tennant Creek (Northern Territory, Australia) **53**
Tennessee (*s.*) (United States) **15**
Tennessee (*r.*) (United States), **14**, 37.04N 88.33W
Teresina (Brazil) **19**
Ternate (Indonesia), **48**, 0.48N 127.23E; **49**
Terni (Italy), **28**, 42.34N 12.44E
Terrain and climate 6
Teshio (*r.*) (Japan), **50**, 44.53N 141.44E
Tete (Mozambique), **42**, 16.10S 33.30E; **43**
Teteven (Bulgaria) **33**
Texas (*s.*) (United States) **15**
Thabana-Ntlenyana (*mt.*) (South Africa), **42**, 29.28S 29.17E
Thailand (*c.*), **48**, 16.00N 101.00E; **5**, **46**, 48, *49*
Thailand, Gulf of, **48**, 11.00N 101.00E
Thai language 49
Thames (*r.*) (England, United Kingdom), **22**, 51.30N 0.05E
Thar Desert *see* Great Indian Desert
Thasos (*i.*) (Greece), **28**, 40.40N 24.39E; **29**
Thimphu (Bhutan), **44**, 27.29N 89.40E; **45**
Thionville (Lorraine, France) **25**
Thira (*i.*) (Greece), **28**, 36.24N 25.27E; **29**
Thjórsá (*r.*) (Iceland), **20**, 63.53N 20.38W
Three Kings Islands (New Zealand), **54**, 34.09S 172.09E
Thule (Greenland), **12**, 77.30N 69.29W; **13**
Thunder Bay (*city*) (Ontario, Canada), **12**, 48.25N 89.14W; **13**
Thuringian Forest (Germany), **30**, 50.40N 10.52E
Thurston Island (Antarctica), **56**, 72.15S 98.00W
Tianjin (China), **46**, 39.08N 117.12E; **47**
Tiber (*r.*) (Italy), **28**, 41.45N 12.16E
Tibesti (*mts.*) (Chad), **38**, 21.00N 17.30E; **5**, **7**
Tibet (*d.*) (China) **47**
Tibetan language 47
Tibet, Plateau of (China), **46**, 34.00N 86.30E; 46
Tien Shan (*mts.*) (Xinjiang, China), **46**, 42.00N 80.30E; **5**, **7**
Tierra del Fuego (Chile/Argentina) (*i.*), **18**, 54.00S 69.00W; **4**, **6**, **10**, 19
Tigre and Kunama language 39
Tigrinya language 39
Tigris (*r.*) (Iraq), **36**, 31.00N 47.27E; **5**, **7**, 36
Tiksi (Russia) **35**
Timaru (New Zealand), **54**, 44.24S 171.15E
Timbuktu (Mali), **38**, 16.49N 2.59W; **39**
Timimoun (Algeria) **39**
Timişoara (Romania), **32**, 45.47N 21.15E; **33**
Timmins (Ontario, Canada) **13**
Timor (*i.*) (Indonesia), **48**, 9.30S 125.00E; **5**, **7**, **49**, **52**
Timor Sea **52**
Tin 10
Tindouf (Algeria), **38**, 27.42N 8.09W; **39**
Tiranë (Albania), **32**, 41.20N 19.48E; **33**
Tîrgu Mureş (Romania) **33**
Tirso (*r.*) (Italy), **28**, 39.52N 8.33E
Tiruchchirappalli (India) **45**
Tisza (*r.*) (Hungary), **32**, 45.09N 20.16E
Titicaca, Lake (Peru/Bolivia), **18**, 16.00S 69.00W; **4**, **6**, **10**
Toamasina (Madagascar), **42**, 18.10S 49.23E; **43**
Tobago (*i.*), **17**, 11.15N 60.40W
Toba Kakar Hills (Pakistan), **44**, 31.15N 68.00E
Toba, Lake (Indonesia), **48**, 2.45N 98.50E
Toba language 19
Tobelo (Indonesia), **48**, 1.45N 127.59E
Tobol (*r.*) (Russia) (Russia/ Kazakhstan), **34**, 58.15N 68.12E
Tocantins (*r.*) (Brazil), **18**, 1.50S 49.15W
Togo (*c.*), **40**, 8.30N 1.00E; **5**, 40, *41*
Tok (*i.*) (Japan), **50**, 37.14N 132.00E; **51**
Tokelau (*isls.*) (New Zealand), **55**, 9.00S 171.45W; 55
Tokushima (Japan) **51**
Tokyo (Japan), **50**, 35.40N 139.45E; **51**
Tôlañaro (Madagascar), **42**, 25.01S 47.00E; **43**
Toledo (Spain) **27**
Toliara (Madagascar) **43**
Tomakomai (Japan) **51**
Tombuka language 43
Tone (*r.*) (Japan), **50**, 35.44N 140.51E
Tonga, (*c.*), **55**, 21.09S 175.14W; **5**, **7**, 55
Tongan language 55
Tonkin, Gulf of, **48**, 20.00N 108.00E
Tonle Sap (*l.*) (Cambodia), **48**, 12.50N 104.00E
Toowoomba (Queensland, Australia) **53**
Topeka (Kansas, United States) **15**
Topography 4
Torbay (England, United Kingdom) **23**
Torne (*r.*) (Sweden), **20**, 65.53N 24.07E
Toronto (Ontario, Canada), **12**, 43.39N 79.23W; **13**
Torrens, Lake (salt) (Australia), **52**, 31.00S 137.50E
Torres Strait, **52**, 10.00S 142.20E
Tortosa (Spain) **27**
Toruń (Poland) **33**
Toubkal (*mt.*) (Morocco), **38**, 31.03N 7.57W
Toulon (Provence-Alpes-Côte-d'Azur, France), **24**, 43.07N 5.53E; **25**
Toulouse (Midi-Pyrénées, France), **24**, 43.33N 1.24E; **25**
Tours (Centre, France), **24**, 47.23N 0.42E; **25**
Townsville (Queensland, Australia), **52**, 19.13S 146.48E; **53**
Trabzon (Turkey) **37**
Trade winds 6
Tralee (Ireland), **22**, 52.16N 9.42W
Trang (Thailand) **49**
Transantarctic Mountains (Antarctica) **56**, 85.00S 165.00E
Transportation 10
Transylvanian Alps (*mts.*) (Romania), **32**, 45.40N 24.40E
Trapani (Italy), **28**, 38.02N 12.30E; **29**
Trečín (Slovakia) **33**
Trelew (Argentina) **19**
Trent (*r.*) (England, United Kingdom), **22**, 53.41N 0.41W
Trenton (New Jersey, United States) **15**
Trieste (Italy), **28**, 45.40N 13.47E; **29**
Triglav (*mt.*) (Slovenia), **32**, 46.23N 13.50E
Trincomalee (Sri Lanka) **45**
Trinidad (Bolivia) **19**
Trinidad (*i.*), **17**, 10.30N 61.15W
Trinidad and Tobago (*c.*), **17**, 11.00N 61.20W; **4**, 16, *17*
Trinidade (*i.*) (Brazil), **18**, 20.30S 30.00W
Tripoli (Lebanon), **36**, 34.27N 35.50E; **37**
Tripoli (Libya), **38**, 32.58N 13.12E; **39**
Tristan da Cunha (*isls.*) (United Kingdom) **5**, **7**, 23
Trivandrum (India), **44**, 8.41N 76.57E; **45**
Trois-Rivières (Quebec, Canada) **13**
Tromsø (Norway), **20**, 69.42N 19.00E; **21**
Trondheim (Norway), **20**, 63.36N 10.23E; **21**
Trondheim Fjord (Norway), **20**, 63.40N 10.30E
Tropic of Cancer **5**, **7**, **14**, **16**, **36**, **38**, **44**, **46**
Tropic of Capricorn **5**, **7**, **18**, **42**, **52**, **55**
Tropics;
tropical climate **6–7**, 6
Troyes (Champagne-Ardenne, France) **25**
Trujillo (Peru) **19**
Tryavna (Bulgaria) **33**
Tsaratanana Massif (*mts.*) (Madagascar), **42**, 14.00S 49.00E
Tsugaru Strait, **50**, 41.30N 140.50E
Tsu Islands (Japan), **50**, 34.30N 129.20E; **51**
Tsumeb (Namibia), **42**, 19.12S 17.43E; **43**
Tswana language 43
Tucson (Arizona, United States) **15**
Tulcea (Romania) **33**
Tulsa (Oklahoma, United States) **15**
Tumen (*r.*), **50**, 42.18N 130.41E
Tundra **6–7**, 6, 12
Tunis (Tunisia), **38**, 35.47N 10.10E; **39**
Tunisia (*c.*), **38**, 35.00N 10.00E; **5**, **28**, 38, *39*
Turfan (*f.*) (Xinjiang, China), **46**, 42.40N 89.00E
Turin (Italy), **28**, 45.04N 7.40E; **29**
Turkana, Lake (Kenya), **40**, 4.00N 36.00E; **5**, **7**
Turkey (*c.*), **36**, 39.00N 35.00E; **5**, **28**, **32**, 36, *37*
Turkish language 25, 29, 37
Turkmenistan (*c.*), **34**, 40.00N 60.00E; **5**, 34, *35*, **36**, **44**
Turkmen language 35
Turks and Caicos Islands (United Kingdom), **17**, 21.30N 71.10W
Turku (Finland), **20**, 60.27N 22.17E; **21**
Turpan (Xinjiang, China) **47**
Tutsi 41
Tuvalu (*c.*), **55**, 8.31S 179.13E; **5**, 55
Tuzla (Bosnia and Herzegovina) **33**
Tuz, Lake (Turkey), **36**, 38.45N 33.24E
Tweed (*r.*) (United Kingdom), **22**, 55.46N 2.00W
Tyrrhenian Sea **28**

Ubangi (*r.*), **40**, 2.00N 19.00E
Ube (Japan) **51**
Ubon Ratchathani (Thailand), **48**, 15.15N 104.50E; **49**
Ucayali (*r.*) (Peru), **18**, 4.40S 73.20W
Udine (Italy) **29**
Ueda (Japan) **51**
Uele (*r.*), **40**, 4.08N 22.25E
Ufa (Russia) **35**
Uganda (*c.*), **40**, 1.00N 33.00E; **5**, **38**, 40, *41*
Uighur language 47
Uige (Angola), **43**
Uist, North (*i.*) (Scotland, United Kingdom), **22**, 57.35N 7.20W
Uist, South (*i.*) (Scotland, United Kingdom), **22**, 57.15N 7.20W
Ujiji (Tanzania) **41**
Ujungpandang (Indonesia), **48**, 5.09S 119.28E; **49**
Ukraine (*c.*), **34**, 49.00N 30.00E; **5**, **28**, **32**, 34, *35*, **36**
Ukrainian language 35
Ulan Bator (Mongolia), **34**, 47.54N 106.52E; **34**, **35**
Ulan Ude (Russia) **35**
Uliastay (Mongolia), **34**, 47.42N 96.52E; **34**, **35**
Ullung (*i.*) (South Korea), **50**, 37.30N 131.00E; **51**
Ulm (Germany) **31**
Ulsan (South Korea), **50**, 35.32N 129.21E
Uluru (*mt.*) (Ayers Rock) (Australia) **52**, 25.23S 131.05E
Umbundu language 43
Ume (*r.*) (Sweden), **20**, 63.47N 20.16E
Umeå (Sweden), **20**, 63.45N 20.20E; **21**
Ungava Peninsula (Canada), **12**, 60.00N 74.00W
Union of Soviet Socialist Republics (USSR) 4, 32, 34
United Arab Emirates (*c.*), **36**, 24.00N 54.00E; **5**, 36, *37*
United Kingdom (*c.*), **22**, 55.00N 3.00W; **5**, **20**, 22, *23*, **24**, **30**
dependencies 17
United States of America (*c.*), **14**, 42.00N 96.00W; **4**, 14, *15*, **16**, 16, **34**
agriculture and fisheries 10
climate 14
dependencies 17
flag **15**, *15*
population 14, 15
states 14, **15**, 15
Unst (*i.*) (Scotland, United Kingdom), **22**, 60.45N 0.55W
Upington (South Africa) **43**
Uppsala (Sweden), **20**, 59.52N 17.38E; **21**
Ural (*r.*) (Russia/Kazakhstan), **34**, 47.00N 52.00E
Ural Mountains (Russia), **34**, 60.00N 60.00E; **5**, **7**, 24, 34
Uranium 10
Urbanization 8
Urdu language 45
Urmia (Iran), **36**, 37.32N 45.02E; **37**
Urmia, Lake (Iran), **36**, 37.40N 45.28E
Uruguay (*c.*), **18**. 34.00S 56.00W; **4**, 18, *19*
Uruguay (*r.*), **18**, 34.00S 58.30W
Urumqi (Xinjiang, China), **46**, 43.43N 87.38E; **47**
Usedom (*i.*) (Germany), **30**, 54.00N 14.00E
Usti (Czech Republic) **33**
Ust Kamchatsk (Russia) **35**
Usumacinta (*r.*) (Mexico), **16**, 18.44N 92.30W
Utah (*s.*) (United States) **15**
Utrecht (Netherlands), **30**, 52.04N 5.07E; **31**
Uzbekistan (*c.*), **34**, 42.00N 63.00E; **5**, 34, *35*, **36**
Uzbek language 35

Vaal (*r.*) (South Africa), **42**, 29.04S 23.37E
Vaasa (Finland), **20**, 63.06N 21.36E; **21**
Vadodara (India) **45**
Vaduz (Liechtenstein), **30**, 47.09N 9.31E; **31**
Vah (*r.*) (Slovakia), **32**, 47.40N 18.09E; **33**
Valence (Rhône-Alpes, France) **25**
Valencia (Spain), **26**, 39.29N 0.24W; **27**
Valencia (Venezuela) **19**
Valenciennes (Nord-Pas-de-Calais, France) **25**
Valladolid (Spain), **26**, 41.39N 4.45W; **27**
Valletta (Malta), **28**, 35.53N 14.31E; **29**
Valparaiso (Chile) **19**
Vancouver (British Columbia, Canada), **12**, 49.20N 123.10W; 12, **13**
Vancouver Island (Canada), **12**, 49.45N 126.00W; **4**, **6**, **10**
Vänern (*l.*) (Sweden), **20**, 58.55N 13.30E
Van, Lake (Turkey), **36**, 38.35N 42.52E
Vanuatu, **55**, 17.45S 168.18E; **5**, 55

Varanasi (India), **44**, 25.20N 83.00E; **45**
Varaždin (Croatia) **33**
Varna (Bulgaria), **32**, 43.13N 27.57E; **33**
Vatican City (*c.*), **28**, 41.54N 12.27E; **29**
Vatnajökull (*mts.*) (Iceland), **20**, 64.20N 17.00W
Vättern (*l.*) (Sweden), **20**, 58.24N 14.36E
Vejle (Denmark) **21**
Venezuela (*c.*), **18**, 7.00N 65.30W; **4**, **17**, 18, *19*
Venice (Italy), **28**, 45.26N 12.20E; **29**
Venice, Gulf of, **28**, 45.20N 13.00E
Veracruz (Mexico), **16**, 19.11N 96.10W
Vereeniging (South Africa) **43**
Verkhoyansk (Russia), **34**, 67.25N 133.25E
Verkhoyanski Range (*mts.*) (Russia), **34**, 66.00N 130.00E
Vermont (*s.*) (United States) **15**
Verona (Italy), **28**, 45.27N 10.59E; **29**
Vesterålen (*i.*) (Norway), **20**, 60.06N 15.50E
Vest Fjorden (Norway), **20**, 68.10N 15.00E
Vesuvius (*mt.*) (Italy), **28**, 40.48N 14.25E
Victoria (*d.*) (Australia) **53**
Victoria (British Columbia, Canada) **13**
Victoria Falls (Zambia/Zimbabwe), **42**, 17.58S 25.45E
Victoria Island (Canada), **12**, 71.00N 110.00W; **4**, **6**, **10**
Victoria, Lake, **40**, 1.00S 33.00E; **5**, **7**
Victoria Land (Antarctica), **56**, 75.00S 163.00E
Victoria (Seychelles), **40**, 4.38S 55.28E
Vienna (Austria), **30**, 48.13N 16.22E; **31**
Vienne (*r.*) (France), **24**, 47.13N 0.05E
Vientiane (Laos), **48**, 18.01N 102.48E; **49**
Vietnam (*c.*), **48**, 15.00N 108.00E; **5**, **46**, 48, *49*
Vietnamese language 49
Vignemale Peak (*mt.*) (France), **24**, 42.46N 0.08W
Vigo (Spain), **26**, 42.15N 8.44W; **27**
Vijayawada (India), **44**, 16.34N 80.40E; **45**
Vilanandro, Cape (C. St.-André, Madagascar), **42**, 16.11S 44.29E
Vila Real (Portugal) **27**
Villach (Austria) **31**
Vilnius (Lithuania), **34**, 54.40N 25.19E; **35**
Vincennes Bay (Antarctica), **56**, 66.30S 109.30E
Vindhya Range (*mts.*) (India), **44**, 22.55N 76.00E
Vinson Massif (Antarctica), **56**, 78.35S 85.25W; **57**
Virginia (*s.*) (United States) **15**
Virgin Islands, **17**, 18.30N 64.40W
    British **17**, 17, 23
    US 15, **17**, 17
Viseu (Portugal) 27
Vishakhapatnam (India), **44**, 17.42N 83.24E; **45**
Vistula (*r.*) (Poland), **32**, 54.23N 18.52E
Vitoria (Spain) 27
Vladivostok (Russia), **34**, 43.09N 131.53E; **35**
Vlissingen (Netherlands), **30**, 51.27N 3.35E; **31**
Vltava (*r.*) (Czech Republic), **32**, 50.22N 14.28E
Vogelsberg (*mts.*) (Germany), **30**, 50.30N 9.15E
Vohimena, Cape (C. Ste.-Marie, Madagascar), **42**, 25.36S 45.08E
Volcano Islands (Japan), **48**, 25.00N 141.00E; **55**
Volga (*r.*) (Russia), **34**, 45.45N 47.50E; **5**, **7**
Volgograd (Russia), **34**, 48.45N 44.30E; **35**
Vólos (Greece), **28**, 39.22N 22.57E; **29**

Volta, Lake (Ghana), **40**, 7.00N 0.00
Vorkuta (Russia) **35**
Voronezh (Russia) **35**
Vørterkaka Nunatak (*mt.*) (Antarctica), **56**, 72.20S 27.29E
Vosges (*mts.*) (France), **24**, 48.30N 7.10E
Vostok (Antarctica), **56**, 78.30S 106.50E; **57**
Vyatka (Russia) **35**

Waddenzee (*b.*), **30**, 53.15N 5.05E
Waddington, Mount (Canada), **12**, 51.23N 125.15W
Wad Medani (Sudan), **38**, 14.24N 33.30E; **39**
Wagga Wagga (New South Wales, Australia) **53**
Waitaki (*r.*) (New Zealand), **54**, 44.56S 171.09E
Wajir (Kenya) **41**
Wakasa Bay (Japan), **50**, 35.50N 135.40E
Wakatipu (New Zealand) **54**, 45.05S 168.33E
Wakayama (Japan), **50**, 34.12N 135.10E; **51**
Wake Island (United States), **55**, 19.18N 166.36E; 15
Wakkanai (Japan) **51**
Walbrzych (Poland) **33**
Wales (United Kingdom) 22, **23**
Wallis and Futuna (*isls.*) (France), **55**, 13.18S 176.10E; 25
Walvis Bay (*town*) (Namibia), **42**, 22.57S 14.30E; **43**
Wanganui (New Zealand), **54**, 39.56S 175.02E
Wanxian (Sichuan, China) 47
Warsaw (Poland), **32**, 52.15N 21.00E; **33**
Warta (*r.*) (Poland), **32**, 52.44N 15.26E
Wash, The (*b.*) (England, United Kingdom), **22**, 52.55N 0.15E
Washington (*s.*) (United States) **15**
Washington, D.C. (United States), **14**, 38.55N 77.00W; **15**
Water;
    irrigation 10
    supply 8
Waterford (Ireland), **22**, 52.16N 7.08W; **23**
Wau (Sudan) **39**
Weathering 4
Wei (*r.*) (China), **46**, 35.00N 105.00E
Wellington (New Zealand), **54**, 41.17S 175.46E; **55**
Wellington Island (Chile), **18**, 49.30S 75.00W
Welsh language 23
Wenzhou (Zhejiang, China) **47**
Weser (*r.*) (Germany), **30**, 53.15N 8.34E
West Australian Current **7**
Westerlies **6**
Western Australia (*d.*) (Australia) **53**
Western Sahara (Morocco), **38**, 25.00N 13.30W; **5**, **39**, 39
Western Samoa, **55**, 13.50S 171.44W
Westerwald (*f.*) (Germany), **30**, 50.40N 7.45E
West Frisian Islands (Netherlands), **30**, 53.20N 5.00E; **31**
West Ice Shelf (Antarctica), **56**, 67.00S 85.00E
West Pakistan *see* Pakistan
Westport (New Zealand), **54**, 41.46S 171.38E
West Siberian Plain (Russia), **34**, 62.00N 80.00E; **5**, **7**
West Virginia (*s.*) (United States) **15**
West Wind Drift **7**
Wetar (*i.*) (Indonesia), **48**, 7.45S 126.00E; **49**
Wewak (Papua New Guinea), **52**, 3.35S 143.35E; **53**
Wexford (Ireland), **22**, 52.20N 6.28W; **23**
Whangarei (New Zealand), **54**, 35.43S 174.20E
Whitehorse (Yukon Territory, Canada), **12**, 60.43N 135.03W; **13**

White Sea **20**
Whitney, Mount (Alaska, United States), **14**, 36.35N 118.18W; **4**, **6**, **10**
Wichita (Kansas, United States) **15**
Wicklow Mountains (Ireland), **22**, 53.06N 6.20W
Wiesbaden (Germany) **31**
Wight, Isle of (England, United Kingdom), **22**, 50.40N 1.17W; **23**
Wilhelm, Mount (Papua New Guinea), **52**, 6.00S 144.55E
Wilkes Land (Antarctica), **56**, 69.00S 120.00E; **7**
Williston Lake (Canada), **12**, 56.00N 124.00W
Wind;
    climate and 6
    erosion by 4
Windhoek (Namibia), **42**, 22.34S 17.06E; **43**
Windsor (Ontario, Canada) **13**
Winnipeg (Manitoba, Canada), **12**, 49.53N 97.09W; **13**
Winnipeg, Lake (Canada), **12**, 52.00N 97.00W; **4**, **6**, **10**
Winnipegosis, Lake (Canada), **12**, 51.30N 100.00W
Wisconsin (*s.*) (United States) **15**
Wollongong (New South Wales, Australia) **53**
Wonju (South Korea), **50**, 37.24N 127.52E; **51**
Wonsan (North Korea), **50**, 39.09N 127.25E
World Trade Organization (WTO) 15
Wrangel Island (*mts.*) (Russia), **34**, 71.00N 180.00E; **35**
Wroclaw (Poland), **32**, 51.05N 17.00E; **33**
Wu (*r.*) (China), **46**, 27.30N 108.00E
Wuhan (Hubei, China), **46**, 30.35N 114.19E; **47**
Wumeng Shan (*mts.*) (China), **46**, 26.00N 105.00E
Würzburg (Germany) **31**
Wuyi Shan (*mts.*) (China), **46**, 26.40N 117.00E
Wuzhou (Guangxi, China) **47**
Wyndham (Western Australia) **53**
Wyoming (*s.*) (United States) **15**

Xai-Xai (Mozambique) **43**
Xánthi (Greece) **29**
Xi (*r.*) (China), **46**, 22.23N 113.20E
Xi'an (Shaanxi, China), **46**, 34.16N 108.54E; **47**
Xiangfan (Hubei, China) **47**
Xiao Hinggan Mountains (China), **46**, 48.40N 128.30E
Xingu (*r.*) (Brazil), **18**, 1.40S 52.15W
Xining (Qinghai, China) **47**
Xinjaing (*d.*) (China) **47**

Yablonovy Range (*mts.*) (Russia), **34**, 53.20N 115.00E
Yaku (*i.*) (Japan), **50**, 30.15N 130.12E
Yakutsk (Russia), **34**, 62.10N 129.20E; **35**
Yalong (*r.*) (China), **46**, 26.35N 101.44E
Yalu (*r.*) (China/North Korea), **50**, 40.10N 124.25E
Yamagata (Japan) **51**
Yamal Peninsula (Russia), **34**, 70.20N 70.00E
Yamoussoukro (Côte d'Ivoire), **40**, 6.49N 5.17W; **41**
Yamuna (*r.*) (India), **44**, 25.25N 81.50E
Yangon (Rangoon) (Myanmar), **48**, 16.45N 96.20E; **49**
Yangtze (*r.*) (China), *see* Chang **5**, **7**
Yaoundé (Cameroon), **40**, 3.51N 11.31E; **41**
Yapen (*i.*) (Indonesia), **48**, 1.45S 136.10E; **49**
Yaqui (*r.*) (Mexico), **16**, 27.40N 110.30W
Yaren (Nauru), **55**, 0.32S 166.55E

Yarkant (*r.*) (Xinjiang, China), **46**, 39.00N 78.00E
Yaroslavl (Russia) **35**
Yazd (Iran) **37**
Yekaterinburg (Russia), **34**, 56.52N 60.35E; **35**
Yell (*i.*) (Scotland, United Kingdom), **22**, 60.35N 1.05W
Yellowknife (Northwest Territories, Canada), **12**, 62.27N 114.21W; **13**
Yellow River (China) *see* Huang
Yellow Sea **46**, **50**
Yemen (*c.*), **36**, 15.55N 48.30E; **5**, 36, 37, **38**
Yenisei (*r.*) (Russia), **34**, 69.00N 86.00E; **5**, **7**
Yerevan (Armenia), **34**, 40.10N 44.31E; **35**
Yichang (Hubei, China), **46**, 30.43N 111.22E
Yi language 47
Yinchuan (Ningxia, China) **47**
Yin Shan (*mts.*) (China), **46**, 41.40N 110.00E
Yokohama (Japan), **50**, 35.28N 139.28E; **51**
Yonago (Japan) **51**
Yonne (*r.*) (France), **24**, 48.23N 2.58E
York (England, United Kingdom), **22**, 53.58N 1.07W
York, Cape (Australia), **52**, 10.42S 142.31E; **23**
Yosu (South Korea), **50**, 34.46N 127.44E; **51**
You (*r.*) (China), **46**, 23.25N 110.00E
Yuan (*r.*) (China), **46**, 29.00N 112.12E
Yubetsu (Japan) **51**
Yucatán (*pen.*) (Mexico), **16**, 20.00N 89.00W
Yugoslavia (*c.*), **32**, 43.00N 21.00E; **4**, **5**, 28, 32, *33*
Yukon (*r.*) (Alaska, United States), **14**, 62.35N 164.20W; **4**, **6**, **10**
Yukon Territory (*d.*) (Canada) **13**
Yumen (Gansu, China) **47**
Yunnan (*d.*) (China) **47**
Yu Shan (*mt.*) (Taiwan), **46**, 23.20N 121.03E

Zadar (Croatia), **32**, 44.07N 15.14E; **33**
Zagreb (Croatia), **32**, 45.49N 15.58E; **33**
Zagros Mountains (Iran), **36**, 32.00N 51.00E
Zahedan (Iran) **37**
Zaisan, Lake (Kazakhstan), **34**, 48.00N 83.30E
Zákinthos (Greece) **29**
Zákinthos (*i.*) (Greece), **28**, 37.46N 20.46E; **29**
Zambezi (*r.*), **42**, 18.15S 35.55E; **5**, **7**
Zambia (*c.*), **42**, 14.00S 28.00E; **5**, **40**, 42, *43*
Zamboanga (Philippines), **48**, 6.55N 122.05E; **49**
Zanzibar (*i.*) (Tanzania), **40**, 6.10S 39.12E; **41**
Zaragoza (Spain), **26**, 41.39N 0.54W; **27**
Zaskar Mountains (Jammu and Kashmir), **44**, 33.15N 78.00E
Zhangzhou (Fujian, China) **47**
Zhanjiang (Guangdong, China) **47**
Zhejiang (*d.*) (China) **47**
Zhengzhou (Henan, China) **47**
Zhongshan (Antarctica) **56**, 69.00S 75.00E
Zhu (*r.*) (China), **46**, 21.50N 112.40E
Zibo (Shandong, China) **47**
Zimbabwe (*c.*), **42**, 18.55S 30.00E; **5**, 42, *43*
Zinc 10
Zonguldak (Turkey) **37**
Zugspitze (*mt.*) (Germany), **30**, 47.25N 10.59E
Zulu language 43
Zurich (Switzerland), **30**, 47.23N 8.32E; **31**
Zwolle (Netherlands) **31**